J. Spencer

Middlebury

1975

9

WEST AFRICA PARTITIONED

Volume I

THE LOADED PAUSE, 1885–1889

West Africa Partitioned

Volume I

The Loaded Pause, 1885–1889

JOHN D. HARGREAVES

MACMILLAN

First published 1974 by
THE MACMILLAN PRESS LTD
London and Basingstoke
Associated companies in New York
Dublin Melbourne Johannesburg and Madras

SBN 333 14485 6

Printed in Great Britain by
Cox & Wyman Ltd, London, Fakenham and Reading

Contents

List of Maps

List of Abbreviations

AE	Archives Entrangères, Paris. (All references to the series *Mémoires et Documents* unless otherwise stated.)
ANSOM	Archives Nationales, Section d'Outre-mer, Paris.
C	'Command' number of Parliamentary Papers.
C. of C.	Chamber of Commerce
CEA	*Cahiers d'Etudes Africaines*
C.M.S.	Church Missionary Society
C.O.	Colonial Office
C.P.	Confidential Print
D.D.F.	*Documents Diplomatiques français*
E.D., ix	*Études Dahoméennes*, ix (1953)
EHR	*English Historical Review*
Econ. H.R.	*Economic History Review*
F.O.	Foreign Office
G.I.L.B.	Government Interpreter's Letter Book (Sierra Leone National Archives)
IFAN	(*Bulletin de l'*) *Institut français [fondamentale] de l'Afrique noire*, Dakar
J.O.	*Journal Officiel*
JAH	*Journal of African History*
JHSN	*Journal of the Historical Society of Nigeria*
M.A.E.	Ministre des Affaires Etrangères
M.M.C.	Ministre de la Marine et des Colonies
P.P.	Parliamentary Papers
P.R.O.	Public Record Office, London
RFHOM	*Revue français d'histoire d'Outre-mer*
R.G.S.	Royal Geographical Society
Sal. P.	Salisbury Papers
S.L.S.	Sierra Leone Studies
S.S.E.C.	Sous-Secretaire d'Etat pour les Colonies
U.A.C.	United Africa Company
W.B.	*Weiss Buch*

I have given full reference to printed books on their first citation, and thereafter have generally used short titles. Where no place of publication is given, books in English are published in London and books in French in Paris.

Preface

This book seeks to make a modest and closely-defined contribution to a subject of great contemporary importance; to the understanding of those extremely complex relationships of inequality among peoples of the world which are commonly called 'imperialism'. The European occupation and territorial partition of Africa during the last two decades of the nineteenth century has always been recognised as an episode of central importance to this problem; some discussions indeed have assumed it to be virtually synonymous with the problem itself. Recently, it has become more usual to recognise that it *was* only an episode; the impact of European power on the lives of Africans did not begin when the Imperial flags were hoisted, and did not and could not end when they were hauled down. But the dramatically sudden transition to a period when white men exercised direct political control did have profound effects, not only on the Africans subjected, but on the societies of the colonisers themselves.

It is a historian's responsibility to study the detailed records left by such events: not without prejudices or moral preconceptions (for it is impossible), but without predetermined conclusions. Because he knows 'what happened next', a historian may feel he is merely recounting the unfolding of the inevitable; he still owes it to the men of whom he writes to remember that they too were moral agents, convinced that they had at least *some* freedom to decide their destinies. In writing this book – and, as is apparent from the title of my earlier volume, in describing the *Prelude to the Partition of West Africa* – I am of course aware of a coming climax in which technological sophistication would exercise a decisive influence. After all, Europeans had got the Maxim gun (or its predecessors); the Africans (though less defenceless than some accounts have implied) had not. But this did not mean that the form of partition or the modes of colonial rule were inevitable. If they were, the chain of causality which required this was extremely complex, incorporating the result of many choices made by Europeans and Africans in quite specific circumstances; in other words, full explanation of the logic of events demands a detailed historical narrative. Even if it is true (and I am not sure that the statement is particularly useful) that by 1885 European political control was already inevitable, was it 'inevitable' that Muslim ruling hierarchies would be destroyed in Segou and preserved in Sokoto? What great historic forces had pre-determined how the Wolof, the Ewe and the Kissi, would be divided amongst the empires of France, Britain and Germany, and the Black Republic of Liberia? These are not unimportant issues, for the Hausa and the Ewe at least. Men's decisions do shape history, though within narrower limits than they like to believe: historians need to understand how and why decisions were taken, as well as the often unintended results to which they led.

For such reasons, there are more details in this book than some whose primary interest is in constructing a general theory of imperialism may care to know. I know that history cannot be written without some theoretical assumptions, and I hope to clarify my own in a later volume of this work. I fully share the hope that deeper theoretical understanding might help our generation to control the intolerable inequalities which it has inherited. But some discussions of the theory of imperialism are a little short of concrete historical detail: there seems to me a need for studies which lean in the other direction, while working on a broader canvass than the normal research monograph.

The version of the partition of Africa which many of us learned as students began with monolithic European states – hardly more clearly delineated than contemporary caricatures of Britannia, Germania and Marianne – striding masterfully on to a Hegelian stage to take control of the destinies of what Keltie called 'the one barbarous continent'. Critics of imperialism sometimes inverted the moral qualities of the characters, but rarely managed to produce any substantially more subtle plot. Such myths of the past continue to poison relationships between Europeans and Africans today. During the last quarter-century historians in every conti-

nent have gradually been replacing this version by one more
faithful to the record, and so infinitely more complex – a process
painful at times, yet potentially therapeutic. The collective effect
of this work – apart from the lengthening of historical perspective
suggested earlier – has been to make even the best of the older
versions unrecognisable by penetrating the surface of events in
greater depth. There are three major directions in which I hope
this book may carry this process further.

Firstly, historians are achieving a more realistic view of what
forces – and what accidental circumstances – lay behind the decisions actually taken by those European monoliths. In the first
place, this involves close studies of the specific interests and aims
of merchants and missionaries active in West Africa before the
1880s, and of the channels through which they might succeed
in enlisting the support of politicians or bureaucrats; these in turn
need to be set in broad contexts of European economic, social and
political history. It is not too difficult to record deputations to
the Foreign Office, Parliamentary Questions, ponderous official
minutes; but to explain in what conditions such initiatives could
lead to decisive action by a European state may raise more complex issues. Most Europeans regarded Africa as a continent of
relatively small and peripheral interest; when governments did
act decisively there it might be because they had perceived some
possible relevance to central questions of the day. In the 1880s,
as more recently, Africa's misfortune may have been not so much
to receive the full impact of Europe malevolence as to be the
incidental victim of measures intended to solve problems which presented themselves to Europeans in some quite different context.

Yet only a partial account of the partition can be based upon
even the most thorough study of the European centres of decision.
A second result of recent researches has been on vastly enlarged
understanding of Afro–European relationships within African
environments. Since the seminal study of Sir Keith Hancock
applied the frontier concept to African history, it has been clear
that a history of European imperialism must incorporate the influence and experience of many diverse local situations. Even
apparently old-fashioned studies of the policies, personalities and
prejudices of individual Governors and Consuls are relevant to
the new historiography; in the short run at least, these could have
some derisive importance. But Governors' decisions were always

made in specific environments, where Europeans had been trading
with, or preaching to, Africans for years, or even centuries; the
goals and interests of the African participants require equally
careful study if the relationship is to be understood. If the immediate aims of Europeans were not everywhere the same, African
responses were even more diverse; the interaction between them
might set the initial pattern of colonial relationships in a particular
territory.

Yet studies of Afro–European relations take on a new significance when related to the much broader reinterpretation of
African historical development which has been successfully began
during the last quarter-century. The Eurocentric emphasis (which
the nature of the sources may still impose, even on African writers)
must eventually give way to much more rounded accounts.
Africans as well as Europeans took decisions which can only be
understood in the context of the whole historical development of
their societies. Behind the reassessment of particular encounters
lies a broader issue still: what difference did the imposition of
European rule make to the course of African history? This vast
question, which I raise explicitly but briefly in my introduction,
repeatedly challenges the historian who seeks to evaluate the
events which he records. But in the foreseeable future there is
unlikely to be a general consensus on the answer.

Although this book is a continuation of my earlier study, *Prelude
to the Partition of West Africa* (1963), it is designed to be read
quite independently by those who prefer to do so. In the first
chapter, which aims to set relationships between West Africa and
Europe at the time of the Berlin Conference of 1884–5 in a broad
historical context, I recapitulate some conclusions of this earlier
work and develop them in light of further studies. The next four
chapters (and parts of the sixth) describe the development of
this relationship in specific parts of West Africa during the next
five years. Sometimes, when events before 1884 were discussed
at length in *Prelude,* I have again referred interested readers back
to that book; in other cases it seemed necessary to give some attention to the earlier period here. The final chapter reviews the advances made by European powers during these years, despite
the absence of sustained or broad-based pressures for the establish-

ment of empire in Africa, and describes the measures they took to apportion their claims among themselves. This prepares for the discussion of more purposeful imperialist pressures, arising in France and Britain successively, which will provide the central themes of my second and third volumes.

An exhaustive re-examination of all the evidence now available which bears upon this subject is probably beyond the powers of one man. To achieve my self-imposed objectives I have been selective in my study of new sources, and it will be clear that in many chapters I am heavily indebted to distinguished colleagues and predecessors. In Chapter 2, for example, I have added little to the researches of Person, Kanya-Forstner and Saint-Martin, apart from a somewhat different context. A bibliographical essay in the final volume of this work will make explicit other obligations, at present acknowledged only in my footnotes.

Some debts cannot wait so long for acknowledgement. First must come the two universities which have provided me with facilities and encouragement during this work: the University of Aberdeen and (during the session 1970–1) the University of Ibadan. In particular their librarians, and their staff, have been unfailing in their assistance. I must also mention my deep gratitude to the Rockefeller Foundation, which not only helped to make my year in Ibadan possible, but gave me the privilege of spending a month in the Villa Serbelloni in order to produce a final version of my manuscript. Only friends who have read my earlier drafts will appreciate how much I owe to the Foundation, and to our hosts at Bellagio, Bill and Betsy Olson.

For facilities for research in their archives or libraries, I also offer sincere thanks to directors and staff of the *Archives Nationales, Section d'Outre-mer*, Paris (especially to Mademoiselle Marie-Antoinette Ménier); of the *Archives Etrangères*, Paris; the Public Record Office; the British Museum; the Sierra Leone National Archives (especially Mrs Gladys Jusu-Sheriff); the Library of the Royal Commonwealth Society (especially Donald Simpson); Lord Salisbury (for permission to consult the Salisbury Papers, and also Dr Mason for assistance in helping me to do so); and to the United Africa Company (whose Secretary, Mr J. D. Keir, kindly allowed me to use their archives and library).

Many colleagues and friends in many countries have helped me with advice, and stimulated me with their conversation. For hospitality and guidance in France I am particularly grateful to Denise Bouche, Marc Michel, Roger Pasquier and Yves Person. For the labour of reading and commenting helpfully on early drafts of parts or the whole of the manuscript, I owe special debts to Emmanuel Ayandele, Tony Hopkins, Tunji Oloruntimehin, Robert Smith, and especially to my friend and valued colleague, Roy Bridges. Among the others, I must especially mention the continued stimulus provided by my students in Ibadan and Aberdeen, both undergraduates and post-graduates; Adam Mboge and Nathan Senkomago may, I hope, soon render parts of this work obsolescent.

For typing my contorted drafts, I owe thanks to Mrs Ann Gordon, Mrs Christine Macleod, Mrs Edna Riddell, but above all Mrs Maureen Carr, who has struggled with the main part of this formidable task with unfailing cheerfulness, and always with eventual success.

I thank my daughter Sara for her care in producing the sketches from which the maps were produced, and my daughter Catherine, who conquered her distaste for historical studies and worked hard and accurately upon the index. My wife has as always contributed much in positive help and advice, and still more in continuing love and forbearance.

1 West Africa and Europe in 1885

NINETEENTH CENTURY RELATIONSHIPS

By the two final decades of the nineteenth century West Africa was changing increasingly rapidly, at least in those regions most easily accessible to the ocean, as influences from other continents interacted with forces already operating within African societies. An earlier study has attempted to detail some of these interactions within the period from 1860 to 1885.[1] It showed that, even though European governments long remained reluctant to undertake political responsibilities in tropical Africa, the activities of their agents and their citizens were in fact exercising increasingly strong influences upon certain African societies. Although colonial imperialism was generally out of favour, the 'informal imperialism' represented by the activities of merchants, missionaries and consuls continued to flourish. Many Africans – rulers, traders, and others – had fairly clear perceptions of this situation, and responded to the European presence with ingenuity, and often with considerable success.

West Africa however was playing a less important role in the international economy than some Europeans who had worked against the Atlantic slave trade expected. Disappointingly, few of the needs of a young industrial economy could be immediately satisfied from African resources. By any quantitative measurement, the European impact before 1880 was modest. There are serious methodological difficulties in measuring the share of trade with West Africa in Europe's foreign commerce, but precision in the decimal places is not too important when all the estimates place the proportion below 1 per cent. Africa's total exports were tending to increase. To the early sources of palm oil the 1840s

[1] John D. Hargreaves, *Prelude to the Partition of West Africa* (1963): cited as *Prelude*.

had added a growing trade in groundnuts; palm kernels were in increasing demand from the 1870s, and that decade also saw the first interest in African resources of wild rubber. A careful estimate of the total trade of those areas for which figures of some sort are available suggests a rise in annual value between 1850 and 1880 from about £3,500,000 to about £8,000,000: since prices of palm oil were falling, the rise in quantities exported was somewhat greater.[2] But the areas affected by trade were still limited; by 1880 the resources of Senegambia, southern Dahomey, parts of the Oil Rivers, were being quite intensively exploited, but elsewhere the frontiers of export-related commerce were expanding only slowly and gradually. In total value of trade, some developing seaports were still less important than inland markets like Kano and Kong, centres of distribution for African foodstuffs and craft products, and for imports arriving across the Saharan routes.[3]

Yet the social and political effects of maritime commerce were potentially great. Producing vegetable oils for export might involve important changes in land use and methods of cultivation, in the use of labour, in commercial organisation, and in the distribution of indigenous and imported wealth. Already the new economy had given opportunities to new types of African entrepreneur, and to Africans educated in Western missionary schools, to launch activities which were having quietly revolutionary effects on African society.

It is now a commonplace that economic change *will* have such effects; that it is part (probably the most important part) of a comprehensive, and essentially progressive, process of 'modernisation' which transforms institutions, attitudes, beliefs and behaviour over the whole field of social existence. The general tendency of this inexorable process is that men everywhere will come to behave more like citizens of the more highly industrialised societies of the north Atlantic area (placing greater reliance on attempts at rational prediction of future conditions, for example, and sub-

[2] C. W. Newbury, 'Trade and Authority in West Africa from 1850 to 1880' in L. H. Gann and P. Duignan (eds.) *Colonialism in Africa, 1870–1960*, Vol. I, *The History and Politics of Colonialism 1870–1914*, (Cambridge, 1969) pp. 76–80.

[3] Newbury, 'Trade and Authority . . .', pp. 66–73; and generally, C. Meillassoux (ed.) *The Development of Indigenous Trade and Markets in West Africa* (1970).

stituting impersonalised bureaucratic procedures for methods of government depending heavily on personal relationships). 'Traditional societies' (to simplify such theories) seek to regulate behaviour according to prescriptive rules, whereas 'modernisers' must innovate; they determine the status of individuals according to the social standing of their kin, whereas it is more 'modern' and efficient to reward achievement. Not all social scientists agree that the characteristics of 'modernity' are so easily defined in human reality, or that processes of change always involves that 'eurhythmic' uniformity which simple versions of the theory seem to imply; but 'modernised' societies always seem to preserve some fossils.[4] Historians often find the whole concept of 'modernisation' too culture-bound to be useful, and select from its voluminous literature only simple reminders that structural change in human societies is a complex process, where those who concentrate on solving simple problems always create new ones.

These are no recent discoveries. In the later eighteenth century, British Evangelicals eager to construct new societies in Africa clearly perceived that this would involve the interaction of many different elements in the social situation. The Sierra Leone Company, instituted to promote 'the establishment of a trade with Africa in the true principles of commerce', therefore wished to encourage cultivation, which in turn implied 'the civilisation of those among whom it is to be introduced. Hoping thus to influence their African neighbours they sent to their settlement instructions covering not merely the administration of justice and the conduct of government, but the introduction of coinage, the provision of schools, the promotion of Christian worship, the fostering of good race relations, and the regulation of a wide range of moral behaviour.[5] Half a century later, T. F. Buxton, seeking 'the deliverance of Africa by calling forth her own resources', likewise argued for a comprehensive campaign in which the British government would co-operate with private agencies to replace the slave trade by 'legitimate commerce' and improved agricultural methods; an essential part of his plan was to import such moral

---

[4] *Cf.* C. S. Whitaker, Jr., *The Politics of Tradition: Continuity and Change in Northern Nigeria, 1946–1966* (Princeton, 1970) pp. 3–15.

[5] Sierra Leone Company to Superintendent and Council, 1791; text in *SLS* xviii (1932).

and religious instruction as would 'elevate the Native Mind' to the level requisite for such activities.[6]

Though more confidently specific in their recommendations and more ethnocentric in their outlook than modern development planners, such men were equally aware that 'modernisation' was a complex process to be approached by differing methods. Hence, in many Victorian minds, Christianity, Civilisation and Commerce were not just three slogans sanctimoniously alliterated, but three facets of a single Providential power. The natural effects of that division of labour which healthy commerce always encouraged would be to civilise – that is, 'to instruct in the arts of life, and thus elevate in the scale of humanity';[7] Christianity, besides providing the spiritual foundation essential to a truly civilised society, would itself stimulate tastes and needs conducive to its further development. Unlike some of their later apologists, few eminent Victorians would have denied that the mainspring of their new activities overseas was provided by economic growth at home. One of the most eminent had already asked the rhetorical question, 'Can mankind fulfil its destiny without a fundamental revolution in the social state of Asia?';[8] applied to Africa, the question, it seemed, could only be answered in the negative. Whether industrial capitalism was regarded as a Providential dispensation, or simply as an unsavoury product of inexorable laws of historical progress, it was widely accepted as a necessary force for economic development and social improvement, which would in God's good time (or History's) transform Africa as it was already transforming Europe.

Whether these characteristically mid-Victorian attitudes can justly be described as 'Imperialistic' is the sort of question which easily lends itself to sterile semantic wrangles. Although state power rarely featured prominently in contemporary prospectuses for economic development, and frugally-minded ministers frequently disclaimed the intention of using it, it remained an ever-present resource which could always be called upon to protect jeopardised European interests. Recent debates among British historians about the so-called 'imperialism of free trade', though

---

[6] T. F. Buxton, *The African Slave Trade and its Remedy* (1840) pp. 518–22.
[7] Johnson's Dictionary, 1866.
[8] Karl Marx, 'The British Rule in India' (1853) in K. Marx and F. Engels, *On Colonialism* (Moscow, n.d.) p. 37.

sometimes tediously pedantic, have at least diverted attention away from general protestations of political intent towards more precise studies of how and in what conditions European governments were in practice prepared to exercise their power. Given sufficient cause or provocation their principles rarely inhibited them from approving acts of naval, military or political intervention to safeguard what they regarded as jeopardised 'national interests' – nor, usually, did their 'anti-imperialist', free-trading, critics suggest that it was inherently wrong to use power in this way. But serious cause did usually need to be shown before British Ministers, at least would willingly depart from accustomed attitudes of masterly inactivity.

THE COURSE OF WEST AFRICAN DEVELOPMENT

The century preceding the Berlin Conference of 1884 was therefore a period when, except in certain localities where Europeans had chosen to try to exercise their power directly, African communities retained considerable freedom for independent development. And developments of considerable political and social significance did take place in many parts of Africa; some in response to the new external influences, others representing the working out of Africa's own history. Taking a continental view, it is not easy to establish verifiable connections between the population movements in southern Africa triggered by the *mfecane,* the expansion of Egypt and Zanzibar, the Muslim revolutions of the Western Sudan, the growth of strong kingdoms in Madagascar and around the great lakes of Eastern Africa, the rise of new commercial complexes on the west African coast. Yet it seems to some observers that most of these movements were in the same general direction, towards 'the growth of a unified and highly centralized state with an absolute monarch unrestricted in his power by any freely elected council'.[9] To others, the most striking effect was the re-structuring of the continental state-system; 'expanding aggressive states', it is said, were effecting a sort of African partition of Africa.[10] Others again are impressed by the flexible

[9] Ivan Hrbek in T. O. Ranger (ed.) *Emerging Themes of African History* (Nairobi, 1968) pp. 47–8.

[10] Christopher Fyfe in Seminar Proceedings, University of Edinburgh Centre of African Studies, *The Theory of Imperialism and the European Partition of Africa* (November, 1967) p. 1.

responses of Africans challenged by European culture and commerce, and by the emerging possibilities for economic growth. Professor Brunschwig believes that Africa was *en voie d'occidentalisation,* just as the Evangelicals had hoped; its new leaders, like Samori or Tippoo Tib, were essentially modernisers (if not designed to Evangelical specifications) who were becoming 'grave diggers of traditional Negro cultures.'[11] Societ scholars describe the changes through their own historical categories, according to which the process of 'overcoming tribal and feudal divisions and the establishment of large centralised states'[12] prepares for the emergence of capitalist methods of production and the ultimate fulfilment of that 'destiny' which Marx had foreseen.

Because the changes which had been induced in African societies had nowhere approached any sort of culmination before the European conquest, it is difficult to say where they were leading. The emergence of larger political units would not in itself imply fundamental social and economic changes nor encourage the growth of any form of autochthonous or autonomous African capitalism. Writers like Mr. Guy Hunter question whether essential conditions for the growth of a modern economy – market exchanges based on division of labour, 'new men' accumulating surpluses to invest for the future, general readiness to reject restrictive sanctions imposed by traditional authority – were anywhere being achieved to the formidable degree necessary for economic 'take-off.'[13] But it is as difficult to speak confidently on the negative as on the positive side: Hunter (whose main African experience has been in the East) seems to under-estimate the extent to which the new commercial economy had allowed Africans well-placed to respond to the European presence to begin to accumulate capital and to adopt the more 'modern' type of outlook associated with the growth of capitalist societies in Western Europe.

This could be seen most clearly in and around existing European settlements, where African entrepreneurs could serve apprenticeships within the new type of commercial economy, and where laws and institutions were designed to assist modern types of economic activity. Since, for much of the nineteenth century,

---

[11] Henri Brunschwig, *L'Avènement d'Afrique Noire* (1964) pp. 176–9.
[12] Ivan Potekhin, *African Problems* (Moscow, 1968) pp. 96–7.
[13] Guy Hunter, *The Best of Both Worlds* (1967) Chap. 1.

there was no great rush of European capital into the African produce trade, there were opportunities for African or mulatto families to enter the market with quite modest amounts of capital; and colonial governments would seek, in general, to encourage their contributions to the spread of Commerce, Civilisation and Christianity. At the end of the century, when something under eight hundred registered *commercants* paid tax in Senegal, at least five hundred of these were Senegalese.[14] On the Gold Coast established trading families (sometimes tracing descent from European as well as African ancestors) established firm bases in the coastal forts, and exercised considerable influence over British colonial policy.[15] On the Sierra Leone peninsula, the society formed by African repatriates from the New World and from intercepted slave ships blended Victorian bourgeois values with elements of several African cultures into a new sort of African society with distinctly capitalistic orientations.[16]

The influence of these communities extended far beyond their deliberately-restricted colonial boundaries. Sierra Leoneans in particular found inadequate outlets for their energies in their own hilly homeland; by the 1870s the Sherbro region was being opened up as 'a kind of Australia'.[17] Though their main activity was to purchase natural palm fruit and rubber gathered by local people, a few, like S. B. Macfoy established plantations where new crops were introduced, and cultivated by Sherbro labour.[18] But Sierra Leonean influence was also powerfully felt in distant areas, from which the recaptives had originally been taken. Henry Robbin, born in Sierra Leone in 1835 and trained in Manchester in the processing of raw cotton under the auspices of the Church Missionary Society, returned in 1857 to manage their cotton enterprises in Abeokuta (probably his ancestral home). Financed by J. P. L. Davies, another Sierra Leonean trading in Lagos, Robbin remained in Abeokuta until 1885, active in the commercial, re-

---

[14] Samir Amin, 'La politique coloniale française à l'égard de la bourgeoisie commercante sénégalaise, 1820–1960' in Meillassoux, *Development of Indigenous Trade* . . .

[15] See, for example, Margaret Priestley, *West African Trade and Coast Society* (1969).

[16] See, John Peterson, *Province of Freedom* (1969); and for ample illustrative examples, C. H. Fyfe, *A History of Sierra Leone* (1962).

[17] C.O. 879/8, C.P. African 82, p. 34, Notes by Darnell Davis (1875).

[18] Fyfe, *History*, pp. 441, 490, 506.

ligious and political life of the Egba state.[19] A younger Sierra
Leonean repatriate, C. B. Moore, who became Treasurer of the
Egba United Government, was said by a contemporary to have
'wielded a powerful influence, second to none, throughout the
length and breadth of the land.'[20] Such individual success stories
were multiplied many times.

The arrival or return of enterprising individuals did not of
course necessarily directly affect indigenous values or behaviour:
Yoruba attitudes towards these returning 'Saro' were complex
and variable. But in general there is no doubt that their presence
stimulated commercial development and innovation. A striking
example of Yoruba response is provided by Daniel Conrad Taiwo,
born at Isheri on the Ogun river, who achieved a dominant position in the trade and politics of Lagos during the second half of
the nineteenth century. Taiwo's commercial opportunities came
through collaboration with the German entrepreneur, G. L.
Gaiser, in opening up trade in palm produce with Egba country;
his political standing came in part from his rise to leadership in
that section of the Lagosian traditional élite associated with the
deposed ruler Kosoko, in part from his employment by Glover
and other governors as an intermediary in dealings within Yoruba
country. Taiwo became the *baba isale* (or resident agent in Lagos)
of his native town, and was able to develop it into an important
market centre for the Lagos trade with Egbaland.[21] Glover's attack
on the Egbas at Ikorudu in 1865 is said to have been instigated by
Taiwo, and it was after this attack that Isheri's independent prosperity began;[22] yet Taiwo maintained amicable correspondence
and business relations with Abeokuta through his brother Sorunke,
Jaguna of Igbein and one of the four leading chiefs of the city.[23]

[19] Jean H. Kopytoff, *A Preface to Modern Nigeria: The Sierra Leonians in
Yoruba* (Madison, 1965) esp. pp. 297–8.

[20] Adeoye Deniga, *African Leaders, Past and Present* (Lagos 1915) II,
pp. 14–15.

[21] See P. Cole 'Modern and Traditional Elites in the Politics of Lagos'
(Ph.D. thesis,) Cambridge, 1970).

[22] 'Kunle Akinsemoyin, 'Taiwo Olowo', *Daily Times* (Lagos) 20 February
1971 – a memorial supplement sponsored by Taiwo's descendants.
Taiwo's interests and influence are not mentioned by Earl Phillips, 'The
Egba at Ikorodu, 1865: Perfidious Lagos?', *African Historical Studies*, III, 1970.

[23] C.O.879/27, C.P. African 345, No. 134, encl. Sorunke to Taiwo, 10
May 1888; C.O.879/28, C.P. African 355, Moloney to Knutsford 234, 31
July 1888.

He remained resident in Lagos until his death in 1901, extending his commercial contacts throughout Yorubaland and beyond. (During the Ekitiparapo war, for example, he supplied Snider rifles to Ibadan, at a high price.) While Taiwo gained respectability within colonial society as a patron of the C.M.S. and supporter of community petitions, his influence extended into such frontier regions as Porto Novo, and possibly Nupe.[24]

Equally impressive cases of Africans responding to new commercial opportunities within the institutional framework of traditional societies can be found in the Oil Rivers, where the expanding demands of Europe led to a continuing redeployment of labour into the gathering of palm produce. There are now many studies of the complex processes of social change within these decentralised and in many ways democratic societies, and all emphasise the degree of social mobility which could be achieved by able entrepreneurs, even if of servile origin.[25] Most attention tends to be focused on men like Jaja who achieved political eminence, but many successful business careers are also recorded in the historical notes compiled by a local historian of Bonny in the mid-twentieth century. One interesting example is Squiss Atobobara Banigo, who in 1869 became head of one of the 'houses' which were the basic social units of this important trading state.[26] Although nominated by his predecessor on account of personal qualities, Squiss was opposed by elders of the house who claimed that they should have been consulted; at this period of Bonny history innovators were often at war with traditionalists. From 1869 to 1873 and 1879 to 1883 we are told that the new head was 'actually in charge of a company of warriors'. But eventually it was his success in the commercial sector which secured his

[24] Akinsemoyin, loc. cit.: S.A. Akintoye, *Revolution and Power Politics in Yorubaland 1840–1893* (1971) pp. 130–1; K. Folayan 'Egbado and Yoruba . . .' (M.A. thesis, Ibadan University, 1967): Kopytoff, *A Preface to Modern Nigeria*, p. 365, N. 87.

[25] E.g. A. J. H. Latham, *Old Calabar, 1600–1891* (Oxford, 1973).

[26] Adadonye Fombo, J.P. *Short Outline History of Bonny.* Typescript deposited in Ibadan University Library (with manuscript emendations up to 1964). Fombo defines a 'house' in Bonny as a collection of different families'; a 'principal house' as one controlling sufficient wealth to man two war canoes and 'satisfactorily participate in any tribal war', numbering 1000 to 5600 members. For a history of the houses of Bonny, see G. I. Jones, *Trading States of the Oil Rivers* (1963) pp. 51–7, 105–32.

standing: Squiss 'enlarged the house in manpower and wealth', built it a new headquarters, 'planted many assorted economic plants and created large reserved fund [sic] for the house'. Squiss survived until 1924 but in 1903 he handed over to his son Walter Finapiri, whose education in England culminated with three years' study of botany. He too 'was responsible for many assorted economic plants planted on the family lands', notably rubber.[27] Walter, of course, reaped his profits under colonial rule; but it seems doubtful how far the colonial administration can claim direct credit for innovating enterprises of the Banigo house.

But how much impact could such 'new men' make upon the fabric of their own societies? How many innovating capitalists are needed to create a modernising capitalism? Against the view that a process of self-modernisation was brutally cut short by colonial conquest, it is argued that established codes of values and patterns of behaviour still worked powerfully in quite different directions. The general argument is inconclusive; for cultural attitudes can be modified, and few 'modernised' societies ever free themselves wholly from their past. Africans did (and do) employ accumulated surpluses in 'cementing social relations for political ends',[28] but such practices were (and are) also common among their European contemporaries. In a negative sense however it may be possible to identify societies – Benin, whose early commercial development was not sustained, may be an example[29] – where the weight of traditional authority deliberately or unconsciously stifled growth. And even in Bonny itself, a more famous entrepreneur, Jaja, had in 1869 found it necessary to separate himself from the old order and found the new trading-state of Opobo.[30]

Possibly more convincing is the argument of scale. The expansion of trade was everywhere financed by credit; large-scale expansion would involve amounts of capital which could only be provided from Europe; and African debts to Europeans involved

[27] Fombo, op. cit. f. 113–14. In the accompanying albums of photographs Chief Squiss appears in Vol. i, p. 26 (posed like a minor self-made Victorian businessman) and Chief Walter on p. 53.

[28] Newbury, 'Trade and Authority . . .', p. 75.

[29] Cf. A. F. Ryder, *Benin and the Europeans, 1485–1897* (1969).

[30] Cf. K. O. Dike, *Trade and Politics in the Niger Delta* (Oxford, 1956) Chap. 10; cf. below pp. 112–3.

increasing risks of European political intervention. In retrospect, it may seem unlikely that 'new men' like Squiss and Taiwo, or African entrepreneurs working within colonial societies like Saint-Louis and Lagos, could ever have generated sufficient capital from the produce trade to free themselves from dependence on Europeans for credit, shipping space, and generally for access to international markets.[31] Under the colonial systems which did develop, African capitalists were to be largely squeezed out, or reduced to dependence upon more highly capitalised foreign firms – and during the 1880s this process was already beginning within the private empire of the Royal Niger Company. But in general the disproportion between the capital resources of European and African merchants still seemed neither extreme nor obvious.

As to the necessary effects of produce trade upon African societies, there is room for endless disagreement. Dr. Newbury, while emphasising the rapid growth of exports of West African produce, tends to see it as essentially an extension of old-established internal trading networks which had long operated within African societies without transforming them; Madame Coquery on the other hand sees in Dahomey (a state whose traditional structures seemed little affected) the gradual rise of a new group of trading nobles. Others, like Dr. Meillassoux, regard the Atlantic trade as more 'predatory' than intra-African commerce, being based on the gathering of wild produce rather than on cultivation; thus the closing of trans-atlantic markets for slaves involved little social change, beyond the redeployment of slave labour for the role of commodity to that of gatherer.[32] Professor Ralph Austen has independently developed the argument that the nineteenth century saw little more than the growth of a small-scale client capitalism on the exterior of the 'archaic trading state'. 'The commodities exported by West Africa to Europe . . . were procured outside the system of agriculture, animal husbandry and handicrafts which constituted the core of the internal African economy,' he argues; 'revolutionary changes in the structure of West African trading

[31] On this point, see A. G. Hopkins 'An Economic History of Lagos, 1880–1914' (Ph.D. thesis, University of London, 1964); also S. Amin, 'La politique coloniale francaise . . .'. On credit generally, see C. W. Newbury, 'Credit in early nineteenth century West African Trade', *J. A. H.* XIII (1972) pp. 81–95.

[32] Meillassoux, 'Development of Indigenous Trade . . .'; on Dahomey, see below pp. 141–3.

states came therefore only with the imposition of full military and civilian colonial subjugation.'[33]

It is difficult and dangerous to generalise about a sub-continent; Austen's argument fails to recognise that in Senegambia and Guinea the growth of trade was essentially in groundnuts. Since these must be planted and cultivated annually, European demands could be satisfied only by changes in land use and in social relations, which potentially at least did have revolutionary effects. The history of the Senegalese state of Cayor provides a striking example of an African ruler trying to control a process of selective modernisation, so as to draw the maximum benefit from the new commerce without relaxing the essentials of his sovereignty. During the 1860s Lat-Dior, pretender to the royal office of *damel,* had faced defeat by rival claimants backed by French armies; (for under Faidherbe the colonial government of Senegal was, exceptionally, prepared to intervene militarily against its African neighbours). Lat-Dior however established his position within Cayor by declaring his conversion to Islam, allying with Maba (the charismatic leader of *jihad* in the Gambia valley), and aligning himself against the rapacious warrior nobility known as *tiedo* both with the *marabouts* and with the ordinary farmers who wanted security and protection in the occupation of new land. This Muslim variant of the 'New African Policy' commanded sufficient Wolof support to enable Lat-Dior to establish his position on the basis of an expanding agricultural economy; as groundnuts poured into colonial ports the French, temporarily disenchanted with African campaigns, found him a desirable collaborator, both commercially and politically. In 1871 Governor Valière recognised him as *damel,* and a decade of mutually advantageous, though uneasy, collaboration followed; temporarily, a new export-based economy seemed capable of satisfying French expectations without inciting new interventions.[34]

In Cayor, the frontiers of oceanic commerce overlapped the frontier of Islam, and there seemed to be some possibility of synthesis. But many West African Muslim societies seemed more likely to follow a different course of historical development. A belt

[33] R. A. Austen, 'The Abolition of the Overseas Slave Trade; A Distorted Theme in West African History', *JHSN*, v (1970) pp. 269, 267.

[34] V. Monteil, *Esquisses Sénégalaises* (Dakor, 1966) Chap. 2, 'Lat-Dior, damel du Kayor (1842–86) et l'islamisation des Wolofs'.

of Islamic states stretched across the savannas from Senegal to Bornu – divided by political conflicts and by divergent traditions, yet connected by the circulation of scholars, traders and pilgrims who professed a common faith; in most of these, innovations to meet the needs of commerce were still subordinated to the maintenance of the Muslim religion and of its laws and customs. Over much of the region external relations were largely directed northwards, across the desert; Europeans were at most occasional visitors from afar until the last two decades of the century. Outsiders sometimes asserted that such great Islamic states as Sokoto and Bornu were declining in power; this can now be seen to be dubious, but their central authorities did remain preoccupied with problems of maintaining internal administrative cohesion, and of relations with their immediate neighbours. While opportunities to extend foreign commerce, under proper safeguards, were always welcomed, there were no strong forces working internally to transform their rather conservative, legalistic structures.[35]

In the western quarter of this great Islamic region – in Senegambia, Futa Jalon, the Tokolor empire and the Mande region to its south – oceanic influences were being more strongly felt. But rarely did they produce such drastic social changes as in Cayor; a more common response of Muslim rulers was to tolerate Europeans under close supervision and regulation – forbidding them, for example, to build erections of stone, which experience showed might easily be turned from factories to forts. A famous letter to Governor Protet from the Tokolor state builder Al Haj 'Umar prescribed a status for Europeans as *dhimmis* or tolerated aliens within a Muslim state:

The whites are only traders; let them bring merchandise in their ships, let them pay me a good tribute when I'm Master of the Negroes, and I will live in peace with them. But I don't wish them to expect permanent establishments or send warships into the river.[36]

[35] On Sokoto, R. A. Adeleye, *Power and Diplomacy in Northern Nigeria 1804–1906* (1971) Part i; M. Last, *The Sokoto Caliphate* (1967); See below pp. 100–3. On Bornu, L. Brenner, *The Shehus of Kukawa* (Oxford 1973).

[36] Quoted P. Cultru, *Histoire du Sénégal* (1910) p. 337; cf. M. A. Klein, *Islam and Imperialism in Senegal: Sine-Saloum 1847–1914* (Edinburgh, 1968) p. 123 and *passim*.

When this letter was written in 1854, 'Umar's new state seemed militarily strong enough to afford such a hard line towards Europeans; unfortunately he had been confronted by a French governor more strongly determined to exercise sovereignty in Africa than any of his contemporaries. Faidherbe found it unacceptable that French citizens should be bound to observe all the rules laid down by their African neighbours; although his military campaigns did not destroy 'Umar's power they did divert it away from the Senegal valley, demonstrating more clearly than ever before that Europeans might not be indefinitely content to promote the peaceful radiation of Christian civilisation by trading along the waterfront.[37] But Faidherbe was an exception in his time; Valière, his successor during the years 1869–76, resumed a more characteristic policy of interfering only intermittently in African states, and there were no new forts in Senegambia until the late 1870s. Under 'Umar's son Ahmadu the Tokolor empire, though greatly weakened by resistance movements among the conquered peoples and by opposition to Ahmadu's authority from other sons and disciples of the founder, was able to survive, making its own cautious attempts to utilise some of the technical resources brought to Africa by Europeans.[38]

Meanwhile a different type of Muslim state was facing the same problem, of what contacts with the European world might safely be accepted or encouraged. The Mandinka empire of Samori was in part the recent creation of a military commander of genius: but it was also, in the phrase of Professor Person, the culmination of a series of '*dyula* revolutions'. Its social foundations went deeply into this trading community, who had long provided bonds of unity through the Mande-speaking regions of the western Sudan; as Person puts it, they were 'sufficiently in contact with the outside world to know how to resist it, but close enough to animist society to work for its salvation and not its destruction'.[39] They could see that the changed pattern of commerce produced by the shift in

---

[37] Cf. *Prelude*, pp. 97–103; for a slightly different interpretation see A. S. Kanya-Forstner, *The Conquest of the Western Sudan: A Study in French Military Imperialism* (Cambridge, 1969) p. 28–44.

[38] The fullest account is B. O. Oloruntimehin, *The Segu Tukulor Empire* (1972); cf. John D. Hargreaves, 'The Tokolor Empire of Segou and its Relations with the French', *Boston University Papers on Africa*, II (1966).

[39] Y. Person, in H. Brunschwig (ed.) *Histoire Générale de l'Afrique Noire*, II, pp. 109–11.

European interest from slaves to produce and by the development of new ports on the Atlantic coast, and the stimulus to the long-established Islam of the *dyulas* provided by the Fulani *jihads*, together required the creation of new political structures.

Samori, a clear-sighted leader who knew the world of the *dyula* from long apprenticeship, combined perception of this need with outstanding organising powers and military skill. About 1861 he and six comrades took an oath together in a village of the upper Milo;[40] twenty years later Samori controlled an empire of 80,000 square kilometres and some 300,000 subjects, including the gold-bearing province of Bouré. From this base he was extending his commercial contacts with the Atlantic coast in order to build up the resources of a powerful and effective military administration.[41] Yet to this time all Samori's contacts with Europeans had been indirect; their trading factories were useful but remote sources of military supplies. No white man had yet appeared in his empire or posed any threat to its independence. During the 1870s it still seemed possible for most African states to draw upon the technical resources of Europe without exposing themselves to imminent domination by European power; Samori, like others, sought to use the opportunity to create a new political structure, capable of utilising wealth accumulated by trade in the pursuit of independently determined goals. There still seemed plenty of scope for such experiments.

NEW EUROPEAN INTERESTS AND ATTITUDES

During the later 1870s, however, Europeans of a somewhat different type, with different attitudes and more ambitious programmes, began to appear in West Africa. Though not numerous, nor clearly representative of the dominant elements of their own societies, their behaviour was frequently sufficiently purposeful and vigorous to upset existing balances in Afro-European relations. It is tempting to regard these new 'frontiersmen' as heralds of a new imperialism, directed towards Africa by some common force within the nation-states of western Europe; but observation of the men involved does not immediately suggest what that common force might be. The new arrivals were a strangely assorted

[40] Y. Person, *Samori: une Revolution Dyula*, I (Dakar, 1968) pp. 273–4.
[41] ibid, p. 346.

lot; they included merchant adventurers, showing greater enterprise than their immediate predecessors, and backed by somewhat
greater capital; missionaries with a more imperious sense of
mission; in the Senegal, railway engineers and soldiers; in the
Congo, well-armed travellers, serving a king who combined keen
capitalist acumen with romantic fantasies about African rivers.
Possibly their only common feature was their use of modern
technologies; and even these were not very recent discoveries. The
steamship, with which some merchants began to modernise their
trading techniques, had been available since the 1820s, and actually used on scheduled services to West Africa since 1852; quinine
had been used as a prophylactic to facilitate European penetration
of the interior since Baikie's voyage of 1854; projects for developing new regions by railway construction had been materialising
in other continents since the 1850s. It is not easy to see a common
motive force behind the new initiatives of the 1870s.

Some grandiose projects for applying technology to African
development were clearly stimulated by two great engineering
achievements of 1869 – the commencement of the Union Pacific
railway and the opening of the Suez Canal. Lesser Lesseps now
proliferated. A French engineer officer called Roudaire proposed
to inundate the Sahara by cutting a canal from the Gulf of Gabes;
an eloquent Scot called Donald MacKenzie based a similar project in the neighbourhood of Cape Juby (where it quickly dwindled
into a more mundane trading project, almost equally abortive).[42]
Big railway developments were freely canvassed during the 1870s
by Chambers of Commerce and Geographical Societies. In particular, patriotic Frenchmen contemplating continental maps
during this decade of defeat were widely attracted by the idea of a
trans-saharan railway, as a means of connecting the Algerian
settlements with Sudanic regions, where it was assumed that there
must exist 'numerous populations, a fertile soil, and undeveloped
natural riches'.[43] Such visionary schemes, planned by railway en-

[42] Henri Brunschwig, 'Notes sur les technocrates de l'impérialisme
française en Afrique noire', *RFHOM*, LIV (1967); F. V. Parsons, 'The
North-West African Company and the British Government, 1875–95',
Historical Journal, I (1958) pp. 136–9.
[43] Report of Preliminary commission on a Trans-Saharan Railway,
12 June 1879, quoted in Ministère de la Marine et des Colonies, *La
France dans l'Afrique Occidentale, 1879–83* (1884) p.8.

thusiasts with premature and ill-informed attention to details, eventually merged into even bolder and less realistic schemes for transcontinental networks.

It is clear that these essays into science fiction did not represent any search by European capitalists for new fields of profitable investment; they were the work of technocrats using eloquent contemporary idioms to call up the capital they lacked. Professor Shepperson has perceptively pointed out how these essays in the poetry of technology had in 1867 been quite precisely anticipated by Ibsen's Peer Gynt:

> ... It wants but a gap, a canal –
> Like a flood of life would the waters rush
> In through the channel and fill the desert ...
> The southland, behind the Sahara's wall
> Would make a new seaboard for civilisation.
> Steam would set Timbuctoo's factories spinning;
> Bornu would be colonized apace.
> The explorer would pass safely through Habes
> In his railway car to the Upper Nile ...
> Skirting a bay, on a shelving strand
> I'd build the chief city, Peeropolis.
> The world is decrepit! Now comes the turn
> Of Gyntiana, my virgin land.[44]

But only two historical Peer Gynts were able to command sufficient funds to realise their fantasies and found eponymous empires: Leopold of the Belgians, who by virtue of royalty had opportunities for raising capital not available to lesser visionaries, and Cecil Rhodes, whose capital (like his Imperial vision) was generated on the mining frontier of South Africa rather than in the heart of industrial Europe.

Those who actually engaged in business on the West African coast had to set their sights more realistically; but some such men too began during the 1870s, not only to expand their horizons, but to take practical steps towards them. The most celebrated of these, George Goldie, had (or acquired) some of Peer Gynt's visionary megalomania; and Goldesia might have been the eventual name

---

[44] H. Ibsen, *Peer Gynt*, Trans. W. and C. Archer (1907) Act IV, Scene v. Another translation is quoted in G. A. Shepperson, 'Africa, the Victorians and Imperialism', *Revue Belge de Philologie et d'Histoire*, XL (1962) p. 123.

of the province he had dreamed of adding to the British Empire. But Goldie's initial achievement was the more modest one of amalgamating small competing trading houses into a company with a nominal capital of one million pounds, and sufficient respectability to acquire a Royal charter; the process of empire building was conducted with hard headed caution and consisted at first simply in the extension and re-organisation of trading factories.[45] The role of Empire-builder was one which grew on him with practice.

In France, Goldie's nearest equivalent was the Marseille merchant C. A. Verminck, for a time his direct rival on the Niger. Verminck, who first went to West Africa in 1844 at the age of seventeen, began in the 1870s to buy out competitors in the Guinea rivers and to broaden his interests in many directions; he began to convert his sailing ships to steam, acquired oil mills in Marseille, sent a substantial expedition to explore the sources of the Niger in 1879, and in 1882 began to trade in the lower Niger also, drawing Sierra Leonean traders into collaboration by liberal provision of credit. In 1881 Verminck transferred his African interests to a new *Compagnie du Sénégal et de la Côte Occidentale de l'Afrique,* which later became the mighty *Compagnie française de l'Afrique occidentale.* He also found an influental patron in Maurice Rouvier, the rising Deputy for Marseille, who in 1881–2 served as Gambetta's Minister of Commerce and Colonies.[46]

In the new German empire, the political defence of West African interests was assumed by the family which had pioneered trade there since 1849. After the death of old Carl Woermann in 1880, his son Adolph, who assumed direction of a growing steamship company and of prosperous trading factories in Liberia, Gabon and Cameroon, became increasingly active in Hamburg's Chamber of Commerce. Germany's industrial expansion was now making available for export increasing quantities of cheap gin, and at the same time developing new uses for palm produce, in margarine manufacture for example. New trading houses, some

[45] John E. Flint, *Sir George Goldie and the Making of Nigeria* (1960); cf. *Prelude*, pp. 272–8, and below pp. 97ff.

[46] P. Masson (ed.) *Les Bouches du Rhône: Encyclopédie Départmentale,* VIII (1962) p. 184, IX (1922) pp. 265ff, 398f. Further details on Verminck may be found in *Prelude* (see index).

founded by former agents of Woermann, opened up.[47] The enterprising and successful merchant G. L. Gaiser, after pioneering the
trade in palm kernels at Lagos, Porto Novo, and neighbouring
ports, extended his interest to include oil mills in nearby Harburg.[48]
Adolph Woermann first spoke for the group politically. It was his
initiative which culminated in the establishment of German control over the Cameroons; in 1884 he was elected to the Reichstag
as a National Liberal, and for a time advised Bismarck on African
policy.[49]

But Woermann remained a free-trader, with an instinctive mis-
trust of the German Imperial bureaucracy; it would be mislead-
ing to regard him as a typical figure of any new phase of North
German capitalism, or as a man whose political importance
equals that of a younger Hamburg shipping magnate, Albert
Ballin.[50] The Woermanns, like Verminck and his fellow townsmen,
Cyprien Fabre, or the honest Liverpool Liberal, John Holt, were
essentially old-style provincial merchants who had made good in
West Africa within the old free-trading system, rather than new
types of capitalist whose interests demanded new political structures. If to reinforce commercial success they now called on their
governments for selective political initiatives, this need arose from
the dialectic of Afro-European relations, rather than from any
structural crisis of European capitalism, or any radically new
development of its manifestations in West Africa.

What was new, perhaps, was that the political climate in
European states increasingly allowed such modest merchants (as
well as more forceful adventurers like Rhodes and Goldie) to
enlist government support for their local interests. Whenever one
such merchant succeeded, his foreign rivals were naturally encouraged to redouble pressure upon their own governments. His
African collaborators in turn might need to react sharply in defence

---

[47] *Prelude*, pp. 316–23; cf. 'Die Woermann'sche Schule', *Deutscher
Kolonialzeitung*, II (1885) pp. 14–17.

[48] Ernst Hieke, *G. L. Gaiser: Hamburg Westafrika* (Hamburg, 1944) pp.
34–45.

[49] H. P. Jaeck, 'Die Deutsche Annexion' in H. Stoecker (ed.) *Kamerun
unter deutscher Kolonialherrschaft* I (E. Berlin, 1960).

[50] G. Jantzen, 'Adolph Woermann' in O. Brunner and D. Gerhard,
Europa und Übersee (Hamburg, 1961) pp. 171–96.

of their independence of action; and so local crises deepened. Few
of the new European 'frontiersmen' were powerful, or indeed ambitious, enough to become the architects of new policies; the
demands which they pressed on their influential friends in government were relatively modest ones, controlled by realistic appreciations of short-term market possibilities, and of the limited degree
of governmental support that was likely to be available. Yet, in
many places, these demands did become the effective trigger
which eventually released European invasions. To understand how
the 'new frontiersmen' became the vanguard of the 'new imperialism' requires careful and complex analysis, embracing both the
broad conditions of contemporary European society and politics,
and the detailed reactions of the African communities whose
development was affected by their demands.

THE ELEMENTS OF THE 'NEW IMPERIALISM'
The oldest and simplest model of economic imperialism emphasises
the direct intervention of interested parties. Before intellectuals
like Hobson, Kautsky, Luxembourg and Lenin had defined the
problems and proposed their analyses, radical politicians and
journalists had already discerned, behind the French invasion of
Tunis or the British occupation of Egypt, the malign influence of
predatory special interests with secret access to the bases of power
– of *les affaires*. But simple conspiracy theories are no longer
accepted as adequate for northern or southern Africa; applied to
tropical Africa they are manifestly implausible. The interests of
'new frontiersmen' like Goldie, Verminck and Woermann were
minor and marginal in relation to the commanding heights of
their countries' wealth. Although – depending on the contingencies of domestic politics – they might be able to *influence* their
governments, nowhere in Europe could merchants, even more
powerful ones than these, aspire to *control* policy and turn it in
an imperialistic direction. The longer historians work on public
archives, the more confirmation they find of this. Dr D. C. M.
Platt, having carefully studied the ways in which economic interests pressed their needs upon British governments, concludes
that throughout the nineteenth century these governments, influenced 'both by their aristocratic tastes and prejudices, and by
the *laissez-faire*, Free Trade, tradition of political economy', sought

to restrict their responses within carefully-defined general limits.[51] In French and German society it was sometimes a little easier for merchants to establish close relations with junior officials who could assist their interests, and there were some possibilities of exercising influence higher up. The political structure of the Third Republic sometimes provided provincial merchants and Chambers of Commerce with means of persuading local Deputies to protect their interests;[52] and even Bismarck might find it expedient to satisfy the wishes of men like Adolph Woermann. But this is not to imply control: nobody knew this better than the often-frustrated merchants. The state where the capitalist *bourgeoisie* exercised power most directly was almost certainly Belgium; but here they used it not to advance but to frustrate the premature imperialism of Leopold II.

Why then *did* government policies change? Messrs Robinson and Gallagher, finding old economic models inadequate to explain the evidence of the archives, have proposed a sort of anti-theory. They claim to have located the secret of British expansion exactly where they looked for it – in the 'files and red boxes' produced by government departments. Action in Africa was determined by 'a complex political arithmetic', reflecting the operation of what they call 'the official mind'; the processes of political decision in which this complicated intelligence engaged, they suggest, may itself have been one of 'the objective causes of the partition of Africa'.[53] But in practice its workings were unpredictable and often irrational. Robinson and Gallagher see British statesmen after 1882 lurching from one improvisation to another as European competition or African resistance produced new crisis along the imperial frontiers; lacking much information about tropical Africa or much interest, they acted by the imperfect light of priori-

[51] D. C. M. Platt, *Finance, Trade and Politics in British Foreign Policy 1815–1914* (Oxford, 1968) pp. xxxxix-xl; also his article 'The Imperialism of Free Trade; Some Reservations', *Econ. H.R.*, 2nd series, xxi (1968) pp. 296–306.

[52] C. W. Newbury, 'The Protectionist Revival in French Colonial Trade: The Case of Senegal' *Econ. H.R.*, 2nd series, xxi (1968) p. 340; cf. *Prelude* pp. 238–9, 275–7, 289, 294.

[53] R. Robinson and J. Gallagher with Alice Denny, *Africa and the Victorians: the Official Mind of Imperialism* (1961) pp. 19–20. Henceforth *Africa and the Victorians*.

ties, assumptions and stereotypes devised to guide policy elsewhere. The African colonies thus acquired were 'little more than by-products of an enforced search for better security in the Mediterranean and the East'; the government stumbled into partition 'not to build a new African empire, but to protect the old empire of India'.[54]

In this diagnosis, students of British policy will recognise much truth. But as an explanation of change it is inadequate. It was nothing new for remote bureaucrats to improvise expedients for dealing with local emergencies, usually created by the incursion into differing cultures of the very British interests which claimed to be endangered; in West Africa as elsewhere this had gone on through much of the century.[55] Such had been the origins of the Asante wars, of French military campaigns in the Senegal valley, of the creeping imperialism of British coastal colonies before 1865. But during the last two decades of the centuries, governments began to face these crises in a new spirit; not merely did the emergencies seem to require more drastic action, but there were elements within the European nations which demanded more positive uses of the power of their states. It is true that these elements did not always win; but their strength and influence during the 1880s seems to be unduly discounted by Robinson and Gallagher. The domestic counterpart of the new 'frontiersmen', with great designs to pursue in Africa, is the new 'imperialist' – the European politician or publicist who openly declares that the extension of his country's power in Africa is something to be welcomed, not avoided.

Those Frenchmen, Germans and Britons who adopted such attitudes during the 1880s were not necessarily concerned to promote personal economic interests, nor even those of a class. But many of them did show some awareness that the free-enterprise capitalism of their countries was running into economic difficulties which might have far-reaching social and political implications. Historians of the European economy have long engaged in technical and complex discussions of these difficulties, and of the appropriateness of describing the period 1873–96 as that of the

54 *Africa and the Victorians*, pp. 463–4.
55 Cf. *Prelude, passim;* also W. D. McIntyre, *The Imperial Frontier in the Tropics, 1865–1875* (1967).

'Great Depression'.[56] Some of the issues involved have become rather difficult for simpler scholars to follow. What does remain clear is that the rapid growth of powerful industrial economies in Germany and the United States (in the first place) raised serious problems, easier perceived than solved; notably the provision of lucrative outlets, both for the actual products of the expanding manufacturing industries and for the profits which continued to accumulate in the hands of the bankers and large-scale entrepreneurs who financed them. A number of contemporary German scholars, of whom the most important for present purposes is Dr H. U. Wehler,[57] have recently re-examined the strains set up within the new German empire by the rapid but uneven development of German industry. But of course the problem of outlets did not affect only new industrial states. Older industrial economies like that of the British (who had long assumed that the world contained a supply of new markets which could in turn be opened without any great exertion of political or military power) equally found themselves affected by rapid fluctuations of international economic activity, culminating every seven years or so in a collapse of prices, the bankruptcy of small enterprises, and widespread unemployment and social distress.

Obviously, these recurrent crises, and the prospects of longer-term difficulties which many prophets foresaw, did not worry capitalists alone. The growing Labour movements in the industrial states, which since 1848 had generally moved towards accommodation with liberal capitalism in return for relatively minor benefits 'spun off' from the wealth it was creating, were liable to adopt more radical or revolutionary attitudes if such benefits ceased to spin their way, or if the curse of unemployment became heavier and more frequent. And political change was giving the working class (as well as the *petite bourgeoisie* of small businessmen and

[56] For a brave but not wholly successful attempt to summarise this complex literature see S. B. Saul, *The Myth of the Great Depression, 1873–1896* (1969).

[57] H. U. Wehler, *Bismarck und der Imperialismus* (Köln, 1969). Its argument is conveniently though somewhat tersely summarised in his article 'Bismarck's Imperialism, 1862–1890' *Past & Present*, No. 48, 1970. Other important contributors to the re-writing of the economic history of Imperial Germany are H. Böhme, *Deutschlands Weg zur Grossmacht* (Köln, 1966) and H. Rosenberg, *Grosse Depression und Bismarckzeit* (Berlin, 1967).

service trades) a weapon which even the traditional political leadership could not ignore. In the Third Republic manhood suffrage had given real political power, if not to the workers and peasants, at least to journalists and local political bosses who knew how to appeal to their prejudices and supposed self-interest. In Imperial Germany executive power still lay with the Emperor, and so with the powerful, moody, and arbitrary Chancellor who had successfully reconciled the leaders of German capitalism to a traditionalist and authoritarian state structure; but Bismarck and his collaborators were becoming increasingly aware that they could only preserve their initiative by ensuring that manhood suffrage returned a manageable majority to the Reichstag. Great Britain had not yet advanced so far along the road to a democratic franchise but from 1885 householders and lodgers could vote in the counties as well as the boroughs, and here too aristocratic politicians were adapting their rhetoric, and to some degree their policies, to suit a new and distasteful pattern of electioneering.

Social and political structures thus required that European governments should be seen to make some response to the economic crisis, as it was commonly perceived. From the end of the 1870s, Germany and France began to impose tariffs which might in some degree protect domestic markets against the competition of foreign industry (and also of foreign agriculture); similar measures were proposed even in Great Britain, although public interest and emotional involvement in the idea of free trade was too strong for this to be practical politics. From here it was a small step, easily justified by appeal to the practice of old mercantilist empires, to the idea of reserving colonial markets for exclusive or preferential exploitation by metropolitan interests. As early as 1877 the French administration in Senegal imposed a differential import duty intended to protect against British competition Pondichery cloths which Rouen manufacturers finished for the African trade; and although French and Senegalese merchants generally opposed this innovation, by 1880 there were signs that the free-trading principles of the Chambers of Commerce were beginning to weaken.[58] And as competitors had long noted, even Britain's free-

The climate is good [wrote the normally cautious Sir Robert

[58] C. W. Newbury, 'The Protectionist Revival in French Colonial Trade: the Case of Senegal', *Econ. H.R.*, 2nd series, XXI (1968) pp. 337–48.

West Africa from imposing much higher rates of duty on spirits (exported chiefly by France and Germany) than on cotton textiles (in which Lancashire still held her lead).

Still, nobody would claim that the application of protective tariffs in those small colonies which Europe held in Africa in the early 1880s could make more than a minute and marginal contribution to solving the crisis of European capitalism. But if the resources of inland Africa were opened up by the efforts of the technocratic frontiersmen, organised and governed according to European notions of 'civilisation', and then subjected to appropriate fiscal regimes, it was permissible to hope (for hope is always free) that the results would be far more dramatic. 'Now that Europe is exhausting itself by over-production, it is to Africa that men look to furnish new markets,' the Negro scholar E. W. Blyden observed in 1880.[59]

As has already been shown, the growth in the trade of coastal regions during the previous half-century gave some modest substance to such hopes. But for Blyden as for many of his European contemporaries, the best was yet to come; it was the populous and well-organised Muslim states of the interior which, when fully drawn into the world economy, would provide it with the greatest stimulus. Even before the publication of Barth's *Travels* in 1857–8, Hausaland and Bornu had been regarded as potential sources of great wealth; and Goldie's argument that a monopoly of trade in the Niger valley would generate the resources to enable him to penetrate these markets lay at the base of his claim for a Charter. Further west, Timbuktu had long been a magic name to Europeans (despite Rene Caillié's disappointment when he at last succeeded in visiting it); similar hopes of untapped wealth in the Muslim empires of the Niger valley had inspired the attempts of Governor Faidherbe to penetrate that region through the Senegal, and their revival by Brière de l'Isle in 1879. Like Goldie, Brière was utilising a myth which had become almost a cliché among well-read Europeans, but which had suddenly come to seem more relevant to Europe's economic problems.

From the general expectation that Africa's undeveloped markets

---

[59] E. W. Blyden, Discourse delivered before the American Colonization Society, May 1880, in *Christianity, Islam and the Negro Race* (2nd ed., Edinburgh, 1967) p. 119.

could help European capitalism resolve its crisis, it was a small step to demand for political control. During the early 1880s many groups of merchants, in Germany as elsewhere, came to accept the argument that, in the words of the Wiesbaden Chamber of Commerce, over-production in the motherland would find a natural outlet in colonies.[60] For if African markets were indeed so important it was logical, in an era of competitive nation-states, to revive the old mercantilist connection between the enjoyment of profit and the possession of power. Leopold II, representing a state whose political strength did not match its industrial development, had precociously recognised this in 1863, declaring, 'We would be happy to see Belgians exploiting and trading in colonies in general, but we think that it is in the interests of the country that it should have its own overseas possessions.'[61] Political experience during the early 1880s made many converts to the hopeful attitude expressed by Jules Ferry, that 'when one founds a colony, one is supplying an outlet for trade.'[62]

Even where attachments to free trade were still strong – as in commercial, as against industrial, centres in France, and in most sectors of the British business world – interest in the political future of Africa was growing. In Manchester it was expressed most persistently by James F. Hutton, a leading figure in the Chamber of Commerce, who sat in the Parliament of 1885–6 as one of the city's Conservative M.P.s. His connection with West Africa went back to his grandfather, founder of the London merchant house of W. B. Hutton & Co.; James visited West Africa as a young man when it fell to him to wind up this business on his father's death, and he had continued to trade with the region from the new family base in Manchester, forming a new partnership with his younger brother, Anthony. A third brother, Thomas, a chartered accountant, lived from 1869 to 1872 in the Gambia, where his ancestors had traded; and it was as an opponent of the cession of that colony in 1875-6 that James first made his presence

[60] Wehler, *Bismarck und der Imperialismus.* p. 130.

[61] Leopold, Duc de Brabant, 26 July 1863, in L. le Febve de Vivy (ed.) *Documents d'histoire précoloniale belge* (Brussels, 1955) (*Mémoires de l'Academie Royale des Sciences Coloniales*, n.s.7) p. 23.

[62] Ferry, speech of 28 July 1885: *Journal Officiel* (Chambre) 29 July 1885. See below pp. 52–4.

felt by the British government.[63] Though he later came to regret this action, Hutton followed up his interest by taking over the business of the Gambian merchant, Thomas Brown, on his death in 1880.[64] By now his horizons were broadening; Hutton began to invest modest sums in the schemes of the great projectors of African development, and became increasingly active in soliciting such political support from the British Government as seemed necessary to ensure their success. In 1878 he subscribed £800 to Leopold II's *Comité d'Etudes du Haut Congo*, and in 1882 invested £500 in Goldie's National African Company – but his principal contribution to both projects was as a political lobbyist, organising Manchester's opposition to the Anglo-Portuguese Congo Treaty of 1884, and mobilising support for Goldie's Charter.[65] He also took an interest in the future of East Africa as early as 1879 and in 1885 was appealing to the shipowner, William Mackinnon, as one of the few men whose purse and imagination could both be touched by bold imperial schemes.[66] Materials for a full study of this important figure appear to be lacking, but on the surface he appears to have become more concerned with long-term prospects of trading in Africa than with his own immediate interests – witness a recent comment that in East Africa he 'invested £5,000 in a company with shaky prospects and a ramshackle organisation'.[67] This readiness to put his money behind his words was not shared by his fellow merchants; as Percy Anderson of the Foreign Office once commented sadly, 'Manchester will not advance a sixpence unless the money is safe.'[68] But this did not prevent their

[63] Family details from J. A. and P. C. Hutton, *Hutton Families* (privately printed, 1939). I am grateful to Roger Anstey for lending me a copy of this. *Prelude*, pp. 183–95.

[64] C.O. 87/134, Lee to Knutsford, 11 October 1888.

[65] R. T. Anstey, *Britain and the Congo in the Nineteenth Century* (Oxford, 1962) pp. 65–7, 114–27. Flint, *Goldie*, pp. 46–51 (which however contains some errors of detail).

[66] J. S. Galbraith, *Mackinnon and East Africa, 1878–1895* (Cambridge, 1972) pp. 75, 92f.

[67] Ibid. p. 237.

[68] Minute of 14 April 1885, quoted from F.O. 84/1737 in ibid. p. 95. A. Redford and B. W. Clapp, *Manchester Merchants and Foreign Trade*, II (Manchester, 1956) Chap. 6, traces the growth of the sporadic interest of the Manchester Chamber of Commerce without noting Hutton's dominant role.

addressing a growing stream of requests to the British government, on the initiative of activists like Hutton.

In Bismarckian Germany, Dr Wehler detects in the statements of pressure groups (notably Chambers of Commerce), and of individual public figures, the emergence of what he calls an 'ideological consensus' in favour of increasing state support for exporters and of founding colonies in order to solve the economic problems of the 'Great Depression'.[69] This may be going rather far; such evidence in its nature tends to emphasise the testimony of interested parties concerned to plead the case, and it is difficult to measure the extent to which their pleas were accepted as legitimate, or even the intensity with which they were sustained. The level of argument of these expansionists was commonly generalised and superficial; those who wanted government action to solve their own and their country's economic problems did not always support their predictions by convincing market research. Africa was not really very likely to offer large markets for exports of those technically-based industries – metallurgical, engineering, electrical or chemical – in which German expansion was increasingly based. Even the fears expressed in many countries that others were about to impose protective tariffs were largely premature; although experience in Senegal made many British merchants apprehensive, France did not adopt a generally protectionist policy until the Méline tariff of 1892.[70] Imperial expansion was a fashionable panacea rather than a proven remedy for the current malaise of European capitalism. It could hardly have achieved such popularity as it did had not its advocates linked the expected economic benefits to considerations of national prestige.

It would be too great a diversion to attempt to chronicle the uses of this concept in modern political argument, or to list the follies which have been sanctioned in its name. Since the Franco-Prussian war many Europeans had been aware of a more stringently competitive atmosphere in international relations, in which failure to act vigorously in defence of national interests could lead to a degrading of national status which would have severe if somewhat indeterminate consequences. Continental states were coming to appreciate (what Palmerston had always understood)

[69] Wehler, *Bismarck* . . . , Chap. 3.

[70] H. Brunschwig, *Mythes et Réalités de l'impérialisme colonial français 1871–1914* (1960), Chap. 6.

that the strength of a truly great power, although necessarily based in Europe, needed to be exercised throughout the world. Colonial empire might thus seem an essential element of national greatness, irrespective of any economic advantages it might bring. This view had never been wholly forgotten in England, even at the peak of Liberal 'anti-imperialism';[71] since Disraeli's deliberate attempt to rehabilitate the concept of Empire it had been frequently expressed in the literature read by the political elite.[72] Thus in 1881 the Earl of Dunraven (an adventurous and well-travelled Irish landlord, who would later serve as Colonial Under-Secretary in Conservative governments) attacked the supposed Little Englander view that Great Britain might, without loss of prosperity 'gradually descend from the position of a first-rate power and a great and growing empire into that of a small fifth-rate nation'.[73] Two years later Sir John Seeley, drawing attention to the vast potential strength of Russia and the U.S.A., reminded a wider readership that 'a small state among small states is one thing, and a small state among large states quite another.'[74]

In Great Britain, the doctrines of 'Imperialism' which began to come into favour in the 1880s generally emphasised the consolidation of relationships with the old colonies of overseas settlement. The British Empire did not need to seize new territories in the tropics to achieve the potentiality of world power (although, as Gladstone began sadly to note about 1883, Jingoism and 'colonial annexation fever' in the Australian and South African colonies themselves were exercising increasing pressure in the direction of tropical expansion).[75] Continental states without such overseas affiliates who felt the need to demonstrate their claim to world power status had no alternative but to establish new colonial dependencies. In Africa during the middle 1880s the association between colonial expansion and the mystical status of a 'first-class

[71] For examples related to West Africa, see *Prelude* pp. 70–1 (Seymour, 1864) and 171 (Knatchbull-Hughessen, 1874).

[72] R. Koebner and H. D. Schmidt, *Imperialism: the story and Significance of a Political Word 1840–1960* (Cambridge, 1964).

[73] Dunraven, 'The Revolutionary Party', *The Nineteenth Century* (August 1881).

[74] J. R. Seeley, *The Expansion of England* (1883) pp. 349–50 of the 1931 ed.

[75] This is a repeated theme in *The Diary of Sir Edward Hamilton* (Gladstone's Secretary) (Oxford, 1972) – e.g. II, pp. 507, 521, 761.

power' was repeatedly asserted. At one level, this implied connection was perhaps already clear enough, without any need to demonstrate specific economic or strategic advantages; it reflected almost atavistic attitudes, of a sort deeply rooted in societies where (as throughout western Europe) the social and political influence of old aristocracies and of military traditions remained strong.[76] But how, in concrete political circumstances, a government came to conceive that national prestige was somehow involved in particular tracts of West African soil is a more specific question. It does not help much to say that, during the international crises of the 1880s and 1890s, 'nationalist feeling struck upon a colonial issue as the symbol of the wider clash of national interests and, identifying prestige with territorial compensation, intervened in imperial policy';[77] the crisis of 1884–5 was largely about African problems in the first place. The growing European involvement in West Africa during the 1880s can only be understood as an interaction between these changing needs and attitudes of Europeans and specific crises and developments which were taking place along the frontiers of Afro-European relations.

THE PATTERN OF THE 'SCRAMBLE'

The results of an attempt to do this in an earlier study may be here briefly summarised and developed. The first clear manifestation of a new European imperialism in West Africa appeared in 1879, when France inaugurated policies of expansion in the Senegal Valley. For the immediate vicinity of the old-established colonial trading settlements of the coast and river, there was a fateful decision to link Saint-Louis with the growing ports of Rufisque and Dakar by constructing a railway through the major groundnut producing state of Cayor. Less easily explicable in economic terms was the colonial government's proposal to link this line with a more ambitious railway which would traverse the upper Senegal valley and reach the Niger at Bamako. The existing trade in gold and hides, carried out by African entrepreneurs, held no promise of sufficient growth to make this scheme viable; here, pressure from local agents with technocratic plans difficult to pursue under existing African regimes was, exceptionally, rein-

[76] Cf. J. A. Schumpeter, *Imperialism and Social Classes* (N.Y., 1951).
[77] R. Robinson in *Cambridge History of the British Empire*, III (1959) p. 180.

forced by ministers in Paris prepared to invest in deliberate programmes of expansion.

The idea of a trans-saharan railway, backed by the influence of the French-Algerian lobby, had won the support of Charles de Freycinet, an engineer who in December 1879 rose through the Ministry of Public Works to become Premier for the first time. But when Paul Soleillet, a restless young admirer of Lesseps in search of possible southern termini, arrived in Senegal in 1878 to explore the Tokolor empire of Segou, he was easily persuaded by Governor Brière de l'Isle to include a Senegal-Niger line in his lavish programme of railway plans.[78] This revived Faidherbe's old schemes for pushing French influence inland, but greatly changed its nature by inserting a technological spine; Faidherbe's own prestige as an elder statesman helped commend the plan to Freycinet and to his former colleague and successor as Governor of Senegal, Admiral Jauréguibery. As Minister of Marine, Jauréguibery was anxious to secure priority over the trans-saharan for this 'infinitely less laborious' project,[79] fearing that the transsaharan line without the Senegal-Niger would pre-empt Senegal's commercial hinterland. In June 1881 the trans-saharan plan was shelved, after the destruction of Colonel Flatters' survey party had shown that there were political as well as technical difficulties; meanwhile the legislature had somewhat reluctantly voted funds for the first stage of the Senegal-Niger, from Kayes to Bamako.

This scheme, costed in blissful ignorance of the real problems of constructing and operating such a line, was to prove a serious financial commitment for the French state; but the political commitment was more serious still. On 6 September 1880 a new military district of the Upper Senegal was created under the command of Lieutenant-Colonel Gustave Borgnis-Desbordes, a forceful officer of the Marine Artillery. As Dr Kanya-Forstner has demonstrated, the officers successively charged with the defence of

[78] J. Gross (ed.) *Les Voyages et Decouvertes de Paul Soleillet* (1881) biographical note by P. Barnal. The fullest account of Soleillet's mission to Segou is Y. Saint-Martin, *L'Empire Toucouleur et la France* (Dakar, 1969) Chap. 6. For the background and progress of the railway projects, see Kanya-Forstner, *Conquest*, Chap. 3; also T. W. Roberts, 'Railway Imperialism and French Advances towards Lake Chad, 1890-1900' (Ph.D., University of Cambridge, 1973).

[79] Jauréguibery, Report to the President, 25 September 1879, *La France dans l'Afrique Occidentale*, pp. 10-12.

French interests on this new frontier became the driving-force of its expansion. Impelled by personal, professional and patriotic ambitions, and by arrogant distaste for their African opponents, the Sudanese military made Faidherbe's imperial vision the medium for re-asserting France's military prestige. In their deliberately isolated command posts they claimed the right to interpret French interests and honour, and to determine when either was threatened; sustained by loyal comrades within the Ministry of Marine they proved remarkably successful in imposing their interpretations in Paris.

This, then, was the first explosion of European imperialism to hit West Africa. Its consequences were to be momentous; but immediately it affected only French policy in one region, and provoked little reaction from other European states. Despite signs of increasing restlessness among the handful of Frenchmen interested in districts beyond Senegambia, the French Ministry responded with extreme caution, until the British occupation of Egypt shattered existing conventions of Anglo–French co-existence, and set the African policies of European powers in a new international context.

During the initial 'scramble' of 1883–5 there was certainly plenty of improvisation and muddle on the part of European governments; but there were also some conscious political decisions which reflected changing attitudes to the use of state power in Africa. One condition for these was the existence of a certain stability in international relations in Europe. Germany, insured by the renewed Three Emperors' League against the dangers of renewed conflict in south-east Europe, could experiment with policies involving risks of collision with Britain and possibilities of collaboration with France. In response Frenchmen who were resigned to the impossibility of doing anything immediate about Alsace or Lorraine could express their deep irritation over British encroachments on their colonial interests, and especially about the occupation of Egypt. Already, especially during the brief Gambetta Ministry of 1881–2, it had become clear that some politicians such as Maurice Rouvier were sensitive to appeals from provincial merchants for the protection of their interests, and perhaps aware that vigorous policies in Africa might have some general appeal to those *nouvelles couches sociales* of small-scale businessmen and rentiers which were becoming the principal beneficiaries of the Third Republic.[80] Such pressure groups now found new opportunities of successful action.

Although Britain's occupation of Egypt eroded the tacit entente which previously regulated Anglo–French relations in Africa, this does not mean that the French initiatives were prompted by 'hope of prising the British out of Cairo'[81]. There were some unrealistic people in the French bureaucracy, but none quite so unrealistic as that. The effect of the Suez Crisis of 1882 was twofold. Firstly, it removed restraints which the Quai d'Orsay had hitherto imposed on unilateral French action in areas of British interests; anti-British acts (like the renewed protectorate of Porto Novo) which French representatives in the area had previously demanded in vain became politically acceptable in the new international environment. At the same time 'Suez' created a highly charged psychological atmosphere in Paris, in which French politicians and journalists suddenly found it advantageous both to abuse British policy more noisily than German, and to champion grandiose programmes of colonial empire. M. Stengers and Brunschwig have indicated the importance of this in relation to the Congo question, the effect 'trigger' of the Berlin conference.[82] The treaty with the Makoko which de Brazza so dramatically secured for his adopted fatherland provided an opportunity for Ministers, Deputies and journalists to wallow in chauvinistic euphoria; the British government, seeing a promising market in jeopardy, tried to insure it by an old-fashioned confidence trick (the treaty with Portugal); Bismarck found in that treaty the pretext for a political intervention in Africa which he had apparently been contemplating for some time.

Bismarck's decision to authorise the acquisition of territorial

[80] On the influence of Gambetta and the Gambettists, see C. R. Ageron, 'Gambetta et la reprise de l'expanion coloniale', *RFHOM*, LIX (1972) pp. 165–204; also T. W. Roberts, 'Railway Imperialism . . .', cf. above p. 18.

[81] *Africa and the Victorians*, p. 162.

[82] Jean Stengers, 'L'impérialisme colonial de la fin du xixe siècle; Mythe ou Réalité', *JAH* III (1962) pp. 469–91. Henri Brunschwig, 'Les Origines du Partage de l'Afrique Occidentale', *JAH* v (1964) pp. 121–5. There was some element of rationality in the reaction. In the 1886 edition of *De la colonisation chez les peuples modernes* (pp. 642–3) the econ omist Paul Leroy-Beaulieu referred to losses of income suffered by French bondholders in Egypt and concluded that overseas investments were safer under French political control.

claims in Kamerun, Togo and elsewhere appears to have been a deliberate act of state; to an unusual degree, it seems that the problem of how German colonisation originated can be approached through the study of an individual's motives. But these are not easily ascertained. International developments, by making it safe to quarrel with Gladstone's government and expedient to seek collaboration with that of Jules Ferry, provided necessary conditions for this change of course; but they cannot be accepted as a sufficient explanation. The most recent interpretation sees Bismarck as responding to the 'ideological consensus' which demanded more resolute state action to assist German capitalism in its crisis; he accepted, not the case for colonies as such, but the expediency of undertaking specific, and as he thought limited, measures to protect German economic interests, even though they involved an extension of sovereignty.[83] This would in the first place meet specific needs of merchants trading to Africa from Hamburg and Bremen (cities whose Senates it was important to conciliate, since they were still in 1884 negotiating their entry into the Zollverein); and it might at the same time reassure worried industrialists – also influential bankers (like Gerson von Bleichröder and Adolf von Hansemann) who had shown an interest in overseas colonisation, and agrarians whose potatoes were used to make the cheap gin which was a growing staple of German West African trade[84] – that the Empire cared for their interests. New protectorates showed the government responsive to the *Torschlusspanik*, to the fears which had been sharpened by misreadings of the Anglo–French agreement on the Sierra Leone boundary in 1882 that France and Britain were in process of pre-empting positions of permanent privilege on the West African coast.[85]

At the same time, Bismarck was conscious that colonial expansion might appeal to the wider electorate which he was struggling to keep loyal to his conservative empire. In 1881 he had written 'Colonies demand a fatherland in which the national feeling is

[83] Wehler, *Bismarck*, Chap. 5, Part IB.

[84] Cf. H. Stoecker, *Kamerun unter Deutscher Kolonialherrschaft*, pp. 17–23.

[85] Jaeck, 'Die Deutscher Annextion' in H. Stoecker, *Kamerun* pp. 52ff Henry Ashby Turner, Jr., 'Bismarck's Imperialist Venture; Anti-British in Origin?' in Prosser Gifford and Wm. Roger Louis (eds.) *Britain and Germany in Africa* (New Haven, 1967) pp. 47–82.

stronger than the hatred of the parties [for each other]'.[86] It is impossible, for contemporary statesmen as well as for historians, to measure precisely when such conditions have been fulfilled; they can only judge intuitively what representative importance to attach to the rhetoric of small minorities, such as the recently-founded *Kolonialverein's* claim to represent a unanimous national drive to assist the regeneration of the Fatherland by rechannelling the forces that were being driven abroad by the crisis of over-production,[87] or the inconsequential assertion at the end of the Hamburg merchants' memorial, that 'it is not just a few firms who want colonies but the whole German people.'[88] But certainly, one assumption underlying Bismarck's change of attitude was that the German electorate of 1884 – and specifically, potential supporters of those Conservatives and right-wing National Liberals who formed the basis of his political system – would welcome a vigorous assertion in Africa of Germany's imperial power.[89] That Bismarck, like many others, shortly became disillusioned about the economic benefits to be derived from the new colonies and about the costs and responsibilities of ruling them did not reverse this new involvement of the German state, and of the infant German imperialist movement, in the developing pattern of Afro-European relations.

Moreover, one argument which Bismarck used in support of his short-term purposes would later command wide and influential support in Germany and other continental states. Developing the idea that great nations could no longer afford to concentrate exclusively on European issues, Bismarck had broached the idea of some sort of continental league to control the behaviour of the British, whose naval and colonial strength allowed them to behave so arbitrarily in Africa. Bismarck's somewhat academic approach

[86] Note by Bismarck, 1881, cit. H. Pogge von Strandman, 'German Colonial Expansion under Bismarck', *Past and Present*, No. 42 (1969) p. 144.

[87] *Deutsche Kolonialzeitung: Organ des Deutschen Kolonialvereins* (Frankfurt, 1884) I, No. 1, 'Unser Programm', 6 December 1883.

[88] Memorial of the Hamburg Chamber of Commerce, 6 July 1883, in Weiss Buch, Deutsche Kolonien, 1. Togogebiet and Biafra-Bai. In *Das Stattsarchiv*, LXIII (Leipzig, 1884).

[89] 'H.H. is enthusiastic about the conference for election reasons'. Wilhelm v Bismarck to Holstein, 1 September 1884. *The Holstein Papers* ed. N. Rich and M. H. Fisher (Cambridge, 1961) III, p. 130.

to this subject was illustrated by his attempt to use the precedent of the Armed Neutrality of 1780;[90] the French Ambassador Courcel, aware of the limitations of what Bismarck actually proposed, was not impressed by this. What *did* come to seem significant to Courcel was that these overtures were made during a period when Germany seemed to be suffering from a crisis of overproduction which was driving her into serious economic rivalry with the British Empire.[91] If this was indeed the shape of the future, European unity against the world power of the British, and the future world power of the Americans, was sufficiently desirable to require European governments to re-assess their traditional continental interests, even perhaps such sensitive interests as were involved in Alsace Lorraine. The logic which in 1884 justified limited Franco–German co-operation in Africa would one day point towards much more serious decisions.

Gladstone, Granville and Derby were genuinely surprised when far-reaching designs were attributed to them. Their involvement in the scramble was primarily a matter of improvisation designed to protect old interests now in jeopardy. Yet even their actions contained germs of new and more vigorously imperialistic policies. Before the French challenges in the Niger area had become fully apparent, members of the Foreign Office were already envisaging 'the possibility of altering the whole system of British policy as regards the native chiefs on the West Coast of Africa, and the abolition of the monopolies which are destructive to trade and productive of endless squabbles and wars.'[92] This movement for an extension of British power within the Niger Delta was given added power and urgency by the perception of French hostility, and by fears that French control would prejudice 'the maintenance of an unfettered trade'.[93] The Cabinet decision in November 1883 to seek protectorate treaties from the delta to the Cameroons did not involve a great revolution in official thinking, but it was a decided step forward which, even if carried out according to plan, would have implied increasing interference by British agents in the lives of Nigerians. When the plan was thwarted by French

[90] D.D.F., 1st series, v, No. 249, Courcel to Ferry, 25 April 1884.
[91] Ibid., No. 410, Courcel to Ferry, Pte. 28 September 1884.
[92] P.R.O. 30/29/135, Memo by Lister, 4 January 1882.
[93] Cabinet Minute, 22 November 1883 – C. W. Newbury, *British Policy towards West Africa; Select Documents 1875–1914* (Oxford, 1972).

and German opposition, new attitudes emerged within the British public, Parliament and even in the Liberal Cabinet. Gladstone himself was deeply disturbed by the whole course of events in 1883–5; because of the damage to relations with France, because the attention of M.P.s was diverted from much important domestic problems, but especially because of the stimulus given to jingoism in Great Britain and in overseas colonies. As the scramble for territory extended to other parts of Africa, he deplored the 'wild and irrational spirit' revealed in quarters formerly unsuspected of imperial chauvinism,[94] but he could not restrain his own Cabinet from seeking pre-emptive protectorates and annexation with considerable vigour.

The years 1883–5 thus saw the appearance in a number of quarters of imperialistic attitudes – of demands for the more effective exercise of state power in Africa, whether to secure present or future economic advantages, or simply to assert the virility of the nation-state. Though most evident in the three great industrialising states, such attitudes were not confined to them; even the underdeveloped monarchy of Portugal, reviving a sort of crusading expansionism never quite dead, attempted to assert a protectorate in Dahomey.[95] Such behaviour might appear hardly rational; it often reflected hasty responses to unforeseen contingencies; yet its effect was clearly to constitute new commitments by European governments to territorial imperialism in West Africa.

THE LOADED PAUSE

It is suggested above that the new initiatives of European governments in West Africa during the early 1880s can best be understood as ill-calculated reactions by harassed politicians to a period of economic, social and political uncertainty. There was little objective possibility that African markets, even if developed under European authority, could make more than marginal contribution towards solving the problems of growth which European

---

[94] Gladstone minute, 26 December 1884, cit. *Africa and the Victorians*, p. 207. Cf. *The Diary of Sir Edward Hamilton*, II, *passim;* also the study of French and British newspapers by W. R. Louis, 'The Berlin Congo Conference' in P. Gifford and W. R. Louis (ed.) *France and Britain in Africa* (New Haven, 1971).

[95] See below, pp. 149–50.

capitalist economies were beginning to encounter; but uncosted hopes of future benefits could rationalise measures which primarily served much more limited purposes. Once it became a matter of actually developing the newly established claims, it could be seen that in the short term they brought more problems than relief. For the very period which saw European governments scrambling to control the African coastline saw the beginning of a sharp cyclical reduction of international economic activity. As the effects of the short-term crisis were felt by merchants and governments, they reacted by relaxing, rather than intensifying, their pressure upon African independence. For like the patent medicines so confidently advertised in the same European and African newspapers, which prescribed doses of expansion as the remedy for sluggish business, imperialism had to be paid for; and it was precisely in times of economic sickness that it was hardest to afford the price.

The cyclical depression which was in its early stages in 1883 hit British industry particularly hard. It was marked by falls in the prices and profits of many industries, notably cotton; increased unemployment in Europe led in turn to falling prices for many primary products. Palm oil, the price of which had long been falling as world production increased, reacted particularly sharply (thus enabling the British soap industry to remain profitable); British import prices in 1886 were little more than half those of 1883.[96] Prices of kernels and groundnuts held up somewhat better, but by 1885 the whole oilseed market was suffering from the combined effects of the depression in Europe and good crops in India. Only rubber, a comparatively new export from West Africa, whose collection was still sporadically organised, continued to enjoy reasonably stable markets.

Low prices for African produce had far-reaching effects within Africa. Where farmers and chiefs had committed the harvest to merchants or middlemen in liquidation of old debts, they came under pressure to renew the obligation on less favourable terms. Where producers retained an independent bargaining position, traders resorted to trickery or tried to by-pass habitual channels of exchange. The result might involve political conflict. In the hinterland of Sierra Leone there was widespread fighting among Africans in the producing areas.[97] In the hinterland of Lagos, an

[96] For some data on the prices of palm produce, see Appendix, Table I.
[97] See below, pp. 172–6.

area already troubled by wars among the Yoruba, the slump is said to have intensified unrest 'by biting into the incomes of the large producers . . . and forcing them to launch slave-raiding and plundering expeditions in order to maintain their position.[98] Merchants with overdrafts and other expansionist colonials blamed the generic African malady of 'tribal war', and urged their local government to hit their way out of trouble by adopting such radical solutions as the elimination of African middlemen or the establishment of effective European overrule.

These developments of the mid-1880s may support a thesis recently argued by Dr. A. G. Hopkins: that the 'great depression' which had affected the international economy since the 1870s, and specifically the deterioration which it brought to the terms of trade of African producers, 'helped to bring the Europeans into Africa' – but because of its effects *in* Africa rather than, as more commonly suggested, upon European capitalism.[99] Intensified competition upset the relatively stable relations between European merchants and African farmers and traders which had been achieved during the nineteenth century, and so opened the road to a European invasion. Nevertheless, such effects required time; there could be no European invasion until European governments were prepared to invade. And their conversion to the methods of political imperialism was still by no means complete. Although the short-term economic crisis made some of their subjects see territorial expansion as a plausible solution to some European problems, this does not mean that it was in fact a necessary solution – or that it offered any solution at all to some of the more profound structural problems, such as the need to find new outlets for investment. In the short run, indeed, tentative measures of political imperialism like 'paper protectorates' or 'punitive expeditions' might provide no relief at all; since they could not affect the terms of international commerce, even success would not provide the merchants with the profits with which to sustain expansion. Moreover, military aggression had to be paid for; unless exceptionally

[98] A. G. Hopkins, 'Economic, Imperialism in West Africa; Lagos 1880–92', *Econ. H.R.*, 2nd series (1968) p. 592; see within pp. 130–4.

[99] A. G. Hopkins, *An Economic History of West Africa* (1973) p. 135. Dr. Hopkins' important book appeared as this volume was about to go to press; only in the present paragraph have I been able to use it directly, although my work has benefited from discussions with Dr. Hopkins over several years.

(as in Western Sudan) the home government could be persuaded to subsidise an expeditionary force, it would be a charge on the local governments. But most of these depended for revenue on *ad valorem* import or export duties which were themselves hit by the slump; most Governors could not help the merchants even if they wanted to.

So, even if prevailing economic conditions can sometimes be used to explain the European offensive of 1884–5, they may equally explain a curious corollary – that this offensive was immediately followed by a pause, a period of hesitation and retrenchment on the part of each of the newly imperialist powers. As metropolitan governments began to appreciate the potential extent of their new commitments, they sought means of applying the brake to enthusiastic expansionists on their new frontiers.

The delegates who met at Berlin in November 1884 were thus aware of the need for prudence, in both African and international policies. Already Ferry had set aside Bismarck's hints about collaborating against British imperialism in a Continental League and framed a programme in 'more modest, concrete and practical' terms, related to the actual prospects of French trade.[100] Britain and Germany adopted similar approaches, and any danger of a real international crisis disappeared. This did not prevent the later growth of a myth (which African writers have tended to take over from distinguished European predecessors) that the conference marked the beginning of a full-blooded drive for African territory. Professor Brunschwig, re-examining this curious misconception, confirms the conclusion of Miss S. E. Crowe's pioneering monograph of 1942. In the Conference programme,

> . . . there was nothing revolutionary. They were not talking about partitioning Africa but rather of ensuring the continuation of the traditional free-trading system on its coasts and its great rivers . . . The General Act may be seen as much as an attempt to apply the brakes to the partition as to accelerate it. Diplomats whose custom was to regard Black Africa solely from the point of view of coastal commerce did not become excited about the interior of the 'mysterious continent'. They were able to hope that . . . they were delaying the moment when govern-

100 D.D.F., v, No. 376, Note by Ferry, August 1884.

ments would be obliged to meet the heavy expenses of occupying new territories.[101]

One of the specific purposes of the Conference was to ensure that, when European governments decided to claim control over African coastline in future, other governments would not only be notified in due form, but their subjects assured of continued protection for legitimate interests. The British, who had the most extensive and important interests to safeguard, were reluctant to agree that the latter responsibility could be discharged only through 'effective occupation'; that could involve dangerously open-ended commitments. Experience made them still reluctant to become too involved in the affairs of African societies which they did not fully understand, and in particular to accept responsibility for suppressing domestic slavery. While public opinion would oppose any toleration of slavery on British soil, officials recognised that some varieties of the institution might still serve constructive purposes integral to the fabric of African societies, and that enforced abolition might arouse formidable resistance.[102] Hence they were anxious to find a method of validating territorial claims without full assumption of sovereignty.

The instrument lay to hand in the conveniently ill-defined concept of protectorate. This term (whose application was well established in the case of protected states to which, as in Tunisia, Europeans had previously recognised some sort of international personality) had already been loosely applied by the British to areas of West Africa where, as on the Gold Coast during Maclean's time, they had exercised a limited 'foreign jurisdiction' within less clearly structured African politics. More recently they had given the term a new application by inviting numerous principalities of the lower Niger to sign the proferred treaty-forms. But these had been expedients improvised to solve specific localised problems; not until the Berlin Conference was opening were the government's legal advisers invited to consider the essential nature of a protectorate. A puzzling discussion was eventually settled, temporarily, by the comforting ruling of Lord Chancellor Selborne that:

[101] H. Brunschwig, *Le partage de l'Afrique noire* (1971) pp. 51, 156–60; cf. S. E. Crowe, *The Berlin West African Conference* (1942).

[102] Cf. J. J. Grace, 'Domestic Slavery in the Sierra Leone Protectorate' (Ph.D. Thesis, University of Aberdeen, 1972) Chap. 1.

Protectorate is the recognition of the right of the aboriginal or other actual inhabitants to their own country, with no further assumption of territorial rights than is necessary to maintain the paramount authority and to discharge the duties of the Protecting Power.[103]

This admirably suited Britain's immediate needs; through protectorates they could exclude foreign intruders without incurring any obligation to act against slavery or instal costly colonial administrations. Since Germans and Frenchmen also were becoming more wary of such commitments, their representatives at Berlin agreed to the British contention that claims to African coastline based upon the assumption of a protectorate need not entail that obligation to ensure the establishment of effective authority which, according to Article XXXV, followed from formal 'occupation'.[104] Yet, though the essence of a protectorate appeared to be an undertaking by an African ruler to grant European state control over his foreign relations, the concept remained broad enough to permit considerable extension; it was possible to insert in a protectorate treaty provisions for the promotion of Christian missions, the abolition of African trading privileges, the enforcement of order on a troubled frontier. From such seeds a relationship based on apparent reciprocity of commitment could grow into one where the protector assumed virtually unlimited authority.[105]

[103] Memo by Selborne, 3 January 1885, quoted W. R. Louis, *France and Britain in Africa*, p. 209.

[104] The relevant clauses read:

Art. XXXIV. Any power which henceforth takes possession of a tract of land on the coasts of the African Continent outside of its present possessions, or which, being hitherto without such possessions, shall acquire them, as well as the Power which assumes a Protectorate there, shall accompany the respective act with a notification thereof, addressed to the other Signatory Powers of the present Act, in order to enable them, if need be, to make good any claims of their own.

Art. XXXV. The Signatory Powers of the present Act recognize the obligation to insure the establishment of authority in regions occupied by them on the coasts of the African Continent sufficient to protect existing rights, and, as the case may be, freedom of trade and of transit under the conditions agreed upon . . .

[105] For an analysis by a lawyer of this development in British East Africa, see H. F. Morris, 'Protection or Annexation? Some Constitutional Anomalies of Colonial Rule' in H. F. Morris and J. S. Read (ed.) *Indirect Rule and the Search for Justice* (Oxford, 1972).

But this was essentially a development of the 1890s. In 1885 the enthusiasm of many imperialists was already cooling; economic prudence was reinforced by political setbacks in both Europe and Africa. At the end of March 1885 Ferry was driven from office by embittered attacks in the Chamber, following a military set-back in Vietnam.[106] French politicians and journalists at once became much less enthusiastic about overseas enterprise and colonial adventures. Although this change in political climate did not reverse the actual advances to which France had become committed in West Africa and elsewhere, it did mean that those who sought popularity through demagogic appeals to national prestige redirected their attention towards France's own eastern frontier. Later in 1885 General Boulanger, a flamboyant soldier of few political ideas, was pushed into prominence by radical politicians; his rise to popularity, being vaguely associated with unrealistic dreams of recovering Alsace, warned French politicians to move cautiously before diverting further national resources into conflicts in Africa from which the Germans might be the principal gainers.

The disappearance of Ferry, whose approach to co-operation with Germany had always been cautious, contributed to Bismarck's growing disillusionment with the fruits of colonial activity. He had already been disappointed to discover that the merchants who had called for state action were reluctant to form companies which might take over the costs of administration, and that his own financial dependence on the Reichstag would thus be increased.[107] Now the popularity of colonies among the public seemed to be subsiding too.[108] In September the crisis in eastern Europe which originated with the union of two Bulgarian states which had been deliberately separated in 1878 undermined the Three Emperors League, and threatened to bring Russia into conflict with Germany's Habsburg allies; it became increasingly important for Bismarck to ensure British co-operation in European affairs. On 28 September he assured a British representative that his complaints about their colonial policy had not been intended seriously and that

[106] See below pp. 51–2.
[107] Cf. W. O. Henderson, *Studies in German Colonial History* (1962), Chap. 2.
[108] Pogge *v.* Strandman, 'German Colonial Expansion . . .', *Past & Present* 42, p. 152.

there were now no points of difference between England and Germany. As far as Colonies went, he had got all he wanted, and more than he believed Germany would digest. He had never favoured the Colonial idea himself, but opinion in Germany ran so strongly in favour of Colonial enterprise that he could not resist it, or rather that he could not refrain from turning the Colonial stream into the main channel of his Parliamentary policy.[109]

The British were very willing to reciprocate. There had never been much real interest in African colonies among the country's rulers; and although a certain amount of instinctive jingoism had been evoked by the miniature dramas of the scramble, the instincts of the leaders of both parties still pointed towards caution and re-trenchment. As early as March 1885 Gladstone, ignoring the more 'wild and irrational' feelings of his colleagues, had declared in Parliament:

> If Germany becomes a Colonizing Power, all I can say is, 'God speed her'. She becomes our ally and partner in the execution of a great purpose of Providence for the benefit of mankind.[110]

Soon after this the ephemeral Penjdeh crisis, arising from Russia's military advance towards Afghanistan, diverted jingoistic feelings to an area long recognised as more essential to Imperial interests.

So, when Bismarck decided to liquidate the embarrassing resi-due of his West African initiatives after Ferry's fall, the British government quickly responded. In an exchange of Notes in April and June 1885 the two powers agreed to fix a boundary between their respective spheres of influence in Kamerun and the Oil Rivers along the supposed line of the Rio del Rey. Bismarck abandoned claims which the enterprise of Gaiser's agents had secured to an enclave of territory at Mahin, some forty miles east of Lagos, and the British promised to withdraw from Ambas Bay in the Cameroons as soon as the Germans could come to satisfac-

[109] Note by Sir Philip Currie of conversation with Bismarck 28 September 1885, quoted R. Greaves, *Persia and the Defence of India* (1959) p 247 from. Salisbury Papers.

[110] Hansard, 3rd series, Vol. 293, 979, 12 March 1885. Note also Glad-stone's privately-expressed belief that 'German colonisation will strengthen and not weaken our hold upon our colonies.' (*Diary of Sir Edward Hamilton*, II, pp. 784, 761).

tory terms with British missionary societies established there. (This was completed in March 1887.) The two governments also exchanged promises not to discriminate against each other's subjects in fixing customs duties.[111] In East Africa, where both governments were beginning to detect interests of greater importance, their disputes were not settled quite so quickly; but even there they would not be allowed to escalate into serious conflict.

These moves by European governments to prevent commitments in Africa from complicating relations in Europe were matched by their renewed anxiety to avoid conflicts with Africans. In December 1884 the Germans had had to land troops in Kamerun to suppress a rising against their *protégé*, King Bell; the warning which France had received from Indo-China was underlined in May 1885 by local successes of Samori; the British knew from long experience with Asante and the Zulus that African resistance could not be taken lightly, and this was further illustrated in February 1885 by the news of Gordon's death at Khartoum. Although it might seem excessive to talk of a reaction against expansion in Africa, everywhere in Europe (except perhaps Portugal) 1885 saw increased caution about the short-term consequences.

This did not however imply a withdrawal of interest, or refusal to consider further extension. The inhospitable Mauritanian coast offered few immediate commercial prospects which might help solve the economic crisis, and the capacity for resistance of its nomadic population was well-known. Nevertheless, in September 1885 the North West African Company (the body formed to develop Donald Mackenzie's projects in the area)[112] asked the British Government to help them follow Goldie's example, by granting a Charter and proclaiming British protectorate over the coasts between Morocco and Cape Bojado and between Cape Blanco and Portendic. (Spain had in January 1885 reasserted old claims by proclaiming a protectorate over the intervening coast.) Colonial Office officials (aware, admittedly, that direct responsibility would lie elsewhere) gave warm support to the proposal.

The climate is good [wrote the normally cautious Sir Robert

[111] E. Hertslet, *The Map of Africa by Treaty* (3rd ed., 1909, reprinted 1967) No. 260. Arrangement between Great Britain and Germany . . . 29 April – 16 June 1885.

[112] See above, p. 16.

Herbert]. The facilities for and prospects of trade appear excellent. And if it is possible as alleged to form a first class coaling station – capable of being defended – at or near Cape Juby. England ought not to delay to secure the place.[113]

When the Foreign Office and Admiralty more prudently concluded that the naval and commercial benefits did not justify the grant of a Charter 'to a small Company which could not exist without effective Imperial support', the Colonial Office grumbled that

This is not the sort of answer which Prince Bismarck would make to a German Company asking for protection and a Charter. But we find obstacles 'insuperable' which he overcomes with ease.[114]

Rumours of British interest did however stimulate the French to send a warship to seek (unsuccessfully) the site of the former settlement at Portendic, and to discuss the re-occupation of Arguin near Cape Blanco; suspicions of Britain thus helped keep alive the French design of controlling Mauritania, even at the height of the anti-colonial reaction.[115]

It is now easy to see that the easing of European expansionist pressure was temporary, almost fortuitous. As a colleague put it to the author, the first act of a Greek tragedy was under way, and its denouement would be the extinction of African independence. But the essence of Greek tragedy is that the denouement is unknown to the protagonists; if Oedipus had *identified* his parents, his story would be fit only for a horror comic. For most West Africans, their experience of the new European policies had been so tentative that the implications of the treaties they had signed, and of the landing of the newcomers, were hardly apparent. The hoisting of German flags on the coast of Togo, the installation at Porto Novo of twenty African soldiers and a French Colonel, the distribution of printed treaty forms for signature by rulers of the lower Niger valley, might be bad news for the Lawsons of Little

113 C.O.87/126 F.O. to C.O., 21 September 1885; Minutes by Hemming, 23 September; Herbert, 10 October.

114 C.O.87/129, F.O. to C.O., 17 February 1886; Minute by Hemming, 18 February.

115 ANSOM, Senegal III/12/a, Cuverville to Seignac, 22 February 1885, [sc. 1886]; Seignac to M.M.C., 12 March 1886; M.A.E. to M.M.C., 22 April 1886.

Popo, for the opponents of Kings Tofa and George Pepple; but it would be hard to discern in such events the dawn of a new era of African history. The writing might be on the wall, but it was still extremely difficult to read.

The shape of future events was perhaps most apparent in Senegambia, where the expansion of the groundnut economy had led the French colonial administration, as well as European and African traders from coastal settlements, into deep involvement in Wolof and Tokolor affairs. When the French decided to build their railway through Cayor, Lat-Dior had initially been tempted by prospects of increasing the resources of his commercially oriented Muslim state; but he quickly realised that the perils outweighed the benefits. For some time already his French neighbours had been eroding his authority, encouraging desertions among the royal slaves on whom his power largely rested; the advent of this 'steamship on dry land', Lat-Dior correctly foresaw, would lead to the intrusion of permanent French establishments, and would finally 'take away my country and despoil me of all I possess'. Already by 1882 his alliance with the French had broken down; having been declared deposed Lat-Dior embarked on a campaign of resistance, which continued until his defeat and death at Dyaqlé, on 26 October 1886.[116]

Rather more difficult for Africans to assess were the implications of the French military presence in the Upper Senegal and Niger. At first the aggressive intentions of the colonial army had seemed clear enough. Under Borgnis-Desbordes the soldiers, using the costly white elephant of the railway as 'a convenient disguise for the mounting costs of military expansion',[117] occupied Bamako, guarded their communications by a line of forts extending back to Kayes, and (in their own minds) took a moral commitment to destroy their Muslim antagonists in the not too distant future. But by 1883 many Deputies began to realise that the railway scheme had been frivolously costed, and that the ever-increasing credits they were being invited to authorise were actually being

[116] V. Monteil, 'Lat-Dior . . .' pp. 94–7; Germaine Ganier, 'Lat Dyor et le chemin de fer de l'arachide, 1876–1886', *Bulletin de l'IFAN* (1965) series B 27, pp. 223–81; cf. F. Renault, 'L'abolition de l'esclavage au Sénégal', *RFHOM*, LVIII (1971) p. 34.

[117] Kanya-Forstner, *Conquest*, p. 106 and Chap. 4, *passim*. Until 1886, the French command at Kayes was known as that of the *Haut-Fleuve;* I use the later title, *Soudan*, or Sudan.

appropriated in aid of megalomania dreams of military glory. On returning to Paris in 1883 Borgnis-Desbordes had been forced to recognise that the political climate was unfavorable to further advances. With Jauréguibery out of office, colonial policy was again under the direction of the Under-Secretary, Felix Faure, a hard-headed businessman from Le Havre – an advocate of colonial expansion but, like Ferry himself, a discriminating one. Although prudent imperialism remained in favour until 1885, priority was given to potentially remunerative expansion, and few people thought that the Sudan could fall into this category in the immediate future.[118]

For the Muslim empires of the Upper Niger, the interpretation of these shifts of policy posed puzzles. The Tokolor ruler Ahmadu, distrustful of the French from the first, was reluctant to commit himself to the risks of open resistance, and remained very willing to interpret deliberately ambiguous French policies in the most favourable sense.[119] Samori, on the other hand, had first encountered the French as military opponents; in February 1882 a battle at Keniera on the right bank of the Niger had demonstrated the menace of France's superior fire-power. Seeing the danger of remaining dependent for the import of arms and horses upon routes which the French might be able to close at will, Samori in December 1883 created a new western military command under Langama-Fali, with the role of opening alternative lines of communication through Futa Jalon to the British colony of Sierra Leone,[120] he continued to give priority to building the strength of his army.

But the French had already been impressed by the military organisation of Samori's Sofa cavalry, which had effectively harassed their movements after Keniera; once the struggle for Bamako was won in February 1883, logistic arguments reinforced the political pressure for prudence. During the campaigning season of 1883–4 (while French agents on the coast were extending their protectorates freely but economically) Lieutenant-Colonel Boilève was directed to exercise restraint, and his successor Combes was

[118] Cf. Person, *Samori*, II, pp. 663–4. For Parliamentary action on the Sudanese credits, see Kanya-Forstner, *Conquest*, pp. 113–20.

[119] Cf. *Prelude*, pp. 253–65; below pp. 59, 67, 72–3.

[120] Person, *Samori*, I, pp. 379-410, II, pp. 663–7, 1033; see also below pp. 56–8, 177–80.

warned to 'proclaim our wish to live in peace with everybody'.[121] Peaceful penetration by informal means was already returning to fashion. Thus the Ministry of Marine leapt naïvely at the opportunity apparently offered by the arrival at Kayes in September 1884 of Si El Haj Abd al-Qadir, who claimed to be an emissary from the 'Sultan' of Timbuctu and offered to establish close relations with France (whose Muslim policy he pronounced preferable to that of Britain). This obliging visitor was invited to France, where the Colonial Department happily elaborated plans for establishing a privileged position in that fabulous city and for encouraging dissident elements within the Tokolor empire which Abd al-Qadir suggested would be prepared to collaborate. In fact the man was almost certainly an impostor, but the prospects he held out of extending French influence without military or substantial financial commitments seemed attractive enough to merit his being entertained as an official guest in France from January 1885 until February 1886.[122]

Both in Africa and in Europe there were thus constraints inhibiting the aggressive instincts of military empire-builders, even before colonial policy became a central theme of controversy with the attacks upon Ferry. The treatment of Abd al-Qadir suggested to observant Africans that, as in the past, it might still be possible to negotiate with Europeans on some basis of equality, even in this one area where they were physically present in some force. The Europeans seemed to have paused before persisting in their new modes of behaviour; it was not easy for Africans to see that it was what, in another context, would later be called a 'loaded pause'.

[121] M.M.C. to Combes, 5 November 1884, cit. Kanya-Forstner, *Conquest*, p. 118.

[122] AE Afrique 84, M.M.C. to M.A.E., 1 December 1884; Afrique 85, Faure to Ferry, 19 January 1885. B. Olatunji Oloruntimehin, 'Abd Al-Qadir's Mission as a Factor in Franco-Tokolor Relations, 1885–1887', *Genève-Afrique*, VII (1968).

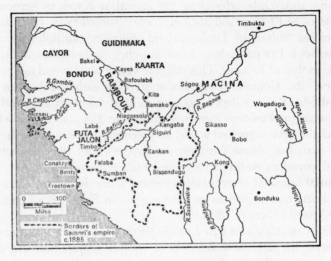

1 Senegambia and the Western Sudan

2 The French Inhibited

FRENCH ATTITUDES TO AFRICA, 1885–6

As the French advance towards the Western Sudan had launched the scramble, so its temporary slowing-down after 1885 marked the relative pause in European activity. The panic which many journalists and politicians experienced after Lang-Son reflected deep continuing doubts about colonial expansion. The military set-back suffered by Brière de L'Isle was not in fact as serious as alarmist reports in the evening papers of 29 March suggested; but it provided a focus for action by Deputies with many different reasons for opposing Jules Ferry. Personal animosity, and resentment of the meagre information supplied to Deputies, counted for much; but perhaps the strongest element was the rejection of Ferry's plea that 'distant enterprises' demanded a united national response in favour of a feeling that colonial campaigns were a luxury which France could not afford. Journalists and deputies who had become euphoric about new overseas provinces acquired by bloodless victories were not so happy about imperialism when it brought humiliating defeats. Clemenceau's charge of treason reflected a view of national priorities shared by many who would shortly support Boulanger's implied promise of a revival of French military power on the eastern frontiers.[1] It was particularly galling that this defeat had taken place while vestiges remained of Franco–German co-operation over West African questions.

With elections due in the autumn, colonial policy became a sensitive issue for French politicians. Some remained convinced advocates of activity overseas; others, on both Left and Right, strongly opposed policies which they variously represented as diverting French power from Europe, identifying the power of the state with the defence of sectional interests, or encouraging

[1] For these debates, see *Journal Officiel*, Chambre, Débats, 29, 31 March 1885, pp. 684–97.

racial attitudes unworthy of the nation which had proclaimed
the Rights of Man. Others again weighed their attitudes in the
scales of political expediency, balancing the risk of attacks on
their patriotism against that of involving their constituents' con-
script sons in more distant, costly, and dangerous campaigns. In
July, Madagascar provided a test case, when the government had
to ask the Chamber for further funds for its long-drawn-out operations against the Hova kingdom. From the Left of the Chamber,
Georges Perin, Camille Pelletan (a Radical henchman of Clemenceau), and Frederick Passy (an economist of the *Centre-Gauche*),
expressed fears that bellicose soldiers and missionaries would
'transform an expedition legitimately undertaken . . . into a
war of conquest'.[2] François de Mahy, Deputy for Reunion and a
former Minister, and the *rapporteur*, J. M. de Lanessan (a former
Radical becoming a colonial specialist) replied forthrightly that
France needed 'a policy of colonial expansion, consisting of an
outward thrust of her force, a spreading overseas of her intellectual
and military powers, a summons to civilisation addressed to new
barbarian peoples, an implantation of ideas among these inferior
peoples'.[3]

At this stage Ferry – who may originally have stumbled into
colonial expansion through the accidents of office, but since his
overthrow had grown increasingly convinced that he had been
right to do so – decided to intervene in the debate 'pour l'honneur
de la politique coloniale'.[4] In the face of intense and virulent heck-
ling from both Left and Right, Ferry strongly defended, not only
the specific policies which had led to his fall, but the legitimacy
and necessity of colonial expansion in general, using more forceful
arguments than had seemed prudent while he was in office.[5]
Parts of this often-quoted speech read like the pleading of a first-
class advocate who had mastered a brief: one historian calls it
'rather a series of defensive arguments than the cogent expression
of a faith'; another says that Ferry still spoke for the *ancienne ecole*

[2] J. O. Chambre, Débats, 26, 28, 29, 31 July 1885 – pp. 1613–23,
1624–8, 1636–47, 1659–72, 1677–88, 1693–4. Quotation from Perin, p.
1616.

[3] Lanessan, ibid., p. 1642.

[4] J. Ferry to Charles Ferry, 26 July 1885; *Lettres de Jules Ferry, 1846–
1893* (Paris 1914) pp. 380–1.

[5] J. O. Chambre, 29 July 1885, pp. 1659–72; also in P. Robiquet (ed.)
Discours et Opinions de Jules Ferry, v, pp. 172–220.

of colonisation (to which he accused Passy of belonging).[6] His economic reasoning was broad and unspecific, his general tone remote and academic. His arguments were met with equal force and vigour by Clemenceau, who declared that French trade would be handicapped, not served, if obliged to pay taxes to support colonial armies and bureaucracies, while the honour of the Republic would in no way be enhanced. 'My patriotism is in Europe', Clemenceau declared.[7] He thus directly challenged the central arguments of Ferry, and of many future imperialists, that the future prosperity of the French nation would be jeopardised if the government failed to assert the prestige of a great power, and that in the new condition of the world this prestige would depend on successful and vigorous colonial expansion.

Since 1871 there had been much rhetorical discussion in France of this intangible 'prestige' and of the means by which it could be secured. At first the prevailing view was that the shame of defeat and the loss of Alsace-Lorraine could be redeemed only by resolute policies in Europe. By 1881 French diplomats were extending this argument from prestige to justify imperialism in Tunisia; if France's passive role in the Berlin conference of 1878 were followed by passivity here, her standing as a Mediterranean power might be jeopardised. The Tunisian question, a French Ambassador to Rome had argued,

> affects not only our various interests in the Regency, the security of our Algerian colony, our prestige on the shores of the Mediterranean (whose inhabitants are so easily impressionable) – it has become a menace to our whole foreign policy . . .[8]

The Mediterranean however was an area of established importance in European diplomacy; 'prestige' had never been so centrally involved with policy in tropical Africa. Government initiatives here still needed to be justified by the prospect of concrete economic benefits, or possibly by some vague 'civilising mission'. True, in the autumn of 1882 attitudes of politicians and

[6] G. Chapman, *The Third Republic of France: the First Phase* (1962) pp. 253–4; H. Brunschwig 'Politique et economie dans l'empire Français d'Afrique Noire, 1870–1914', *JAH*, xi (1970) p. 406.

[7] J.O. 31 July 1885, 1677–85, cf. R. Girardet, *L'idée coloniale en France, 1871–1962* (1972) pp. 55–62.

[8] D.D.F. 1st series, iii, No. 405, Noailles to St. Hilaire, 19 March 1881; No. 406, St. Vallier to Noailles, Pte., 21 March 1881.

journalists towards de Brazza's successes in the Congo had suggested that vicarious compensation might be found there for the damage which French prestige had suffered in Egypt.[9] But Ferry's open assertion that failure to vote funds for Madagascar might set France into decline towards the status of a third- or fourth-rate power seemed to propound a significantly new doctrine on the importance of African colonies.

Although the Chamber accepted the necessity of voting the Madagascar credits by 277–120,[10] it did not thereby accept this new doctrine. In the election of October 1885 advocates of colonial activity had to go on the defensive. Although it is difficult to analyse the results in terms of attitudes to imperialism when most Deputies thought either of particular proposals or of quite different things, it seems that most of those who formed the new and more conservative majority still regarded French prestige as something to be defended in Europe. After the election new colonial estimates were approved by a majority of only three votes; and this experience naturally increased ministerial reluctance to approach the Chamber for even quite modest appropriations in aid of overseas enterprises.[11] The argument of endangered prestige could still serve to resist demands for sudden withdrawals; 'if one is free to choose not to make new acquisitions, one is not free to scuttle', declared that supple politician Freycinet, to public applause, in September 1886.[12] But the political case for colonial expansion had not yet been convincingly established, and there was still no real weight of private economic interest behind it. Ferry had unveiled a line of argument which imperialists would develop in the future, but the economic depression did not provide a favourable climate in which to do so.

As a recent study re-emphasises, the French merchants engaged in West African trade were still relatively small fish in the world of French capitalism; though anxious to use the influence of the Chambers of Commerce to protect established interests

[9] J. Stengers, 'L'impérialisme colonial de la fin du XIXᵉ siècle; mythe ou réalité?', *JAH*, III (1962) pp. 469–91.

[10] J. O. Chambre, Débats, 31 July 1885, pp. 1693–4.

[11] C. M. Andrew and A. S. Kanya-Forstner 'The French "Colonial Party": its Composition, Aims and Influence, 1885–1914', *Historical Journal*, XIV (1971) pp. 99–100.

[12] Speech by Freycinet at Toulouse, reported in *Le Temps*, 30 September 1886; copy in C.O. 96/177, F.O. to C.O., 11 October 1886.

they showed little concrete interest in the tempting prospects for investment and development held out by the technocrats of the 1870s.[13] Even in the Senegal valley, where the soldiers saw them- selves as laying military foundations for future commercial expan- sion, most French merchants preferred pacific policies which avoided disturbing such business relations as they had established with African traders from the interior; they still preferred to regard Senegal as *un vaste comptoir* rather than a true colony.[14] Those few merchants who had challenged British dominance on the oil-palm coast south of Senegambia controlled limited re- sources and sought limited political objectives. Arthur Verdier of La Rochelle had indeed started a coffee plantation on the Ivory Coast, which produced its first crop in 1886; but essentially he remained a minor provincial merchant, uneasily sharing a mono- polistic position in a limited sector of the palm oil trade with the British firm of Swanzy. His imports to the Ivory Coast were in 1885 officially estimated at 750,000 francs, his exports 845,000 francs.[15] Verdier, having been entrusted since 1871 with official responsibility for these French settlements, used his office to pro- tect his monopoly; when Charles Bour was sent out to create a more regular administration in February 1885 Verdier's agents objected to paying duties until the protection they were supposed to finance had already become effective. They obstructed Bour's maladroit proceedings so effectively that this attempt at more direct French control was abandoned within eighteen months.[16]

There was a similar story elsewhere. Marseille merchants – Victor Régis (his interests now merged in the firm of Mantes Frères de Borelli ainé) and Cyprien Fabre – had secured the pro- clamation of French protectorates in Porro Novo and Great Popo chiefly to protect modest trading fortunes against threats of British control. Their local representatives might dream dreams of inland penetration, but their principals provided little cash with which to back such projects. Even Verminck's Senegal Company had

[13] Brunschwig, 'Politique et economie . . .'.

[14] Quoted by R. Pasquier in H. Brunschwig (ed.) *Histoire Générale de l'Afrique Noire*, II (1971) p. 70.

[15] ANSOM Senegal III/13/c, Report by Lt. Hiart on a visit to the Ivory Coast, October–November 1887; AE Afrique 83, Note pour le Ministre 14 April 1887.

[16] P. Atger, *La France en Côte d'Ivoire de 1843 à 1893* (Dakar, 1962) pp. 92–109; AE Afrique 83, Verdier to M.M.C., 30 September 1886.

preferred to use its available capital to develop groundnut processing in France rather than to peg out claims for the future by
maintaining its independent presence on the Niger. When Goldie
offered to buy out its interests, and those of the *Compagnie
française de l'Afrique Equatoriale*, the weak resistance they offered
had infuriated patriotic agents like Commandant Mattei and
Edouard Viard.[17] And, as Viard discovered in 1886, the growing
depression of trade made the French business world generally
reluctant to venture even modest sums in West Africa.

The episode is quite instructive. Early in 1886 this young enthusiast secured an interview with Freycinet, again Premier and
Foreign Minister, and offered to forestall British designs on the
Fulani empire by leading an expedition from Porto Novo through
Boussa.[18] Freycinet was sufficiently interested to offer Viard a
grant of 20,000 francs, on condition that the balance of his estimated expenses of 100,000 francs was raised from commercial
firms. But six weeks later Viard submitted a discouraging report:

> For forty days I have done nothing but pay visits, make repre-
> sentations and requests, and write letters to the French business
> world, which is undergoing such difficulties and has such a need
> for new impetus. I tried to rouse it from its torpor and interest
> it in my journey and the advantages which it would bring; I
> made requests to everybody, not for merchandise but merely
> for collections of samples. I obtained no response; or those
> replies which I did receive drove me to despair. Some told me
> that it was the State which ought to take complete responsibility
> for the expenses of the expeditions; others that they did not
> know the country through which I was to travel, and that
> consequently it did not interest them. I left the world of
> commerce and directed my enquiries to that of banking and
> finance. That was even worse; I saw nothing but dirty schemes
> of avarice, and unmentionable appetites.[19]

Viard did his best to remain optimistic about French enterprise.

> Although I have had no success, I do not despair of my country-
> men. They fall back too much upon the State because they are

[17] *Prelude*, pp. 275–8, 310–12, 330; E. Viard, *Au Bas-Niger* (3rd ed.
1886) p. 15.
[18] AE Afrique 85, Viard to Freycinet, 12 February 1886.
[19] AE Afrique 85, Viard to Freycinet, 26 March 1886.

ignorant, because they are still too timid. But who knows the limits of the energy they will display when they find before them great new productive markets, secured for their profit by the State. . . .[20]

In looking to the State rather than to private capitalism to finance expansion in Africa, Viard correctly appreciated the mood of French business in 1885–6; but he was over-optimistic in expecting more than token encouragement from French governments at this period.[21] The Slave and Ivory Coasts aroused interest only in limited commercial and missionary circles; and even the commitment in the Sudan generated more suspicion than enthusiasm.

THE CRISIS OF SUDANESE IMPERIALISM:
FRANCE AND SAMORI

By 1885 French soldiers understood that Samori's still-expanding empire represented not only a tempting prize (controlling much of the upper Niger basin, including the gold of Bouré), but also a formidable military problem. Boilève, observing the restraining instructions which Borgnis-Desbordes drafted for him, had resisted the temptation to attack Samori during the campaign of 1883 and 1884. His major preoccupations were to construct forts (using Chinese coolie labour) in territories already occupied, and to assemble the prefabricated gunboat *Niger* – a striking and ominous innovation, but directed against Ahmadu rather than Samori, since it was launched downstream of the rapids of Sotuba. So co-existence continued, though somewhat precariously. Samori regarded the French with suspicion and by 1884 was increasing his purchases of arms in markets outside their control;[22] but these guns were primarily intended to be used in support of his campaigns in the Bagoue valley, where his expansion was meeting resistance from another rising African state, Kenedugu, under its able leader Tiéba. Although the bitter antagonism of these two men would later be increased by French intrigues, their original conflicts antedated French access to the area. Samori, who in July 1884 assumed the title of Alimani, was in process of enforcing a more rigorous Islamisation of his conquered peoples; this

[20] Ibid, Viard to Charmes, 26 March 1886.

[21] Cf. Brunschwig, 'Politique et Economie', pp. 410ff., for the comparable experiences of Dr. Colin.

[22] See below, pp. 177–9.

was resisted by many small Bambara states in the Bagoue valley, and Tiéba (though a Tijani Muslim) made himself the champion of traditional religion and culture in order to diminish his rival's power.[23] These preoccupations ensured that Samori, who had acquired a heathy respect for French armaments, responded to Boilève's restraint and maintained a 'tacit truce' with the French through 1884.[24]

Lieutenant-Colonel Combes, appointed in 1884 to continue Boilève's defensive holding operations, mistook Samori's restraint for weakness, and was led by vain dreams of glory into a flagrant violation of his instructions. In February 1885 he began work on the construction of a new fort at Niagassola; in March he advanced southwards into Bouré, seeking support from elements opposed to Samori. He greatly under-rated the strength of his enemy; Samori moved all available forces northwards, and late in May launched a counter-offensive which placed the French forces in grave peril of a new Lang-Son. Although Combes was able to conduct a fighting retreat to Niagassola without serious losses, 'this tactical success did not obliterate the humiliation he had suffered, and African opinion rightly saw this affair as a victory for Samori.'[25] Samori, arriving personally in Bouré, sent his brother Manigbe-Mori to occupy Mandinka districts in the upper Senegal which the French had lately detached from Tokolor rule, hoping to gather recruits and supplies, and also to strengthen his negotiating position. Blockading Niagassola but avoiding other French forts, the Sofas occupied much of the Bafing valley, and by August 1885 were within forty miles of Bafoulabé. Samori, had he chosen to give priority to resisting the French, was already powerful enough to present a formidable military challenge; but he was too conscious of their technological superiority, and too preoccupied with continuing revolts on the Bagoue, to wish to provoke a direct confrontation. Nevertheless, the French forces were in a dangerously exposed situation.

Nor was Samori the only threat. It was after all the Tokolor empire which was the original target of French expansion, and

[23] Person, *Samori*, I, pp. 502–12, II, 749–55.

[24] Ibid. II. pp. 663–7.

[25] Person, *Samori*, II, pp. 673, 667–84, gives the best account of this campaign; the notes contain devastating criticism of French colonial historiography.

against Ahmadu that Borgnis-Desbordes had originally hoped to win successes. His advance to Bamako had indeed accelerated the decline of Ahmadu's authority; by occupying lands which he claimed for his empire, the French encouraged resistance by other discontented subjects, and insubordination by the kinsmen on whom Ahmadu's system of government so heavily depended. There could be no effective resistance to the French until such revolts were more effectively controlled. Hence late in 1884 Ahmadu personally led an army through the turbulent district of Beledugu into Kaarta, and after defeating his rebellious half-brother Muntaga established his own headquarters in Nioro in 1885.[26] This offensive revived Ahmadu's prestige, and placed him in a better position to threaten French lines of communication around Kayes. When the French in September 1885 signed a treaty at Nyamina on the Niger, and later expelled the Tokolor garrison, Ahmadu replied by forbidding his subjects to trade with the French; and so increased the preoccupation of the colonial army.[27]

As it was realised in Paris that the conquest of the Western Sudan could not be a speedy, and might be a hazardous, operation, fears of being forestalled by the British intensified. (The old enemy Rowe, who had returned to Freetown as Governor of Sierra Leone and the Gambia, was showing a definite interest in the area.) The Colonial department had lost such enthusiasm it had even had for the Faidherbian myth of a rich empire in the upper Niger basin; during the Berlin Conference they were quite ready to grant Britain full rights of trade and navigation under an international commission for the upper basin of the Niger if they could thereby secure an equivalent status for the lower basin of the river.[28] This showed a just perception of the relative economic potential of the two regions; but the Foreign Ministry knew that the British would not willingly concede the point, and Ferry was not prepared to rely on German collaboration in order to contest it. Once Goldie had brought out the French competitors it was

[26] Y. Saint Martin, *L'Empire Toucouleur et la France* (Dakar 1967) pp. 316–22; B. O. Oloruntimehin, *The Tokolor Empire of Segu* (1972) pp. 259–65. There is a convenient account of Franco-Tokolor relations by A. S. Kanya-Forstner in M. Crowder (ed.) *West African Resistance* (1971) pp. 53–79.

[27] Saint Martin, *L'Empire Toucouleur et la France*, pp. 323–8.

[28] AE Afrique 109, M.M.C. to M.A.E., 12 December 1884.

difficult to challenge his effective monopoly. But it seemed to French diplomatists that the Berlin Conference was creating an instrument by which they could, with relative ease, redeem their prestige by reserving a substantial area (though of unproven value) for their empire. By applying Article 34, defining the procedure for obtaining international recognition of European protectorates over African coastline, to inland areas, the French could turn against the British their own juridical device for painless pre-emption of political control. In July 1885 therefore the Foreign Ministry invited the Ministry of Marine to provide such treaty texts as would justify a French protectorate over the upper basin of the Niger.[29]

Unfortunately, this method was not immediately usable: France had no valid treaties which would debar the British from penetrating the empires of Ahmadu or Samori. She had not ratified the somewhat ambiguous document which Gallieni secured from the Tokolors in 1881; and Samori had just demonstrated a capacity for resistance which could only suggest to French politicians the danger of another setback comparable to Lang-Son. And in the prevailing climate there was little hope of strongly reinforcing France's position on the ground. Armand Rousseau, Under Secretary for the Colonies in the Brisson ministry which had succeeded Ferry, was a believer in colonial expansion; but he realised that the Chamber would not approve heavy new expenditure on railway construction or military advance in the Sudan, and that to ask for this would only jeopardise more important enterprises in Indo-China and Madagascar. After the electoral successes of the Right in October 1885, when Rousseau lost his seat, no successor was appointed; for three months political responsibility vested in a Minister of Marine, Admiral Galiber, with little interest in colonies.[30] A young colonial officer, Captain P. L. Monteil, later claimed that in December 1885 he and Major Archinard had to plead France's obligations towards her *protégés* and the need to maintain security and prestige in Senegal itself, in order to dissuade Galiber from proposing complete withdrawal from the Sudan.[31]

[29] AE Afrique 85, M.A.E. to M.M.C., 27 July 1885.

[30] F. Berge, *Le Sous-Secretariat et les Sous-Secretaires d'Etat aux Colonies* (1962) pp. 37–8; cf. Person. *Samori*, ii, p. 682.

[31] P. L. Monteil, *Souvenirs Vécus*, pp. 36–40.

This story may be exaggerated; Galiber had already decided on a somewhat less drastic change of policy. In October 1885 Lieutenant-Colonel Frey was reluctantly sent to the Sudan with instructions (which he had helped to draft) to conduct such operations as would re-establish French prestige, without being drawn into any policy of conquests on the right bank of the Niger. 'Our object is to pacify the upper Senegal – not to make conquests.' A brusque admirer of General Boulanger (to whom he dedicated a sour volume of memoirs), Frey was thoroughly disillusioned with the 'fever' of colonisation which since 1876 had enmeshed the country in unrewarding African adventures; his main concern was to get through his term of duty without calamity, and on this understanding he persuaded Rousseau to provide additional troops, armament and equipment, including 20,000 bottles of wine to maintain the morale of his European personnel.[32] Provided that his forces could avoid any disgrace or debacle Frey was prepared obediently to try to protect French interests (and exclude the British) through diplomacy.

More generally, it was clear that Paris was reluctantly falling back on a policy of reserving future rights by negotiations with African rulers. When in February 1886 the Foreign Ministry came to draft a notification to the powers of French protectorates in the region, they realised that, even if taken at face value, their list of treaties could never exclude a British challenge. In order to cover the French possessions in Senegambia, keep open the route through Timbuktu to Algiers and prevent the British establishing some alliance with Samori, a much greater diplomatic effort in Africa would be needed.[33] This necessity, comments Person, 'might have led a different country from France into a system of zones of influence and in direct administration.'[34] But few French officers had the temperament to take collaboration with large African states seriously, except as a short-term expedient; and the colonial army

[32] H. Frey, *Campagne dans le Haut Sénégal et dans le Haut Niger 1885–1886* (1888) – especially the opening sections and the conclusion.

[33] AE Afrique 122, M.A.E. to M.M.C., 8 February 1886; De la Porte to Freycinet, 1 March 1886; draft notification, 27 May 1886. Most of the correspondence in this file concerns the French attempt to build up a comprehensive system of treaties during the years 1886–9. Cf. Kanya-Forstner, *Conquest*, pp. 138–41.

[34] Person, *Samori*, II, pp. 683, 729 (n. 126) quotes Frey's instructions from ANSOM, Senegal IV/84.

had already taken up positions and acquired commitments hardly
compatible with such a policy.

Samori, however, being anxious to concentrate his forces in
the east, was ready to explore the possibilities. In November 1885
he had already sent a letter offering peace to Lieutenant Péroz,
the French commandant at Niagassola, and he followed this by
ordering Manigbe-Mori to withdraw from the upper Senegal
to Siguiri, in Bouré. On 17 January 1886 these retiring forces
were attacked by Frey at Fatako Dyinko – a relatively minor
battle, but one which allowed the French, too, to negotiate with
the prestige based on recent military success. By 5 February discussions at Niagassola between Péroz and Samori's envoy Amara-
Dyeli had sketched out a draft treaty defining the Niger as the
frontier between the two empires. But Amara-Dyeli had no powers
to conclude such a treaty: and on receiving his report Samori asked
that a French delegation should be sent to negotiate a definite
agreement at Kenieba-Koura.[35]

By the time this delegation, led by Captain Tournier and Péroz,
began its negotiations on 26 March 1886, France's military and
diplomatic position had been gravely weakened by the withdrawal
of troops to protect Kayes against Mahmadu Lamine.[36] It now
became doubly urgent for the French to get a treaty which would
protect them against the danger of war on two fronts in the
Sudan, and at the same time provide some basis for notifying
a claim to the upper Niger. 'The mission may not accept the risk
of a rupture,' Frey wrote urgently to Tournier, '. . . Do not waste
time on secondary questions. . . . We must content ourselves with
getting Samori's signature. For the rest, make any concessions,
but have done with it quickly.'[37]

The treaty agreed at Kenieba on 28 March 1886 not only
carried Samori's agreement to peaceful co-existence, but gave the
French some reason to hope for a favoured commercial position
in his empire. Beyond this, Samori had insisted on introducing
reservations and supplementary provisions which were extremely

[35] Person, *Samori* II, pp. 68ff., gives the only satisfactory account of these
negotiations. B. O. Olorontimehin, 'The Treaty of Niagassola 1886',
JHSN, IV 4, 1969, pp. 601–12, relies too heavily on French colonial
publications and so fails to clarify some important points.

[36] See below pp. 65–7.

[37] Frey to Tournier, 23 March, 4 September 1886, cit. Person, *Samori*,
II, p. 734 (n. 161) from ANSOM Senegal IV/105.

disappointing to French imperialists. Not only did the treaty fail
to define French rights of protection in any form which could
command recognition by other European powers; but Samori
refused to abandon his rights over Kangaba and Bouré on the left
bank of the Niger; he agreed only not to maintain troops there
nor prevent the French from procuring provisions.[38] Bouré, which
had long enjoyed commercial relations with Freetown, thus remained vulnerable to the supposed designs of Sir Samuel Rowe.[39]
But although French colonialists frankly regarded the treaty as
a temporary expedient,[40] the text conceded rights which they
could subsequently extend by imposing literal interpretations of a
sort quite foreign to Samori.[41] He evidently intended to implement
its terms – as he understood them – in good faith, and readily
agreed that his son, Dyaulé-Karamoko, should make an officially-
sponsored visit to France. This Frey hoped might so impress the
young man as to make him a willing agent of French rule in the
future.[42] Other French soldiers did not look so far ahead; they
regarded the treaty as a disagreeable charade, but conceded that
it secured France's frontiers with Samori at a time of real peril.

FRANCE AND ISLAM IN THE SENEGAL VALLEY, 1885–6

The constraints imposed from Paris interacted with African resistance to inhibit French penetration, not only on the Niger but
within the territorial limits of their Senegalese colony. Although
Faidherbe claimed to have established French sovereignty over
Futa Toro and the Wolof and Serer states which lay to the south,
in practice French power outside the 'four communes' of the
coast remained dependent on isolated forts and garrisons. Their
capacity to intimidate backed up the heavy-handed and often
erratic diplomacy, sometimes cemented by mutual commercial
interests, which was still the real basis of French control. Through-

[38] For French objections and a text of the treaty, AE, Afrique 122, de la
Porte to Freycinet, 14 September 1886.
[39] See below, pp. 176–80.
[40] E.g. J. Méniaud, *Les Pionniers du Soudan* I, p. 255.
[41] Cf. Person, *Samori* II, p. 689: the treaty 'opposed two mentalities, one
moulded by written law, the other – despite a most juridicial spirit –
remained determined by empiricism and the spoken word. It is certain
that the detailed drafting of these articles had little meaning for Samori,
and that the clauses agreed to were in his view to inspire the actions of
the two parties, not to serve as an exact law.'
[42] Person, *Samori* II, pp. 691–5.

out the 1870s many Senegalese Muslims still acted on the old theory that, while the French were welcome as traders, their presence in permanent structures on African soil was unacceptable. French military encroachments almost invariably met resistance: sometimes by arms, sometimes by migration to 'Nioro', as the empire formed by Al Haj 'Umar was locally called.[43] After 1880 France's commitment to expansionist policies, based on railway construction and military penetration of the Sudan, obliged her to make new demands within the Senegal area – for help in the passage of troops and supplies, the construction of a telegraph line through Futa Toro, as well as for the railway concessions themselves – which greatly increased the disquiet of Muslim patriots.

It was Lat-Dior who first received the full weight of the new French policies, and so became the first leader of Senegalese resistance.[44] But as their campaign against him continued into 1885, French officials came to fear the hostile influence of two other Senegalese rulers of widespread influence, who at that time showed signs of forming a Muslim alliance against them. Lat-Dior's cousin, Al-Bouri Ndiaye (1842–1902), who since 1875 had ruled Jolof as a client of the French, had been converted with him by Maba in 1864; despite recurring conflict over internal issues of Wolof politics, the cousins had often collaborated against French encroachments. Although during the crisis of French expansion the government of Senegal made a separate peace with Al-Bouri on 18 April 1885, they were never confident of his 'loyalty' and continued to fear his widespread influence among kinsmen and fellow Muslims like Niokhorbaye Diou in Sine.[45] Governor Genouille in 1887 believed that he was preparing a sort of feudal host by presenting horses to Muslim neighbours in return for promises of military service.[46] The other man the French feared

---

[43] I take this point, like several others, from the thesis of D. W. Robinson, Jr., 'Abdul Bokar Kan and the History of Futa Toro, 1853 to 1891, (Ph.D., Columbia, 1971).

[44] See above, pp. 12–47.

[45] See V. Monteil 'Le Dyoloff et Al-Bouri Ndiaye' in his *Esquisses Sénégalaises* (Dakar, 1966), and compare his uncle's view in 1879 – 'a very fine man, with handsome features – alert and intelligent, with a great reputation for gallantry'. P. L. Monteil, 'Un Voyage d'Exploration au Sénégal en 1879', *Bulletin de l'IFAN*, xxx B (1968) p. 1216.

[46] ANSOM, Senegal IV/105/a, Genouille to Etienne, June 1887. I am grateful to Mr. A. Mboge for a transcript.

was Abdul Bokar Kan (or Abdul Bubakr), chief of Bosséa, a shrewdly realistic contender for power within the much-divided confederation of Futa Toro. Less closely identified with the Islamic cause, Abdul Bokar had strengthened his reputation by skill and resolution in negotiating with the French; like Al-Bouri he secured favourable treaty terms as a condition of his co-operation during the crisis of 1885.

The general tendency of French policy during these years was to resist 'Muslim fanaticism' in Senegambia by collaborating with non-Muslim or tepid Muslim leaders, such as Sambala of Khasso and other Mande chiefs in the upper Senegal, the Mboge brothers in Saloum, or M'Backe Deb Ndiaye in Sine. It would be an over-simplification to describe France's attitude as anti-Islamic; Islam was too strongly implanted within her settlements, and the pre-judices held by many officials were controlled by the self-interest of Senegalese merchants such as Gaspard Devès, who had capital tied up in the fortunes of Muslim rulers.[47] But in the long run the logic of her own imperialism brought France into conflict with Muslims committed to maintaining the independence of their states.

At the end of 1885 however France briefly acquired a real common interest in collaborating with Al-Bouri and Abdul Bokar against a charismatic Muslim leader whose rise threatened many established authorities within the region. This was Mahmadu Lamine (Muhammad al-Amin), a Sarakulé born in Khasso during the 1830s, who had gained inspiration and prestige during a pro-longed pilgrimage to Mecca and other great Islamic centres. The priorities of Lamine's mission were greatly influenced by his ex-perience while returning; he was detained in Segou for several years by Ahmadu, who saw in his *baraka* a threat to his own authority. When Lamine returned to Khasso in 1885, French

[48] E.g. Servatius to Brun, 8 April 1883, quoted in G. Ganier, 'Lat-Dior et le chemin de fer d'arachide, 1876–1886', *Bulletin de l'IFAN*, B xxvii (1965) pp. 272–3. In a note of 1887 (AE Afrique 85) Viard condemned the methods of peaceful penetration adopted by the commercial houses. Besides combining to exclude new competitors, 'their other tactics consist of involving the chiefs of the country in debt; hence the chiefs bring pressure upon their subjects, so that the crops of these poor wretches, the objects of exchange which they possess, go to one firm or another to fulfill the obligations of the chief. The death of the Damel of Cayor . . . has, it seems, meant a loss to one Saint Louis House of 150.000 francs.'

officers believed he intended to use his religious authority to create a Sarakulé state in the upper Senegal, preferably with French support. He repeatedly declared that he would direct the force of *jihad* against Ahmadu ('ce méchant homme',)[48] and that his territorial ambitions centred on Guidimaka (in the Tokolor empire) and Tenda (whence they might point towards the British sphere in the Gambia).[49] But from December 1885, Lamine began to intervene in the disputed succession in Bondou, a state of great importance to French diplomacy. Colonel Frey now feared that his half-formed policy of playing off Lamine again the Tokolors might prove dangerous; he moved troops from Kayes to Bakel, and on 13 March 1886 seized members of Lamine's family as hostages. The French thus made the first moves in a military campaign which proved far more formidable than they had expected. Lamine continued to emphasise that he wished for peace with the French, if only for practical reasons – 'for powder, shot, guns and munitions of war, as well as paper, are all French articles, which we can only obtain from you, with your consent and for that peace is necessary.[50] But no French commander welcomed the idea of arming Muslims; and indeed, even if Lamine was sincere in his friendly overtures towards the French, this was not true of other Sarakulé with closer and more recent experience of dealing with them.[51] To maintain prestige among their clients in the Senegal valley the French had to resist Lamime's movement, and this absorbed their major military effort until his defeat and death in December 1887. They were thus obliged to seek, besides the truces with Samori and the Senegalese leaders, a more or less active alliance with the Tokolors against this formidable common enemy.[52]

Although aware that the Foreign Ministry urgently needed a

[48] Lamine to Governor, August 1885, quoted in D. Nyambarza, 'Le marabout El Hadj Mamadou Lamine d'après les archives françaises', *CEA*, IX (33) p. 130; cf. Méniaud, *Pionniers*, I, pp. 216ff.

[49] This paragraph owes much to the chapter by B. O. Oloruntimehin in M. Crowder (ed.) *West African Resistance* (1971). Early traditions are analysed by Humphrey Fisher, 'The early life and pilgrimage of Al-Hajj Muhamad al-Amin', *JAH*, XI (1970) pp. 51–70.

[50] Mahmadou Lamine to Governor, translated 24 September 1886; text in Nyambarza, loc. cit., pp. 141–2.

[51] Nyambarza, pp. 132–8, 144.

[52] Oloruntimehin, loc. cit.; also his 'Muhammad Lamine in Franco-Tukolor Relations, 1885–7', *JHSN*, IV, 3 (1968).

protectorate treaty which could be used to avert British claims, Frey had initially inherited the military tradition of hostility towards Ahmadu; an invitation of January 1886 to sign such a treaty was peremptorily worded, and combined with a ban on the arms supplies which the Tokolor state needed.[53] Frey had been warned by Tokolor dissidents that 'Ahmadu is working to form a vast league against the French, in which not only Abdul Bubakr but the chiefs of Jolof, of Cayor, and even fanatical Muslims from Saint-Louis are to participate';[54] and he seems to have taken this version of the familiar 'Muslim' peril seriously. During the early stages of the campaign against Mahmadou Lamine his troops entered Guidimakha without regard to Ahmadu's territorial claims. But the prolongation of this campaign emphasised that France and the Tokolors had short-term interests in common: Frey began to wonder whether his hostility was necessary or justified. His distaste for service in Africa was increased when his operations were sharply criticised by the trading community of Saint-Louis and their Deputy Gasconi, who seemed more interested in resuming the export of arms to Ahmadu than in opening inland markets by conquest.[55] So Frey ended the campaigning season completely disenchanted with the Sudan; in a book published in 1888 he proposed an abandonment of military advances beyond Medine, and a return to Valière's policy of 1872 'based on the constitution in the Western Sudan of a vast empire in the firm hand of a single native chief', [56] namely Ahmadu. Gallieni, who succeeded him as *Commandant Superieur* in 1886, was not ready to effect quite such a drastic change of policy; but he came prepared to carry out substantial reorientations.

GALLIENI AND THE MUSLIM EMPIRES

J. S. Gallieni, who was to become one of the heroes of French colonialists – and, in 1914, of the whole French nation – was a complex and mutable person. Although he was to quarrel sharply with his fellow officers in the charmed circle of the colonial military establishments – the account which he published in 1891 of his 'two campaigns' as commander in the Sudan, between

[53] Text in Saint-Martin, *L'Empire Toucouleur et la France*, p. 329.
[54] Frey, *Campagne*. . ., p. 206.
[55] Kanya-Forstner, *Conquest* . . ., p. 136, quoting ANSOM Senegal iv/85/a, Frey, 22 June 1886: cf. Frey, *Campagne* . . .. pp. 318–20, 471–3.
[56] Frey, *Campagne*. . . . , pp. 495–503.

November 1886 and May 1888, is in places a direct critique of their policies[57] – he was nominated for command by Borgnis-Desbordes, who seems to have been largely responsible for drafting instructions which required him to follow a 'firm, prudent and peaceful' policy.[58] In fact he did bring the military crisis under control; he pushed the wretched railway line up to Bafoulabé; and he gave the areas already conquered a sufficiently stable administration to permit some revival of agriculture and local commerce. But he left the Sudan a strong critic of the whole railway enterprise (which had served as the warrant for military autonomy), and came to advocate substantial reorientations in the whole strategy of Sudanese imperialism.

The framework of French policy was still largely governed by considerations of internal and international politics. Although supporters of the Sudanese enterprise managed to avert the danger of withdrawal which had threatened in 1885, and even to shelter its finances from further attacks by incorporating them more closely in the general budget of the Ministry of Marine,[59] they could not hope to obtain support for new commitments. Those politicians who had come to favour imperialist policies in principle were in no position to advocate them openly. Ferry remained a suspect figure; and imperialist disciples of Gambetta, such as Maurice Rouvier, were preoccupied by the threat to Republican institutions which they saw developing from General Boulanger, who was appointed as Minister of War in January 1886. After the enthusiastic reception which Boulanger received from the crowd at the Bastille Day parade of 1886 there was an evident danger that demagogic politicians might try to ride to power on a tide of patriotic enthusiasm, stimulated by vague hopes of some sort of action over Alsace-Lorraine.

It was apparent to prudent bourgeois politicians that the international implications of this domestic instability might be very serious. The crisis in eastern Europe had broken the Three Emperors' League and ended Bismarck's experimental policy of co-operation with France in African questions. It seemed possible that Germany might use provocative behaviour by the Boulangists as a pretext for some sort of preventative attack, confident

[57] J. S. Gallieni, *Deux Campagnes au Soudan français* (1891).
[58] AE Afrique 85, De la Porte to Genouille, 20 October 1886.
[59] Person, *Samori* ii, p. 696.

that Alexander III would be reluctant to take Russia into alliance
with such an ideologically distasteful regime. Although it is unlikely that Bismarck seriously considered such action, he did use
the argument of a revanchist threat to secure a majority for a
Conservative/National Liberal alliance in the Reichstag election
which he called in January, and so for his new seven-year Army
law. In April 1887 a frontier incident, created when German
police arrested a French customs officer, Schnaebélé, in Alsace,
underlined (and in fact exaggerated) the danger. On 30 May 1887
Rouvier, putting aside his former interest in Africa, formed a
government from which Boulanger was excluded – a move to
defend the peaceful Republican regime of peasants and middle-
bourgeoisie, which involved dependence for support on right-
wing politicians still basically hostile to colonial expansion.[60]

In these conditions, it was clearly prudent to try and prevent
colonial commitments from determining France's general policy.
But this did not mean abandoning colonial policy altogether.
Francis Charmes, a Republican politician and journalist who was
brought into the Quai d'Orsay as *directeur politique* by Freycinet
in 1885, and remained there until his re-election to the Chamber
in 1889, was a professed supporter of colonial expansion; but,
like his brother and collaborator Gabriel, he believed it could only
be safely practised on the basis of the liberal alliance with Great
Britain. The rupture over Egypt, as Gabriel clearly saw, made
French colonial policy dependent upon a partnership with Germany for which there was no real foundation of long-term common
interest;[61] Francis had drawn the logical conclusion by moving
the resolution which led to Ferry's defeat in the Chamber after
Lang-Son. But despite these Anglophil credentials, Charmes's
behaviour as an official left the British Embassy with a strong
impression that he was 'prejudiced' on Egyptian questions, and
generally influenced France's dealings with Britain in a 'very
chauvinist' sense.[62] While the Rouvier ministry could not profess

[60] The international background may be studied in W. L. Langer,
European Alliances and Alignments (N.Y., 1931) and in A. J. P. Taylor, *The
Struggle for Mastery in Europe* (Oxford, 1954) chap. 14.

[61] Gabriel Charmes, *Politique Extérieure et Coloniale* (Paris, 1885) esp. the
essay on 'La Politique Coloniale', dated November 1883: cf. F. Pisani-
Ferry, *Jules Ferry et le Partage du Monde* (Paris, 1962) pp. 257–8.

[62] Newton, *Lord Lyons* (1913) II, p. 387, Lyons to Salisbury, 18 February
1887; Sal. P. A57, Lytton to Salisbury, 27 January 1888.

policies of colonial expansion, neither could it afford to let its diplomatic handling of colonial issues appear neglectful of French interests or French pride.[63]

For French national pride was not easily divisible; since 1883 British slights could raise indignation as easily as German threats. Even a ministry like Rouvier's, anxious to avoid colonial adventures and to improve its diplomatic relations with Britain, had to avoid any appearance of feebleness over colonial issues. Moreover, promoters of colonial expansion were still active beneath the surface. As Under-Secretary for the Colonies, Rouvier appointed Eugène Etienne, Algerian-born Deputy for Oran and a former associate of his own both in politics and business – an able and ambitious politician who, with his Prime Minister's support, began to work to free the Colonial Department from the direct supervision of the Ministry of Marine and to give it a more active role in the formation of policy.[64] Etienne could not succeed in controlling or changing the course of French policy in Africa during this first period of office but it provided opportunities for him to become acquainted with the needs of the various French settlements and to build up relations with interested parties which would later fortify his position as one of several former followers of Gambetta prominently identified with colonial causes. Although Marseille merchants like Fabre carried less weight politically than some of the interests involved in promoting railway contracts and other enterprises in his native Algeria, Etienne took the affairs of tropical Africa more seriously than any of his predecessors. He used such influence as his still relatively minor office possessed to ensure that they were not ignored by his senior colleagues, and to protect the Sudanese enterprise against anti-colonial critics.

In this ambiguous political context, Gallieni proved skilful in advancing French power with minimum military risks. Though no less professionally ambitious than Desbordes or Archinard, he did not share their obsessive need for the meretricious martial glory of spectacular *faits de guerre,* but was happy to proceed by intelligence and guile. His first priority however was the military defeat of Mahmadu Lamine, with whom no secure compromise

---

[63] Ibid., A56, Lyons to Salisbury, 7 June 1887; A59 Salisbury to Lyons, 20 July 1887.

[64] H. Sieberg, *Eugène Etienne und die französiche Kolonialpolitik* (Köln, 1968) esp. pp. 20–39.

seemed possible; to this operation Gallieni had to devote much of his energy and resources during his early months in Africa. But this problem, though difficult, was controllable; since Lamine's *jihad* had rested on a somewhat exclusive ethnic basis, he had isolated himself from possible African allies. Gallieni could concentrate his forces, which he did with skill and panache. His first campaign drove Lamine into the middle Gambia valley at the end of 1886; his second culminated in the prophet's defeat and death in December 1887.[65]

This prior commitment of military forces ensured that the second urgent task facing Gallieni – to secure the western Sudan, and in particular Samori's empire, against any intrusion by the British – would have to be achieved by diplomacy. Specifically, Gallieni was required to supply the Foreign Ministry with the documentary basis for claiming protectorate rights which they had been asking for since mid-1885. Again, Gallieni was well-fitted by temperament and experience to play the temporary role of diplomatist; unlike some of his colleagues he did not regard negotiations with Africans as a demeaning charade. As Person notes, he had arrived in West Africa in time to be influenced by the preexpansionist ethics of Valière and Boilève; his vacillations at Nango in 1880 had shown that he was 'open to the idea of penetration based upon negotiation and the search for transitory partners among the Africans'.[66]

But the partners *would* be transitory; to envisage Gallieni as a potential Lugard, devising a French version of Indirect Rule, was too vigorous an exercise of historical imagination.[67] The most intelligent of all the Sudanese officers, Gallieni suffered from the intellectual's tendency to see both sides of problems which simpler soldiers might solve by direct assault. Too much of a disciplinarian to deal with Africans in a spirit of real equality, too much involved in the Sudanese empire to adopt the indifferent attitudes of Frey, Gallieni was, by 1886, a convinced imperialist – though, as Person adds, a humanistic imperialist. As a French patriot he

[65] The most recent account is by B. O. Oloruntimehin in M. Crowder (ed.) *West African Resistance*. For Gallieni's own account, see *Deux Campagnes* . . .

[66] Person, *Samori*, II, p. 701; cf. *Prelude*, pp. 256–62.

[67] John D. Hargreaves, 'The Tokolor Empire of Segou and its Relations with the French', *Boston University Papers on Africa*, II (1966) p. 145.

regarded empire in Africa as a potentially vital element in his country's power.[68] As a good Republican, he envisaged the essential purpose of empire as the assimilation of Africans to a French way of life, but only after a period of subjection which would last for the foreseeable future. 'He certainly did not regard Africans with the racist arrogance of other colonizers, but he inherited the French illusion that individuals can be liberated by first being deprived of their personality and culture,' writes the Breton scholar, Person. 'That is why his policy was always to be basically hostile to Islam, which he judged a greater threat than animism to his assimilationalist dreams.'[69]

In the book which justified his policies to the French public, Gallieni repeatedly suggests a simple French imperial mission to liberate the peace-loving peasants of the Sudan from the oppression of Muslim conquerors or oppressors, the Tokolors or Moors. Thus he writes that the voyage of a French gunboat down the Niger,

> aroused, among the Bambaras and Fulas, ideas of securing independence from their oppressors, and the desire to shake off a detestable yoke in order to indulge in the peaceful practice of trade and agriculture.[70]

Yet the same work contains passages justifying the negotiation of treaties with 'great protected states', to which Islam had in his view brought a 'veneer of civilization'.[71] And the political result of his 'campaign' during the dry season of 1886–7 was represented principally by the long-desired protectorate treaties with Ahmadu and Samori.

Although neither treaty can be taken at its face value, Gallieni may have regarded that with Ahmadu with a certain limited seriousness. Although his memories of Nango were neither happy

[68] Cf. *Deux Campagnes* . . . , p. 615. 'Il est permis de supposer cependant que peut-être un jour l'Europe, expulsée de l'Asie, où s'étale en ce moment toute son activité industrielle, par l'envahissement progressif et intense de la race jaune, trouvera son dernier point d'appui en cette Afrique qui, de nos jours seulement, ouvre ses secrets si longtemps gardés, et la nation la plus forte sera celle qui aura pu prévoir cet avenir.'

[69] Person, *Samori*, II, pp. 699–702.

[70] Gallieni, *Deux Campagnes* . . . , p. 221 (cf. p. 429).

[71] Ibid., pp. 618–33 (and extracts translated in John D. Hargreaves, *France and West Africa* (1969) pp. 161–3).

nor glorious, they had taught him that it was possible to negotiate agreements with the Tokolors in expectation that they would be carried out. Gallieni addressed Ahmadu in a disdainful and imperious style (employing the second person singular, as was customary in France's African diplomacy); he waited for the Tokolors to take the formal initiative in negotiation, and insisted that they should accept all extensions of French power and rights since 1880 as *faits accomplis*.[72] Yet Gallieni and Ahmadu clearly had reciprocal interests – in disposing of Mahmadu Lamine, and also in reviving trade. Ahmadu needed to replenish the supply of arms on which his jeopardised authority depended; Gallieni was anxious to give the new French colony some shred of economic viability. So, when Ahmadu responded amicably to the news of Gallieni's appointment, the Commandant was quick to authorise the renewal of trade in gunpowder and flintlocks, and to draft a new treaty. On 12 May 1887 Ahmadu affixed his seal to this, at Gouri.

This text ignored most of the reservations which Ahmadu had tried to insert in the Treaty of Nango; and, apart from an annual 'indemnity' in lieu of customs duties payable on the gum trade, there was no longer any question of the French government paying a stipend or directly supplying firearms. In the principal clause Ahmadu placed his 'present and future states' under the protectorate of France – or, according to the Arabic version, under her 'protection and aid'. (This variation, and those relating to the conditions of trade and of navigation on the Niger, suggest to M. Saint-Martin that the Arabic draftsman may have wished to favour the Tokolors.)[73] The main anomaly, however, is not to be found in the text of the treaty, but in discrepancies between its terms and Gallieni's behaviour. In the treaty – a diplomatic document, shortly to be produced to the British in accordance with the procedure agreed at Berlin – Gallieni was careful to maintain the title of his new *protégé* to an empire extending from Dinguiraye to Timbuktu; but in reality he recognised the decay of the central authority within this empire. Not only had Gallieni no intention of restoring Ahmadu's power, but he had already begun to reduce it still further.

[72] Y. Saint-Martin, *L'empire toucouleur et la France*, pp. 343–5, gives the texts of Gallieni's letters of 6 November 1886, 5 February 1887.

[73] Ibid., pp. 352–64, for a comparison of the French text with a French translation of the Arabic text.

In the west, Captain Oberdorf had already, in March 1887, made a separate treaty of protection with Ahmadu's half-brother, Aguibou, who had governed the district of Dinguiraye on his behalf with lukewarm loyalty since 1878; Aguibou had been making overtures to the French since 1884.[74] On the Niger, Captain Caron and his gunboat were sent by Gallieni to negotiate with Tidiani, another half-brother who ruled Macina, and with the authorities of Timbuktu; though unsuccessful, this voyage through the heart of the Tokolor empire was a clearly hostile act which aroused considerable excitement among the Tokolors of Segou.[75] Gallieni was indeed preparing to move against Segou itself as a preliminary to eventual penetration down the Niger; a second French gunboat, the *Mage,* was already under construction at Bamako, and Gallieni had authorised the signature of protectorate treaties and the discreet distribution of firearms among the small Bambara principalities of Beledugu 'in order to permit them, on the one hand successfully to resist Ahmadu's advance and to close his route to Segou, on the other to turn him away from our own supply-line and to engage him in continuous warfare on the borders of Beledugu'.[76]

If Gallieni took the treaty of Gouri seriosly enough to envisage any future for Ahmadu within France's Sudanese empire, it can thus only have been as ruler of Kaarta, the remote and impoverished province where he had concentrated his efforts since 1884.[77] Even such an arrangement could not have been stable; Gallieni's idea that the *grands protégés* should eventually pay tribute in acknowledgment of French sovereignty[78] would inevitably have aroused fierce resistance from Muslims who believed that it was for Christians to pay *jizya* if they came to reside in Islamic territory. It is therefore only to a very limited degree that Gallieni's intentions towards Ahmadu can be considered honourable; he

[74] There is a good account of this episode, including the text of the treaty in Yves Saint Martin, 'Un fils d'el Hadj Omar; Aguibu, roi du Dinguiray et du Macina', *CEA*, VIII, 29 (1968) pp. 144–77.

[75] Gallieni, *Deux Campagnes . . .* , pp. 191–221.

[76] Gallieni to Monsegur, 20 November 1886, cit., Saint-Martin, *L'Empire Toucouleur*, pp. 347–9. This supply of arms was envisaged in Gallieni's instructions.

[77] But cf. the reference to the need to occupy Nioio in Gallieni, *Deux Campagnes . . .* , p. 633: cf. p. 619.

[78] Gallieni to Rivière des Borderies, 1888, cit., Saint-Martin, p. 370.

envisaged at most a *mariage à la mode du pays*, a union with rules essentially determined by the needs of the French partner, who would remain free to terminate it when it ceased to be convenient.

With Samori, Gallieni had had no earlier liaison to leave lingering bonds of affection; his immediate need was to obtain a treaty which, unlike that of 1886, could be effectively used by the diplomatists. His initial instructions had emphasised the inadequacy of Tournier's treaty, and the need for the French to become 'Samori's allies, and at the same time the inspirers of his foreign policy'. If Samori were to grant the British rights over lands bordering any tributary of the Niger, they might claim that the upper Niger had become an international waterway, to be subjected to the international safeguards laid down in Berlin. In view of current rumours about British intentions it was absolutely essential to obtain an undertaking, suitable for publication in Europe, establishing French control of Samori's foreign relations: there was no need however to obtain any right to intervene within his states.[79] In fulfillment of these instructions Gallieni, on arriving in Senegal, despatched Captain Péroz on a mission to Samori's capital of Bisandugu, where he arrived on 15 February 1887.[80]

Samori's position had weakened since his negotiations with Tournier. During 1886 he had continued to accentuate the Islamic character of his empire; in November he proclaimed his intention of prohibiting the consumption of alcohol and the practice of animist religion, and of enforcing the Shari'a. Such radical proselytisation provoked widespread reactions among those attached to traditional ways, even within Samori's own family. At the same time Samori resolved to attack Tiéba in his fortified capital of Sikasso, in order to end his support for rebellious Bambaras of the Bagoue valley, and to secure the routes to the east and northeast on which, since the appearance of the French at Bamako,

[79] AE Afrique 85, De la Porte to Genouille, 20 October 1886; M.A.E to M.M.C., 5 December 1886.

[80] The most recent and best account is in Person, *Samori*, II, pp. 698–701. Péroz's original report appears lost, but see his published versions in E. Péroz, *Au Soudan Français* (1891) and in Gallieni, *Deux Campagnes . . .*, pp. 223–94.

his cavalry depended for supplies of horses.[81] In setting out on this campaign, Samori unavoidably accepted a risk of losing control over Bouré. Yet he was reluctant to make the formal renunciation of sovereignty implied by granting the French permission to build a fort there; he was, says Péroz, 'torn between the fear of a renewed struggle against us, and that of damaging his prestige and his resources by officially becoming our vassal, and especially by abandoning the left bank of the Niger to us'.[82] Moreover, he was determined not to cut himself off from the connection with Freetown, on which his arms supply increasingly depended. Although an attempt in 1885 to establish a definite treaty relationship had been declined by Sierra Leone, Samori maintained communications through known and trusted messengers.[83] In February 1887 his kinsman Lansana Touré denied rumours that Samori had ceded his country to France; he added, 'Sierra Leone is their trading post because he has faith and confidence in the English Government.[84]

But in May the next messenger, Nalifa Modu, (although he asked that a representative of Sierra Leone should visit Samori to negotiate a treaty) did not repeat Samori's assurance about his relations with the French;[85] and it seems likely that he started his journey only after a new agreement had been made. After a month of difficult negotiations Samori, presented with an imperious letter from Gallieni, had given way and on 25 March 1887 accepted an agreement supplementary to the treaty of 1886; he renounced his rights to all lands on the left bank of the Niger below the confluence with the Tinkisso, and placed his present territories and future conquests under a French protectorate.[86] The first concession enabled Gallieni, during the next campaigning season, to construct a fort at the key point of Siguiri; the second closed the most vulnerable gap in the diplomatic defences of the French

[81] Person, *Samori*, ii, pp. 808–18, 887ff, for the Islamization of the empire; pp. 747–9 for the campaign against Sikasso.

[82] Péroz, *Au Soudan*, pp. 371–4.

[83] See below, pp. 176–81.

[84] Sierra Leone Archives, G.I.L.B., Statement by Allanssanah Tooray, 18 February 1887.

[85] C.O. 879/24, C.P. African, 318, No. 55, Hay to Holland, 191, 15 May 1887.

[86] Text in E. Rouard de Card, *Les Traités de Protectorat conclus par la France en Afrique* (Paris, 1897) pp. 230–1.

empire. All this, Gallieni believed, had been obtained in return from assurances which 'do not in any way limit our liberty of action . . . Their sole objective is to extend the boundaries of our future commercial domain, and to close these countries on the Niger against foreign intrusion.'[87]

Why then had Samori agreed to such great concessions? Partly, perhaps, because the French had emphasised their commercial purposes. Samori had no objections to encouraging French trade, especially if this included trade in the arms he needed for his eastern campaign. It seems that Gallieni and Péroz had been able to temper their threats of force with enough sweet reasonableness to permit Samori to expect moral and physical support in the campaigns which he now realised would be needed to suppress internal resistance to Islamisation and to defeat Tiéba. To secure this he was persuaded to surrender important provinces (which were nevertheless becoming more difficult to hold) and to accept some form of exclusive relationship, as implied by the term 'protectorate'. But it seems certain that Samori imagined this relationship as one of alliance rather than dependency; that he had no intention of abating his internal sovereignty; and that in return for promising this exclusive relationship, which seemed to mean so much to the French, he expected them to offer substantive support for his own ambitions.

It is now clear that this was a vain hope. Even though France might have gained commercially by the extension of Samori's empire, Gallieni had no intention of actually strengthening any African state, and was in fact already encouraging Tiéba as a counter-weight to Samori. The unsuccessful siege of Sikasso to which Samori devoted the bulk of his resources in 1887–8 cost him heavy casualties and a considerable loss of prestige. The French presence encouraged his subjects to protest again his requisitions of soldiers and provisions as well as against the new Islamic policies; by the rainy season there was a widespread revolt which Person sees as marking the decisive turning point in the history of the empire.[88]

Meanwhile Gallieni's distrust of Samori was hardening into positive hostility. In October 1887 Lieutenant Binger had sent

[87] Note of 24 September 1887, quoted Kanya-Forstner, *Conquest*, p. 149. from Senegal IV/90/a.
[88] See below, Ch. 5. pp. 189–90.

him an over-gloomy appreciation of the survival prospects of the empire; when in early 1888 reports of a British mission to Bisandugu coincided with rumours that Binger had been murdered by Samori's agents, Gallieni declared bitterly:

> Samori is an evil man (*un personnage néfaste*) who, like all the false prophets of the Western Sudan, causes depopulation and ruin in the countries he controls. For several years he has been the greatest supplier of slaves to the *dyula* caravans, which go to spread their wretched merchandise throughout the lands of Senegambia.[89]

Gallieni therefore began a policy of active though clandestine intrigues designed to weaken Samori's power; this culminated on 18 June 1888 with a treaty with Tiéba, which, as the Colonial Department smugly observed, 'assures us of all the advantages of a protectorate without imposing any of the burdens'.[90] Without planning any immediate military attack, Gallieni devoted his second tour of duty in 1887–8 to an encircling strategy intended to weaken Samori's power and consolidate French control of the upper Niger basin.

FRENCH PENETRATION OF SENEGAMBIA

Control of the upper Niger also implied intervention in the regions through which the *dyula* trade routes maintained contacts with the coast, Futa Jalon and the Gambia valley. Since 1865 France had occupied small forts, and claimed treaty rights, in the estuaries of the Nunez, Pongos and Mellacourie rivers; but no great commercial development had taken place, and politically her hold was insecure. These ports (together with the oversight of French possessions at Porto Novo and on the Ivory Coast) were under the direction of an old associate of Gallieni, the Provençal army doctor, J. M. Bayol, whose post as Lieutenant-Governor of Senegal and Dependencies had recently been given increased status. Gallieni's second priority in the campaign of 1888 (following the erection of the fort at Siguiri and the consolidation of French influence in Bouré) was to open communications with

[89] ANSOM, Senegal vi/18/b, Gallieni to Governor, 102, 30 April 1888,
[90] Person, *Samori*, ii, 709–10; AE Afrique 122, M.M.C. to M.A.E., 8 February 1889.

these coastal bases, to protect them against possible intrusion, and so to consolidate a new axis of French penetration.[91]

The key to this strategy lay in the mountainous district of Futa Jalon, where the first of the eighteenth-century Fulani *jihads* had established an interesting form of loose Islamic federation in which power alternated every two years between two Alimamies representing the families of the *jihad* leaders. Though the state was neither politically cohesive nor militarily strong, its great religious prestige was recognised in the small trading states of the seaboard, where rulers of states supposedly under French protection – and others – sent tribute to the Alimamies and often referred disputes to their arbitration. Freetown Muslims also looked to Timbo as a source of learning and authority, and British Governors had somewhat intermittently made payments during the nineteenth-century; in their minds at least these were in return for the encouragement of trade. The British shared this interest in the trade routes with Samori, many of whose supplies were brought by *dyulas* who carried slaves, gold, ivory and hides through Futa Jalon territory to various Atlantic ports between the Rio Grande and Sierra Leone.[92]

As far as the ruling aristocracy of Futa Jalon were concerned, however, taxes on trade and stipends brought a welcome enlargement of their wealth, but did not fundamentally affect the basis of their power, which rested on religious and social prestige and on the ownership of slaves. They were accustomed to signing treaties of trade and friendship with British emissaries – most recently with Administrator Gouldsbury of the Gambia in 1881 – knowing that no adverse consequences would follow, and that with luck their stipends would be paid. When later in 1881 Bayol had persuaded the Alimamies to sign the somewhat ambiguous text of what he claimed was a protectorate treaty, granting exclusive trading rights in return for annual stipends of 10,000 francs, together with a letter purporting to grant France extensive rights in the tributary states of the seaboard, they undoubtedly regarded their assent as one more relatively insignificant gesture of good will towards the white men. These documents were not interpreted

[91] Etienne to Governor, 16 November 1887, cit., Saint-Martin, *L'empire Toucouleur et la France*, p. 365.

[92] On Futa Jalon, see J. Suret-Canale, *La Republique de Guinée* (1970); on Samori's interest, Person, *Samori*, I, pp. 100–1, 329–30.

as involving any alienation of sovereignty, but as a mutually advantageous alliance, based on the assumption that Futa remained the land of the Fulas, as France was the land of the French.[93] Although their treaty might have some diplomatic value against the British, the French knew in 1888 that they still counted for little in Futa Jalon and that their control of the coastal districts was still far from uniformly secure.

Gallieni therefore launched a series of diplomatic and topographical missions into Futa Jalon, and into surrounding countries; by displaying the forces which France had established in the upper Niger valley he hoped to impress the Alimamies and their neighbours with French power, and to exclude any remaining danger that they might turn to the British. Captain Oberdorf, who had made the treaty with Aguibou in March 1887, was instructed to return to Dinguiraye, to proceed to Futa Jalon and secure a more effective treaty than that of 1881, and to return by the French post of Benty, in the Mellacourie estuary. Oberdorf died early on the journey, but his mission was carried through by Lieutenant Plat, who – despite the disdainful arrogance which he showed towards the Fula aristocracy – on 30 March 1888 secured Alimami Ibrahima Suri's assent to a new protectorate, affirming the terms of 1881 but suppressing the stipends.[94] To reinforce Plat's diplomacy, and to reconnoitre alternative routes from Siguiri to Benty through Futa Jalon, Gallieni sent after him a column of 120 riflemen under Captain Audéoud; its requisitions of food aroused some hostility to France among the peoples of these not very productive areas.[95] These displays of activity however did not in reality much improve the French position. After discussion Etienne judged it expedient to continue to rely on Bayol's treaty for the present, while strengthening France's physical power in the neighbourhood and exploiting conflicts within Futa Jalon as opportunity offered.[96]

Other French missions marched towards the coast by more northerly routes, thus staking out claims in the upper valleys of

[93] Thierno Diallo, 'La mission du Dr. Bayol au Fouta-Djalon . . .' *Bulletin de l'IFAN*, xxxiv B (1972) pp. 131–50; cf. *Prelude*, pp. 265–71.

[94] Plat's narrative is printed in Gallieni, *Deux Campagnes* . . . , pp. 449–552.

[95] ANSOM, Senegal iii/12/i, Gallieni to Audéoud, 24 March 1888; Audéoud's 'Journal de marche', cf. Person, *Samori*, ii, pp. 708–9.

[96] AE Afrique 122, Etienne to Spuller, 14 May 1889; Note pour le Ministre, 21 June 1889.

the Gambia and Jeba rivers, linking France's posts in the lower Casamance to the rest of her West African empire, and in the process restricting Portugese Guinea and British Gambia to small coast enclaves. In May 1886 Portugal had recognised French claims to Futa Jalon, and accepted frontiers restricting Portuguese Guinea to a small quadrilaterial of territory. Gallieni proceeded to beat its bounds by sending Lieutenant Levasseur to travel from Bakel through the Falémé valley to Labé, in the north of Futa Jalon, and back to Sedhiou in the Casamance.[97] Liotard, a dispenser attached to the colonial army, studied the commercial prospects of the upper Casamance valley, where Gallieni during operations against Mahmadu Lamine, had already established relations with rulers of Fuladu.

This rising state was founded about 1867 when Alfa Molo, a former elephant hunter, led a revolt of Fula pastoralists against the Mandinka rulers of the states where they had settled; this affected a wide area east of the Koulountou river, between Futa Jalon and the Gambia. Alfa Molo was a Muslim, linked in tradition with Al Haj 'Umar; but the organisation of the state was largely the work of his son and successor, Musa Molo, an able and unscrupulous opportunist. From 1883 Musa Molo decided to use French support to further his dynastic ambitions and resist pressure from more zealous Muslims; he joined wholeheartedly in Gallieni's campaigns against Mahmadu Lamine and could claim credit for his death in December 1887. France thus became drawn even more deeply than before into a complex set of conflicts involving the whole lower valley of the Gambia.

Musa Molo's principal opponent was Foday Kabba, a disciple of Maba from Bondou, who from about 1874 until his death in 1901 led a Mandinka counter-offensive in the country between the Gambia and the Casamance.[98] The rivalry of these two men, ethnic, political and religious, had profound effects on the Gambia valley as a whole. Both parties needed arms, and sought to obtain them by trading at MacCarthy's Island. Both sought alliances.

[97] Convention between France and Portugal, 12 May 1886, Hertslet, *Map of Africa* (3rd ed.) II, pp. 673–5; Gallieni, *Deux Campagnes* . . . , pp. 576–85.

[98] Charlotte A. Quinn, 'A Nineteenth Century Fulbe State', *JAH*, XII (1971) pp. 427–40; C. Roche, 'Portraits de chefs casamançais du XIXᵉ siecle', *RFHOM*, LVIII (1971) pp. 451–67; cf. *Deux Campagnes* . . . , pp. 338, 363, 574–6.

Foday Kabba, representing the party of Muslim orthodoxy, looked first to Badibu (or Rip) on the north bank, the former home of Maba, whose *jihad* in the 1860s had immensely advanced the Muslim cause. Traditions show Foday Kabba, on his father's advice, seeking support and counsel from Maba's brother and successor, Mahmoud N'Dari Ba, and receiving eighty-three recruits who took part in the launching of his own *jihad*.[99]

But political unity in Badibu had depended heavily on Maba's charismatic prestige, which Mahmoud N'Dari lacked – as the British authorities at Bathurst were well aware. Although vitally interested in maintaining strong rule in the state which made the greatest contribution to the colony's groundnut trade, they had not recognised Mahmoud N'Dari until 1873, six years after his brother's death. They then granted him a stipend in return for promises of protection for traders, not only in Badibu but in other states which had followed Maba, including Niani and Saloum. But four years later Mahmoud N'Dari's authority was challenged by a revolt of some of Maba's former generals, led by Biram Cissé.

The British and French thus found themselves involved in a complex pattern of religious, political and economic conflicts extending from Fuladu to the gates of their own colonial settlements. Fighting to establish an independent authority on the lower Gambia around his trading wharf of Kau-ur in Saloum, Biram Cissé allied with the Molos in the south and in the north with the Mboge brothers – tepid Muslims struggling to establish their own authority in northern Saloum. But this area, like the neighbouring state of Sine, was already solidly established within the expanding frontier of the Senegalese groundnut trade; the French, already committed to war against Lat-Dior and suspicious of his Muslim allies, backed the Mboges in Saloum and Mbacke Deb Ndiaye in Sine.[100] Their alliance with Musa Molo in 1883 completed a system of alignments with African rulers opposed to the more militant tendencies of Islam.

Success for this coalition would gravely jeopardise British interests in the Gambia. But there was no thought of forming any general Muslim alliance against France. Still largely influenced.

[99] Roche, 'Portraits de chefs . . .' , p. 452.

[100] M. A. Klein, *Islam and Imperialism in Senegal* (Edinburgh, 1968), esp. Chaps. 5, 6, 7; J. M. Gray *A History of the Gambia* (Cambridge 1940) Chaps. 30, 31.

by anti-Muslim attitudes, most officials feared the influence of Foday Silla (leader of the 'Marabout' party in Combo, which pressed dangerously on the very frontiers of British territory); they were alarmed, not encouraged, by reports in 1886 that both he and Foday Kabba were in correspondence with Mahmadu Lamine.[101] Despite the extremely tough and militant line taken by Musa Molo, Administrator Hay and his Legislative Council hoped to make a treaty with him, and British traders worked to win him over from his French connections (as they eventually succeeded in doing in 1903).[102]

On the north bank of the Gambia however, this same concern to back the strong was by the mid-1880s pointing towards an alliance with the 'marabout party'. This new British attitude partly reflected an economic and financial crisis in the colony, which will be more fully examined later. But it was directly prompted by the growing influence of Maba's son, Saer Mati, now nearly thirty years old and of an age to claim power. Though recalled as 'impulsive, cruel and uncompromising',[103] Saer Mati had inherited some of his fathers *baraka*; early in 1885 he began fighting in Badibu and Saloum, claiming that 'the kingdom of my father should be given up to me.'[104] Mahmoud N'Dari Ba, having failed through the years to establish a clear-cut supremacy over Biram Cissé, now faced a more dangerous challenger. By July 1886 Administrator Carter concluded that Britain might have backed the wrong horse; linking the decline in groundnut exports a little too closely to the disorders, he suggested that Saer Mati should be recognised and subsidised as ruler of Badibu in place of Mahmoud N'Dari Ba, on condition that he recognised Biram Cissé as ruler of his own sphere of influence.[105] On 10 December Saer Mati, accompanied by an army of 300 cavalry and 2,000 foot-soldiers, came to the British post at Albreda and appeared to

[101] C.O.87/127, Hay to Granville, 16 April 1886.

[102] C.O.87/128, Rowe to Granville, 90, encl. Hay to Rowe, 165, 20 April 1886, Topp to Hay, 19 April 1886; cf. U.A.C. Library, Gambia, Miscellaneous 1858–1903, King Moussa Molloh to A. D. Temple, 19 June 1903.

[103] Klein, *Islam and Imperialism* . . . , p. 133n.

[104] C.O.87/126, Letter from Saer Mati, 30 September 1885, in Rowe to Stanley, 160, 31 October 1885.

[105] C.O.879/26, C. P. African, 341, No. 1, Hay to Granville, 165, 11 August 1886, encl. Carter, 287, 16 July.

receive these terms sympathetically. Subsequent correspondence revealed considerable hesitation and ambiguity in Saer Mati's position; nevertheless by February, Carter, satisfied by his assurances that he would protect trade, respect the position acquired by Biram Cissé and spare the life of Mahmoud N'Dari Ba, signed treaties with both rulers recognising the new arrangements in Badibu.[106]

It is difficult to say whether Carter's view that Mahmoud N'Dari Ba was 'permanently snuffed out'[107] would have proved justified if the people of Badibu had been left to work out their future government without external interference. Given the close proximity of French officers profoundly hostile to Muslim militancy, it proved a disastrous miscalculation. The government of Senegal, with their long-standing fear of general Muslim hostility, were worried about the opposition to their *protégés* in Sine and Saloum of leading 'marabouts' from Badibu; already in 1884 Bayol had clashed with Saer Mati over the latter's demand that Guédel Mboge, the French-backed ruler, should become a Muslim. In 1885 French fears of a 'Tijani league', a great hostile Muslim coalition, were much increased when Saer Mati appealed for support to their *bêtes noires*, Al-Bouri Ndiaye (who was his uncle) and Abdul Bokar Kan. Early in 1886 Abdul Bokar visited Badibu in an attempt to mediate; in fact his enquiries led him to switch support from Saer Mati to Biram Cissé, and this weakened his entente with Al-Bouri, who had sent military aid to his nephew[108] But this did little to allay French apprehensions, which were increased by rumours that Saer Mati was sheltering and aiding Mahmadu Lamine.[109] Carter's recognition of Saer Mati

---

[106] Ibid., Nos. 12, 17, 18 (encls.); Carter to Hay, 4, 8 January, 33, 26 January, 38, 17 February 1887.

[107] Ibid., No. 18a, Carter to Hay, 38, 17 February 1887.

[108] P.P. 1887, LIX, C4978, Thomas to Carter, 18 January 1886; C.O. 87/127, Hay to Rowe, 49, 15 February 1886, encl. 'Abdoul Boobacere' letter, D. W. Robinson, 'Abdul Bokar Kan . . .', pp. 237ff; cf. Klein, *Islam and Imperialism* . . ., pp. 134–9.

[109] ANSOM, Senegal IV/105/a, Genouille to Etienne, May 1887; C.P. African, 341, No. 35, Flourens to Lyons, 17 May 1887; cf. B. O. Oloruntimehin, 'Anti-French Coalition of African states . . ., *Odu*, n.s. 3 (1970). Dr. Oloruntimehin takes some of the fears expressed by French officials too literally; but Dr. Robinson may go too far in discounting the 'panic element' in French policy during this period of stress after 1885.

connected these anti-Muslim fears of French officials with their habitual anglophobia.

By renouncing the treaty of 1873 with Mahmoud N'Dari Ba, Carter had provided a legal opening for French intervention. About 1 April 1887 Saer Mati attacked Kahone in Saloum; Governor Genouille responded by authorising the invasion of Badibu and aligning himself with Mahmoud N'Dari, its former legitimate ruler. This action (taken without consultation with Paris) was intended not merely to protect France's clients and reduce the power of the 'turbulent' Al-Bouri but to consolidate the French empire by linking up with Wuli, a state further up-river where Gallieni had been operating against Mahmadu Lamine. 'In this way', wrote Genouille, 'we should close off all Senegambia on the one hand, and on the other should reach Bakel by a different route from the Senegal river and this might in certain circumstances present considerable advantages.[110]. By mid-May the French had advanced to within two miles of the lower Gambia, raised the tricolour over Mahmoud N'Dari's fortress of Nioro, obtained his signature and that of Biram Cissé to protectorate treaties, and driven Saer Mati to take refuge with the British. This gave them a strong *de facto* position from which to negotiate over the future status of the British enclave in the Gambia, which had so long seemed a desirable and logical appendage to France's colony of Senegal.

TOWARDS THE GULF OF GUINEA

While Gallieni necessarily gave priority to securing the western borders of 'France's future commercial domain' against British intrusion, he also took the first steps towards the lands between the great Niger bend and the southern forests – a vast area, drained by the various branches of the Volta river, where traditional monarchies of which Mossi was the prototype had largely resisted the pressures of Islamisation.[111] Although the region lay at the junction of major internal trade routes, it was still hardly known to Europeans. They had long assumed that it was separated from

[110] ANSOM, Senegal IV/105/a, Genouille to Coronnat (undated, *sc* April 1887); also Genouille to Etienne (undated 1887). I am grateful to Mr. A. Mboge for transcripts; cf. Klein, *Islam and Imperialism* . . ., pp. 138–42.

[111] On them, see E. P. Skinner, *The Mossi of the Upper Volta* (Stanford, 1964).

the Ivory Coast by the 'mountains of Kong' marked on many contemporary maps; the dense forests of the Ivory Coast hinterland, bordered to the east by the formidable state of Asante, had inhibited exploration. The British victory over Asante in 1874 had not been sufficiently conclusive to open up the northern routes to European penetration; the government in London feared to get involved in another such formidable war but remained willing to encourage desultory diplomatic attempts by the Gold Coast administration to find ways of removing the Asante obstacle.

The bases of this policy were attempts to weaken the solidarity of the inner core of *amantoo* states by playing on the disaffection of Juaben towards the power of Kumasi; and to detach the outer ring of *amansin* from the Asante altogether, thus freeing routes which would bypass Kumasi to east and west.[112] Neither policy achieved sustained success. In the north-west John Smith of Accra went to Bonduku in May 1879 in an attempt to detach Gyaman from Asante and place it in direct relations with the coast: but Asante's prestige was still too strong, and the Gold Coast government found it could only exercise a remote and indirect influence. After visiting Bonduku in June 1882, Captain R. Lonsdale suggested that British Consuls should be stationed in the area, but this was rejected by the Administrator, C. A. Moloney, who rightly doubted whether the Liberal Government would support any steps which would 'support any steps which would pledge the Government to interference in matters occurring in foreign and barbarous countries'.[113]

The British set more hopes on developing a northern trade up the valley of the Volta, and specifically through Salaga, long a key centre for Asante's kola trade with Mossi and Hausaland. After 1874 Salaga rebelled against the control formerly exercised by Asante officials, and was encouraged by its southern neighbours of Krachi, who hoped to profit from a reorientation of trade; the British encouraged the supply of arms to Salaga and in 1876 sent up a mission under Captain V. S. Gouldsbury, who went on

112 See esp. F. Agbodeka, *African Politics and British Policy in the Gold Coast, 1868–1900* (1971) Chap. 4; British relations with Asante will be treated more fully in Vol. ii.

113 P.P. 1883, xlviii, C.3687, Further Correspondence regarding Affairs of the Gold Coast, No. 23, Moloney to Kimberley, 12 September 1882, encl. Lonsdale, 2 August; No. 53, Report by Lonsdale of his mission to Ashanti and Gaman, April–July 1882, cf. Agbodeka, pp. 87–91.

as far as Yendi, in Dagomba.[114] Their general aim was to weaken
Asante influence and to encourage the growth of the 'Brong
confederation' under the leadership of the religious authorities
of Kete Krachi. But Asante replied by encouraging an alternative
market for their kolanuts at Kintampo (so crippling Salaga's
trade) and by obstructing subsequent British reconnaissances towards the north.[115] Lacking the will to undertake any more forceful northern policy, the British had made little progress when a
new element was introduced by the installation of the Germans
in Togo in 1884.

The first demonstration of German vigour came from a private
citizen of humane and scholarly interests. Starting from Accra
on 12 May 1886, G. A. Krause passed unaccompanied through
Salaga to Wagadugu and eventually reached Macina, on the
middle Niger. This great journey, though devoid of political purpose, revealed to Europe a whole range of African societies still
untouched by the imperial frontiers, and so stimulated the interest
of colonial officials of all the powers.[116]

Lieutenant Gustave Binger was an ambitious and patriotic
Alsatian whose linguistic studies in Africa had earned him a
posting as aide-de-camp to General Faidherbe (now a Senator,
Grand Chancellor of the Legion of Honour, and elder statesman
of African policy). Late in 1886 Binger approached the Minister
of Marine with a plan to forestall the supposed designs of Goldie's
newly-chartered Niger Company (who were falsely rumoured to
have sent an agent to Timbuktu) by traversing this same region
from the north. Binger argued that, as France's gunboats prepared to sail down the Niger to Timbuktu, the time was ripe to
penetrate the area of Mossi and Kong, where he believed the
relative weakness of Islam should give French influence good
chances of success. The flourishing internal commerce of the

[114] F. Wolfson, *Pageant of Ghana* (1958) prints extracts from Gouldsbury's
report in C.O.96/119.

[115] P.P. 1882, xxvi, C. 3368, Further correspondence regarding
Affairs of the Gold Coast, No. 44, Report by Lonsdale of his mission to
Coomassie, Salaga, Yendi, 2 October 1881–February 1882; cf. Agobodeka,
pp. 84–7, 161–3; also I. Wilks, 'Asante Policy towards Hausa Trade' in
Meillassoux, *Development of Indigenous Trade* . . .

[116] P. Markov and J. Sebald, 'Gottlob Adolf Krause', *JHSN* ii (1963)
pp. 536–44; R. Cornevin, *Histoire du Togo* (1959) pp. 138–9. See within
pp. 208–23.

region Binger hoped to divert towards the Ivory Coast; he cited
a report collected in 1850 by Bouet-Willaumez which suggested
that the Comoe river rose quite near a navigable tributary of the
Niger, and so that the mountains of Kong might prove a less
formidable obstacle than was commonly believed.[117]

The Minister of Marine was Admiral Aube (1826–90) a distinguished officer who had served under Faidherbe in Senegal
and married his wife's sister. Aube was no enthusiast for colonial
expansion *per se;* he repeatedly voiced apprehension lest the precarious footholds on the Slave Coast which his department had
inherited might involve the French state (as represented by his
own Service) in dangerous, humiliating and purposeless conflicts.
But the Sudanese enterprise was another matter; here Aube had
supported the deployment of gunboats on the Niger as a salutary
demonstration of French power in an area of legitimate interest.[118]
Impressed by Binger's plan, Aube commended it to the Colonial
Department with military brevity:

> M. Binger, at present aide-de-camp to General Faidherbe, is
> imbued with the ideas of the illustrious former Governor of
> Senegal; to the realisation of the ideas he sets out he would
> bring all the qualities of a man of action, a traveller and a
> scholar which he has displayed in his previous missions. I trust
> that this officer's request will be received as favourably as
> possible.[119]

When De La Porte found difficulties in raising the grant of 35,000
francs for which Binger was asking, Aube again intervened to
urge speedy action to forestall the supposed activities of the British
on both upper and lower Niger. [120] By the middle of February the
Colonial Department and the Foreign Ministry had each agreed
to provide 17,500 francs for a mission whose primary object was

[117] ANSOM, Missions 12, Projet d'un Voyage d'Exploration dans le
Boucle du Niger, 18 December 1886. Cf. AE Afrique 85, Binger to Aube,
6 January 1887, Faidherbe to De La Porte, 27 December 1886.

[118] Cf. below; also Kanya-Forstner, *Conquest* . . . , pp. 137, 142, 151. F.
Berge, *Le Sous-Secretariat et les Sous-Secretaires d'Etat aux Colonies* (1962)
pp. 40–3.

[119] ANSOM, Missions 12, Minute by Aube, 22 December 1886.

[120] Ibid., Binger to Aube, 3 January 1886 (*sc.* 1887); Minute by Aube,
3 January 1887.

now defined as 'opening a new route to link our posts on the Niger to our possessions on the Gold Coast'.[121]

There was now renewed activity at the southern end of this route. In November 1886 Lieutenant-Governor Bayol visited the Ivory Coast; besides bombarding African trading towns on the Ebrié lagoon which had been resisting Verdier's attempts to enforce his monopoly, he began to study reports about routes to the interior and realised that the caravan centre of Kong might be reached without too much difficulty through Bonduku in Gyaman. The isolation of the French settlements on the coast had perhaps been due less to the 'mountains of Kong' and other physical impediments than to the astute attempts of Amatifou, the recently deceased King of Kinjabo, to control their access to the interior.

Bayol's new perspectives were probably influenced by Treich-Lapleine, an impulsive and adventurous young patriot who in 1883, while a student, had married Verdier's niece and come out to Assinie in his service.[122] Like all Verdier's employees, Treich-Lapleine believed that the Gold Coast government, having failed to impose an inequitable frontier through the abortive Boundary Commission of 1883,[123] was trying to hem in the French by other means. The Colonial Office had indeed cautiously approved Governor Griffith's proposal to establish a protectorate over Sefwi, another former *amansin* state, on the grounds that its position in the Bia valley would bar the best French route towards Asante and would increase Britain's own opportunities for 'intercourse with the interior tribes'; in February 1887 Captain Lonsdale duly concluded such a treaty.[124] Such activities not only threatened to cut off France's access to Bonduku and the north but increased their fears of British intervention within Kinjabo, whose new king, Akasamadou, did not enjoy the uncontested authority or share the apparent devotion to France of his predecessor. So in April, when Bayol was again at Assinie, Treich-Lapleine secured

[121] AE Afrique 85, Note pour le Ministre, 24 January 1887 (with note of approval by Flourens); De La Porte to Flourens, 28 January, 5 February 1887; De La Porte to Binger (copy) 15 February 1887.

[122] P. Atger, *La France en Cote d'Ivoire de 1843 a 1893* (Dakar, 1962) pp. 115–20.   [123] *Prelude*, p. 288.

[124] C.O.879/25, C. P. Africa 333, Nos. 7, 9, 63, Griffith to Stanhope, 345, 14 September, 1886; Stanhope to Griffith, 95, 19 November 1886; Griffith to Holland, 134, 11 April 1887.

his approval for an official mission up the Comoe valley towards Bonduku with the aim of forestalling the British.

> It is indispensable [wrote Treich] that we should act promptly if we do not want to be driven into a political and commercial *impasse,* and so reduced to abandoning, or giving away for nothing, a colony which possesses the only direct route to central Africa; the English covet it and are working to make it untenable for us.[125]

His journey was only partially successful. Ill health, added to political difficulties, prevented Treich-Lapleine from reaching Bonduku before the rains; although he claimed that the appearance of a Frenchman in this area made a great impression, Treich also admitted that the influence of the British was still strong. Treaties were secured only after long negotiations and the presentation of unbudgeted gifts. Whereas the king of Bettie signed the draft treaty placing his country under French protectorate, the ruler of Indenie would only *accepte l'amitié et la protection du gouvernement français*: in countries bordering the Gold Coast the word *protectorat* had already acquired undesirable connotations.[126] But Treich had shown that Binger would be able to find a road through the forests to the Ivory Coast. Verdier, who had already tried to persuade Binger to begin his journey from Grand Bassam, now agreed to send Treich-Lapleine to meet him in the southern savanna during the dry season of 1888–9, and to provide goods valued at 10,000 francs with which to pay for the last stages of his journey through the forest.[127]

Meanwhile, Binger was already well launched upon the last of

[125] ANSOM, Senegal iv/118. Treich-Lapleine to Verdier, 5 April 1887; Bretignère to Bayol, Bayol to Bretignère, 16 April 1887. Senegal iii/12/g, Etienne to Genouille, 20 June 1887; cf. M. A. Bretignère, *Aux temps héroiques de la Côte d'Ivoire* (1931) Chap. 4; F. Bullock, *La Fondation de la Colonie française de la Côte d'Ivoire* ((London, 1912) pp. 7–16; A. Verdier, *Trente-cinq Années de lutte aux colonies* (Paris, 1897) pp. 138–73.

[126] ANSOM, Senegal iii/12/g, contain texts of these treaties and reports from Treich-Lapleine during his journey. His final report is in Senegal IV/118/b, Verdier to Etienne, 24 October 1887, cf. Atger, *La France en Côte d'Ivoire* . . . , pp. 121–2.

[127] Atger, *La France en Côte d'Ivoire* . . . , pp. 122–6; cf. Verdier *Trente-Cinq Années* . . . , pp. 173–8.

the epic European explorations of West Africa.[128] He left Bamako on 30 June 1887; spent some time with Samori's forces besieging Sikasso (making rather disdainful reports which encouraged Gallieni to underrate the continuing strength of Samori's empire);[129] reached Kong in March 1888; and proceeded to Mossi. In Wagadugu, Binger heard reports of approaching Europeans (whom he assumed to be British, though it was actually a German mission under von François) and tried unsuccessfully to persuade Mogho Naba Sanum to accept a French protectorate. Thence he travelled southwards to Salaga and on 5 January 1889 met Treich-Lapleine at Kong. This time, Treich's journey had gone well; at Bonduku on 15 November King Agyeman had signed a treaty placing Gyaman 'under the protection and friendship of France' in return for a promised stipend of 3,000 francs. This, Treich claimed, laid the foundations of a new French empire whose prospects equalled those of Gabon-Congo. At Kong the two travellers jointly concluded another treaty before returning to Grand Bassam, which they reached on 20 March 1889. Even before they arrived, Verdier was echoing their euphoria:

> A route is opened towards this unknown country of Kong, which we now know to be inhabited by a population of higher civilisation than that of the coast, which is consequently capable of offering outlets for our manufactured products. By happy coincidence, this new market opens at the very moment when a French shipping company is going to help French products arrive on the African coast.[130]

But it would still be several years before the undoubted economic potential of the Ivory Coast could be fully realised. For the present, the heart of France's West African empire remained in the Sudan. Here it was clear that, despite the restraints which had

[128] It can be best studied in his published account: L. G. Binger, *Du Niger au Golfe de Guinée* (two vols., 1892). A few of the reports which he sent back during his journey are in ANSOM, Missions 12; cf. L. G. Binger, *Souvenirs extraits des Carnets de Route ou notes sous la Dictée par son fils Jacques Binger* (1938) – a badly edited work of small value.

[129] Person, *Samori*, II, pp. 766–7.

[130] AE Afrique 125, M.M.C. to M.A.E., 11 March 1889, encl. Treich-Lapleine to Verdier, 15 November 1888, Verdier to De La Porte, 14 January 1889.

been placed upon the policy of military expansion, Gallieni had both consolidated and extended French control. Even in the upper Senegal, despite Gallieni's disillusionment with the route, French power was more solidly based than ever before – Mahmadu Lamine had been eliminated, the railway had at last been made of some limited value, and it would be feasible to resume operations against the Tokolors whenever that seemed expedient. More generally, Gallieni had in January 1888 summarised a series of objectives which he could justly claim were on the way to achievement:

    (i) to allow us to give our Sudanese possessions natural frontiers (*des limites naturelles*)

    (ii) to permit us to establish ourselves, within a short period, in Futa Jalon

    (iii) to assure all lines of communication between our establishments on the upper Niger and those in the southern rivers

    (iv) to procure for us the commercial and political possession of the immense geographical triangle bounded by the Atlantic Ocean, the Scarcies, the Tinkisso, the upper Niger, the Sahara and the Senegal

    (v) finally to permit us to constitute a compact colony with the unity it needs – thus replacing this confused group of small native states, all entangled without any unity, and often placed under the influence of the foreign powers whose enclaves are such a great obstacle to the development of our country's commerce in the Senegambian region.[131]

To this programme, Binger now added the opportunity to secure profitable new outlets to the Gulf of Guinea. For Frenchmen with faith in the future of an African empire the prospects were as attractive as they were ominous for independent African rulers like Ahmadu and Samori.

[131] ANSOM, Senegal vi/19/a; Note by Gallieni, 20 January 1888.

3 The Foreign Office and the Niger

In Great Britain too there had been a pause in government-sponsored expansion, once the frenzied activity of 1884–5 had provided title deeds to the Nigerian coast which provisionally satisfied rival claimants. Reactions in London to Gordon's death at Khartoum in February 1885 were more complex and more enduring than French responses to the lesser debacle of Lang-Son; although peace-loving, or timid, politicians resolved that nothing similar should be risked again, others felt it a humiliation which an Imperial power would have to avenge. But immediately, politicians were soon diverted to other matters – to an international crisis over Afghanistan, to the economic recession, and then overwhelmingly to Ireland. To Joseph Chamberlain in March 1886 it was the Home Rule issue, not any African dispute, which would decide whether the U.K. was destined to decline to the status of a 'third rate power'.[1] And at the level of day to day politics, the dominance of the Irish question was even clearer. Directly and indirectly, it was responsible for Gladstone's resignation in June 1885; for the uncertainty surrounding the minority Conservative 'caretaker' administration which Lord Salisbury led until January 1886; for the agonising divisions of the Liberals during the Gladstone ministry which followed, and for its disastrous defeat in the Home Rule Bill in June 1886. Until Salisbury's second Cabinet had secured a strong electoral majority in August 1886 politicians could spare little time for Africa. But even then no demand appeared for any policy of deliberate expansion.

Despite the popular stereotype of 'Tory Imperialist', Conservative squires had rarely been enthusiasts for colonial empire. The maintenance of the Union with Ireland (and of the rights of landlords, some of whom were literally their own kith and kin)

[1] P. Fraser, *Joseph Chamberlain: Radicalism and Empire* (1966) pp. 88.

was the Imperial question about which they cared most deeply (although Disraeli had taught them that India was equally and more obviously essential to the maintenance of British greatness in the world). The did have deep-rooted prejudices about national honour and prestige which could easily be converted into support for specific acts of imperialism; it is dangerous to generalise about their attitudes on the basis of statements approving such general objects of policy as peace and economy. The Commons debate on the Address in 1887, where one writer finds evidence that 'the Jingo fever appeared to be at its very lowest ebb',[2] was opened by a classically Imperialist justification of the recent Burma campaign from a Tory back-bencher.[3] But it is probably true that few Conservatives yet regarded the extension of British rule in Africa as a purpose which could in itself justify any considerable expenditure of British lives or money, and that such 'Jingo Fever' as survived was more likely to be found among radical businessmen intoxicated by the prospect of wielding state power – Liberal Unionists like Joseph Chamberlain who, having broken with Gladstone over Home Rule, now sustained Salisbury's government from outside.

The Prime Minister's approach was more sober and discriminating. Salisbury had long accepted it as inevitable – and essentially desirable – that Asian and African societies would undergo erosion and drastic change under the impact of what he once called 'the pacific invasion of England'.[4] 'Living nations', as he was to put it in 1899, were destined to take over from the 'dying nations' that failed to adapt themselves to the political and technological realities of the modern world. Salisbury took no pleasure in this prospect (knowing that in the process many unscrupulous and unsavoury Europeans would benefit), but the decease of the

---

[2] R. E. Robinson in *Cambridge History of the British Empire*, III, p. 156, quoting A. B. Winterbotham, 3 February 1887.

[3] '. . . while a new and vast area has been opened out to British trade and commerce, we have the satisfaction of knowing that the Native population are already reaping the fruits of the civilized Government which replaced a barbarous and besotted despotism, and that a country of rich resources has been reclaimed to honest industry and secure cultivation.' Viscount Weymouth, Hansard, 3rd series, Vol. 310, col. 79, 27 January 1887.

[4] Quoted by G. N. Uzoigwe, *Lord Salisbury and Tropical Africa* (D.Phil. thesis, Oxford University, 1967) pp. 53ff.

senile was no occasion for sentimental regret. As a British minister his concern was to decide what action was needed to protect British interests, so that his own 'living nation' might continue to flourish.

When he returned to the Foreign Office in 1885, Salisbury found that the old Slave Trade Department had been replaced by an African Department under an able and forceful official of decided views, H. Percy Anderson. Anderson recognised that the old liberal vision of African states progressively opening their lands to the trade of the world as they came under modernising influences had been called in doubt by the recent scramble, and particularly by France's adoption, since 1882, of 'a settled policy in Africa . . . antagonistic to us'.[5] One necessary consequence, Anderson thought, was that Britain should be more accommodating to the new African policies of Germany – a power whose friendship had become necessary in a wider context also, especially since the occupation of Egypt.[6] Salisbury soon drew similar conclusions from the changed situation, as regards both the need for good relations with Germany and the need for some more vigorous measures in Africa itself. Former experience at the India Office had made him sceptical about soldiers and officials who called for forceful initiatives; and in Africa the economic and strategic interests at stake were clearly less vital. But Salisbury came to recognise that such interests existed – though more conspicuously in the East[7] and South of Africa than in the West – and would need protection against other 'living nations' who had begun to follow their own interests there. Salisbury regretted the complications which African disputes with France had introduced into Britain's foreign relations; he always hoped to allay her hostility over Egypt, and was reluctant to add to it by provocative action over minor issues. But increasingly it seemed that French hostility to British colonial interests had initially to be assumed; and where commercial or political interests existed – or might reasonably be anticipated – Salisbury recognised a responsibility to act, though

[5] F.O.84/1654, Memo by Anderson, 11 June 1883.

[6] Wm. Roger Louis, 'Sir Percy Anderson's Grand African Strategy, 1883–1896', *EHR*, LXXXI (1966), also in *Britain and Germany in Africa*, pp. 10 ff.

[7] Cf. M. E. Chamberlain, 'Clement Hill's Memorandum and the British Interest in East Africa', *EHR*, LXXXVII (1972) for discussion of British interests in East Africa.

with the minimum expenditure of force and of money necessary
to secure essential objectives.

And he would himself decide which objectives were essential.
Earlier experience had given Salisbury a low opinion both of the
discretion and commonsense of British colonial governors and of
the capacity of the Colonial Office to control them. Hence, in the
prolonged rituals of correspondence in which British government
departments engaged over West African affairs, Salisbury used
the traditional primacy of the Foreign Office to ensure that the
actions finally taken would reflect national interests in the world
as a whole.[8] He did not at this time find this too difficult. After
short periods under two undistinguished Tory notables, Frederick
Stanley and Edward Stanhope, the Colonial Office, from January
1887 was headed by Sir Henry Holland (1825–1914), who after
serving in the Department as legal adviser and Assistant Under-
Secretary had gone into Parliament as a Conservative in 1874.
Holland (created Lord Knutsford in 1888) was an affable and
conscientious man, but his interests lay in established colonies of
settlement rather than in imperial expansion; as Secretary of State
his concern for financial regularity and equitable administration
was more conspicuous than any great dynamism.[9] His son
described him as a 'singularly modest man with little trust in
himself', and quoted a Colonial Office subordinate:

> Lord Knutsford is always right. He leaves the office for a Cabinet
> Meeting determined to press for this or that, but he comes back
> without it.[10]

There was thus substance in the complaint that the interests of the
British Crown Colonies in West Africa were often sacrificed by
Salisbury's Foreign Office to secure Imperial interests elsewhere.
Indeed, according to his biographer, Salisbury actually welcomed
French expansion in parts of West Africa as presenting 'the most
tangible hope of detaching her from her Egyptian dream'.[11]

[8] G. Cecil, *Life of Salisbury*, III, pp. 217 and *passim;* cf. *Africa and the
Victorians*, pp. 256–7.

[9] For a personal impression of his congenial and accommodating
personality see G. E. Marindin (ed.) *Letters of Frederic, Lord Blachford*
(1896) p. 264; cf. B. L. Blakeley, *The Colonial Office 1868–92* (Durham
N.C. 1972) p. 17n.

[10] Sidney Holland, *In Black and White* (1926) p. 211.

[11] Cecil, *Salisbury*, IV, p. 252.

The principal centre of British interest in West Africa, however, still contained no Crown Colony; the valuable commerce of the Niger had developed under the supervision of Consuls directed by the Foreign Office, which therefore assumed direct responsibility for the protectorates proclaimed in 1884. Here Salisbury did recognise substantial British interests, though of a secondary order, which would have to be protected from the intrusion of either France or Germany. Even on the Niger, London was not actively seeking to expand Imperial power; Salisbury still hoped to delay any extension of direct administrative responsibility. But here, as on other frontiers of British influence, local agents, both of the Imperial government and of private interests, were taking decisions and making commitments which effectively determined the pace and method of British expansion.

THE EMPIRE OF THE ROYAL NIGER COMPANY

Although the well-populated states of Hausaland and Bornu were still widely believed to represent the richest prizes in the scramble for West Africa, neither the British nor their rivals yet had ready means of attempting any direct exercise of power so far inland. In July 1886 Goldie's National African Company received from Gladstone's government a Charter authorising it, as the Royal Niger Company, to administer those territories to which it had acquired rights in the Niger basin. Since the Berlin Conference it had been clear that there was no preferable way for the British to provide some rudimentary political umbrella over these regions. There had been controversy (under both Liberal and Conservative governments) as to the degree of control to be reserved to the Foreign Office; the compromise eventually reached on this point was rather favourable to the Company, which now became established as a sort of autonomous frontier baron of the British empire.[12] In return, however, the Foreign Office African Department expected the Company to pursue a vigorous policy of expansion. Accepting without great alarm that the French were likely soon to control the Western Sudan up to Timbuktu, they expected the Company not merely to secure and develop the area of established trade on the lower Niger, but to advance to protect the approaches to Hausaland. If claims could be established before Frenchmen reappeared physically on the scene, their validation ought not

[12] Flint, *Goldie*, Ch. 4.

to raise serious diplomatic difficulties. 'The contest for the Middle Niger between the French on the Upper and the British on the Lower will be interesting,' Anderson rather smugly noted.[13]

Initially, however, Goldie could spare resources for territorial expansion only if faced by immediate foreign threats; and since his success in buying out French competitors, these came primarily from Germans. Although Bismarck had no intention of involving the German empire in further territorial annexations, his initiatives of 1884 had stimulated the appetites of private citizens. In particular G. L. Gaiser, the pioneer of Lagos's palm kernel trade, had attracted to his service some patriotic young Germans who were anxious to peg out claims for the future in the Niger area. Some of these had inspired the treaty ceding Mahin beach in January 1885, which Bismarck traded away during the boundary negotiations with Britain;[14] others were already looking to inland trade by the great rivers.

E. R. Flegel first went to Lagos in Gaiser's service in 1875; more recently he had carried out exploratory journeys on the Benue and in the Sokoto empire. In August 1884 he issued from Lagos the last of three eloquently argued appeals 'to the friends of African studies in Germany, of colonial endeavour and of the extension of German trade'. Perhaps with the precedent of Leopold's International Association in mind, Flegel emphasised the need to establish permanent stations for carrying out scientific observations and exploration, but he linked this argument with others based on Germany's economic interests in what he called a 'new and more promising era in our national position in the world'. And he suggested concentrating the nation's endeavours in the Niger-Benue area, still unappropriated by any other power, which offered possibilities of communication with the new German colony of Kamerun, with the Congo area, and with Lake Chad.[15] In October 1884 Flegel returned to Berlin, accompanied by two Hausa traders from Nassarawa emirate, and began not only to

[13] F.O.84/1787, Minute by Anderson on W.O. to F.O., 21 July 1886; cf. Flint, *Goldie*, p. 100.

[14] Ernst Hieke, *G. L. Gaiser: Hamburg-Westafrika* (Hamburg, 1949) pp. 46–60; cf. above p. 44.

[15] 'Dritter Brief an die Freunde Deutscher Afrika-Forschung, Kolonialer Bestrebungen und der Ausbreitung des deutschen Handels' in K. Flegel (ed.) *Vom Niger-Benue* (Leipzig, 1890) pp. 93–104.

collect funds for his scientific proposals but to circulate plans for a new Niger Company which, while concentrating on the Benue, would compete with Goldie by methods very like his own.[16] This scheme was taken up by the Hamburg firm of Jantzen and Thormählen, who were deeply interested in Kamerun, and the *Deutsche Kolonialverein*, a recently-founded public pressure group, undertook to raise 150,000 marks by public subscription. The notion of linking Kamerun with Adamawa and the Benue also attracted the attention of the Auswärtige Amt, which still felt free to seek advantages in Africa at British expense. In hope of securing the goodwill of the overlords of the region they entrusted Flegel with gifts and letters from Wilhelm I to the 'Sultans' of Sokoto and Gwandu. Before sailing from Hamburg in April 1885, with five German companions and a new river steamer called *Heinrich Barth*, Flegel had conversations with Bismarck himself, as well as other political leaders, and was formally presented to Wilhelm I.[17]

Goldie, having failed to buy Flegel into his own service,[18] determined to prevent him from establishing any political stake in Nigeria. While agents of the National African Company harassed the German expedition at Loko,[19] Joseph Thomson, a young Scottish naturalist who had recently distinguished himself in East Africa, was despatched on a hastily and secretly organised mission to the capitals of the Sokoto caliphate. Sultan Umar of Sokoto was the legal, and in large measure effective, sovereign of the great theocratic empire of 'Uthman dan Fodio; the Emir of Gwandu, since the death of the founder, had been recognised as viceroy of the western provinces, though the Sultan exercised not only ultimate sovereignty, but direct supervision of state security and foreign relations.[20] Despite a somewhat trying journey

---

[16] Note by Flegel, 29 November 1884; Ibid., pp. 106–12.

[17] For details of these plans, see Flegel to *Kolonialverein*, 23 March, 16 April 1885; ibid., pp. 114–23, Also Flegel to his brother 2 March 1885 (ibid., pp. 112–13) and P. Staudinger, *Im Herzen des Haussaländer* (Berlin, 1889) pp. 105–6.

[18] Flegel, op. cit., pp. 5–6.

[19] Staudinger, op. cit., pp. 51–5, 70–2, 78.

[20] For the institutions of the Empire, see D. M. Last, *The Sokoto Caliphate* (1967). On the position of Gwandu, S. A. Balogun, 'Gwandu Emirates in the Nineteenth Century, with Special Reference to Political Relations' (Ph.D. thesis, University of Ibadan, 1971) esp. pp. 320–1.

Thomson, normally sceptical about immediate economic prospects in Africa, returned an enthusiastic believer in the potential of Hausaland. He also brought treaties dated 1st and 13th June 1885, in which rulers of Sokoto and Gwandu respectively conferred on the Company their 'entire rights, absolutely, to the country on both sides of the River Benue and Kworra for a distance of ten hours journey inland, or such other distance as they may desire, from each bank of both rivers throughout my dominions'.[21]

The authenticity of these treaties, by which powerful rulers seemed to concede so much, is clearly questionable. When Staudinger, a young German naturalist deputising for Flegel as bearer of the Kaiser's gifts, was received by the Sultan on 30 December 1885 he was told that, when Thomson's party

> had wanted to acquire land, he [the Sultan] had roundly refused this demand. He would not sell one inch of the lands under his sovereignty which were inhabited by Muslims, still less would he relinquish the right to trade to any single person; his markets would be free for all peoples.[22]

It seems clear that, though Thomson did bring some sort of negotiation to fruition in Sokoto, Sultan 'Umar had no intention of renouncing any sovereign rights. Some misunderstanding might be explained by ambiguous translation; although negotiations took place in Hausa the treaty was eventually signed in English and Arabic texts. Only the English text is available, and, as Dr R. A. Adeleye has emphasised, it differs sharply in form and content from treaties more spontaneously negotiated by the Caliphate, such as that granted to the Arabic-speaking Barth in 1853.[23] On the process of negotiation we have only Thomson's own account,

[21] E. Hertslet, *The Map of Africa by Treaty* (3rd ed. London, 1909) Vol. I, pp. 122–4. The text quoted is that of the Gwandu treaty; the Sokoto text differs only slightly. Thomson's journey: see R. I. Rotberg, *Joseph Thomson and the Exploration of Africa* (1971) chap. 8; J. B. Thomson, *Thomson, Joseph Thomson, African Explorer* (1896) chap. 7.

[22] Staudinger, op. cit., p. 321.

[23] R. A. Adeleye, *Power and Diplomacy in Northern Nigeria, 1804–1906* (1971) pp. 119–23, 334, 132–6. The following account, drafted before the publication of Dr. Adeleye's analysis, arrives at broadly similar conclusions.

which is consciously and perhaps deliberately sketchy.[24] It is impossible to be certain of what passed; but an attempt to reconstruct the assumptions and aims of each negotiator may throw some indirect light on a transaction of considerable importance for Britain's future claims.

The Company's position seems clear enough. They knew their actual position in northern Nigeria to be far more vulnerable, both juridically and physically, than they had dared to admit at Berlin. On the Benue they traded as far as Adamawa, but the Emir refused to allow them to disembark and establish shore-based factories; and lower down that river, as a British Commissioner discovered in 1889, there were large gaps in the system of treaties on which their claim to be the protecting power rested. Even when authenticated treaties purported to convey sovereign rights, the general interpretation of the African signatories was that

> They had not *sold* their country to the Company, neither had they given the land, but they quite understood that they were under the protection of the Company, and the Company would, and in some cases had, protected them against the attacks of their enemies.[25]

On the Niger itself the Company was well-established in the large

[24] Thomson, normally a prolific writer, published only relatively brief accounts of his journey. The most detailed, 'Up the Niger to the Central Sudan' (*Good Words*, 27 (1886) pp. 24–9, 109–18, 249–56, 323–30) takes the form of reprinted letters to a friend, 'added to and altered considerably', and explains that Thomson's journals were stolen during his return journey. His other accounts are a brief but optimistic note about commercial prospects in the Western Sudan in *Proceedings, Royal Geographical Society*, n.s. VIII (1886) pp. 734–5; a paper, compounded of these two, read to the British Association and printed in *Scottish Geographical Magazine*, 2 (1886) pp. 577–96; and a paper read to the Manchester Geographical Society on 27 January 1886 and printed in that Society's *Journal*, 2 (1886) pp. 1–18. The text of this address was censored by Goldie, who deleted Thomson's excessively (and for him unusually) enthusiastic picture of commercial prospects. Goldie realised that 'Not one half of the territories supposed to be under British protection are really secured by treaties, the remaining interspersed territories being thus still open to annexation by foreign nations, whose cupidity it would be impolitic to arouse.' (C.O. 96/177, Goldie to Meade, 19 January 1886, with deleted passages.)

[25] F.O.403/131 (Conf. 5913). Report by Major Macdonald of his visit as Her Majesty's Commissioner to the Niger and Oil Rivers, January 1890, p. 9.

and important Emirate of Nupe; but Etsu Maliki clearly regarded
them as traders operating at his discretion – as *dhimmis* of a
particularly useful sort – and consistently refused to allow them
to proceed further up-stream.[26] Thomson's treaties with the overlords of the region were thus intended to provide a diplomatic
trump which could be played against European rivals who might
succeed in exploiting the Company's precarious local position.
They could be used to nullify any coup which Flegel might achieve
on the pattern of Mahin beach; and they also would justify the
Company in continuing to regulate foreign commerce on the
rivers if the local Emirs should decide to withdraw the privileges
they had conceded.

The Company's central purpose, to control the commercial
relations of northern Nigeria with the outside world, is clarified
in a passage from his instructions which Thomson later quoted
to the Manchester Geographical Society:

> Your chief object will be directed towards obtaining for us
> complete monopoly (as far as foreign trade is concerned, for
> we must not in any way interfere with native trade) of the
> commerce of the two empires. This would in no way form a
> hindrance to trade in those regions, as we shall then become
> an organising company, who would rent out to various com-
> mercial companies the right to trade, mine &c. throughout
> these regions, while the native governments would reap the
> benefit of an extensive opening up of trade and of mineral
> development, which would hardly take place without the im-
> pulse being given to it by us....[27]

There is of course a good deal of casuistry here, for Goldie showed
no eagerness to encourage such sub-concessions; but this emphasis
on arrangements which would not exclude other traders able to
contribute to development was likely to commend itself to the
Fulani rulers, as well as to appease Manchester Free Traders.

For Thomson's arrival cannot have seemed any sort of menace
to the rulers of Sokoto and Gwandu; nothing in their experience
could yet suggest that individual white men might pose a threat
to their states. Their immediate preoccupations were with the
enforcement of an authority based upon the Shari'a, and with the

[26] See within, pp. 107–8.
[27] See Note 24 above.

collection of tribute, throughout their very widely dispersed dominions. The Niger Company were already well-known in both capitals as traders on the Niger, though whom guns[28] and other valuable articles might be obtained which would be of assistance in this task; it is significant that the Wazir's first action after Thomson's arrival at Sokoto was to ascertain that he represented the Company and not the Queen.[29] Once satisfied on this the Sultan, while certainly not assenting consciously to the presumptuous suggestion that he should alienate any part of his sovereign rights, was clearly quite disposed to try and accommodate these merchants, from whom future benefits (besides the relatively lavish gifts which Thomson presented) might be expected. Subsequent correspondence with the Niger Company shows that a Sierra Leonean agent, David Ashford King, secured the Sultan's confidence; he was used to convey, for example, the Sultan's wishes as to the exact composition of the goods to be provided in payment of his stipend of '3,000 bags'.[30] In return the Sultan (albeit ineffectively) instructed the Emir of Adamawa to concede the trading privileges which he was denying the Company.[31] But it is incredible that 'Umar could have thought of conceding any element of sovereignty to mere traders; indeed, Staudinger's report raises doubts whether the phrase 'entire rights' was, even in a purely commercial context, adequately translated into Hausa or Arabic. Whether Thomson's failure to clarify his purposes further should be attributed to fraud, discretion or inadvertence, it is impossible to say.

For Goldie's purpose of scaring off foreign competition, vague formulae which he was still in no position to apply in practice were sufficient. The French had no representatives in the area

[28] But not modern firearms; cf. F.O.84/1940 Goldie to Macdonald, 12 June 1889,' . . . it is vital that no rifles should be included in the presents [to the Emirs] – *not even one*. We have had a standing fight on the subject with most of the Emirs, and have steadily refused to give even a single rifle.'

[29] Thomson, *Good Words* (1886) p. 327.

[30] U.A.C. Library, bound volume of correspondence, 'Royal Niger Company, 1885–90'. Sultan to R.N.C., 22 September 1887; 17 October 1883; 3 September, 1889 (Letter states that King is authorised to receive annual presents. 'We know him personally and have confidence in him.')

[31] See below p. 107.

who could test the true position, and Flegel died in 1886, disappointed by lack of support. The *Kolonialverein* had raised only a small fraction of the 150,000 marks it had promised to Flegel;[32] and more crucially, had failed to persuade Bismarck to run any risk of conflict with Britain.

We wish to eliminate any source of future ill feeling between the two nations, which might arise from the endeavours of companies or individuals to open unknown territories to the influence of their fellow-countrymen [wrote Bismarck. He therefore sought] to conclude a demarcation agreement, before unilateral occupations give the territory to be partitioned an importance which will make subsequent agreement over points in dispute more difficult.[33]

Thus in July 1886, the Germans agreed to extend the demarcation line of 1885 in a way which would leave the key Adamawa town of Yola in the British sphere;[34] while continuing to insist on rights of navigation[35] they showed no disposition to press any queries about Britain's rights in Sokoto which Staudinger's reports might have suggested. European governments were beginning to realise that, if they submitted African treaties made by their rivals to close critical scrutiny, they risked a general devaluation of that currency of paper claims on which their own imperial pretensions still largely rested. From this self-denying ordinance, Goldie was able to benefit.

But if the political framework on which Goldie's monopoly rested remained fragile, the commercial returns were also disappointing. The Company's profits were still derived largely from tapping the palm resources of the forest belt, and hopes of opening up rich new resources in the interior gradually abated. In 1886 the London Office opened a large minute-book entitled 'Extract from Coast Letters re New Products', into which were copied reports

[32] Staudinger, pp. 104–5, cf. Flegel to his brother, Bakundi, 14 October 1885: Flegel op. cit., 14 October 1885.

[33] Bismarck to Münster, 16 October 1885, quoted Wehler, *Bismarck und der Imperialismus*, p. 319.

[34] Hertslet, op. cit., III, pp. 880–1; Exchange of notes, Rosebery–Hatzfeldt, 27 July–4 August 1886; cf. above pp. 44–5.

[35] Flint, *Goldie*, p. 91.

of varying degrees of enthusiasm. Agents despatched samples of plants from the bush, whether identifiable or not, and hopefully analysed the prospects for increased exports of gum, wax, hemp, pepper, chillies, indigo, shea-butter, 'Calabar beans' and many other natural products. Josué Zweifel, an enegetic Swiss who had formerly worked for Verminck in Sierra Leone, sent detailed descriptions of arrow poisons, among other more or less plausible commodities.[36] But the forest contained no magic herbs of unrealised commercial possibilities.

Rubber seemed more promising. This natural product of tropical forests had been in increasing commercial demand for a variety of uses since the development of vulcanising processes in the 1840s, and was already providing a strong incentive for European invasion of the Congo Basin. During the 1880s rising prices in the international rubber market stimulated several attempts by merchants to extract increased supplies from West African forests.[37] In the Niger valley rubber was obtainable both from a tree, *Funtumia Elastica, and,* more commonly, from various species of the *Landolphia* vine. But its extraction required a reasonably cheap labour force of Africans trained to tap the vines without damaging their future productive capacity, which with *Landolphia* is all too easy. Zweifel took a keen interest in this problem, which he had already faced in Sierra Leone, and circulated to his colleagues detailed instructions about the most efficient methods. He favoured a more extensive use of the credit system, so that tobacco and other trade goods carried out from the Company's stations by small African traders would tempt local people to enter the market economy; but Goldie preferred not to encourage independent African traders, and in any case local farmers proved reluctant to redirect their labour into this somewhat arduous work.[38] The Company imported labourers from the Congo; but Zweifel deplored their workmanship,[39] and after the rains of 1887 he returned to Lokoja with a party of 160

[36] This volume is in the Library of U.A.C., London; Zweifel, 10 June 1886.

[37] R. Dumett, 'The Rubber Trade of the Gold Coast and Asante in the nineteenth century . . ., *JAH*, XII (1971) 80–3.

[38] U.A.C. Library, 'New Products . . .', Zweifel, 10 April, 13 April, 24 April, 5 June 1887; McIntosh, 21 July 1887.

[39] Ibid., Zweifel, 6 December 1886; 5 July 1887; Hewby, 20 July 1887.

Temnes who had experience of rubber tapping near Sierra Leone. These men, if more skilled, were also more conscious than the Congolese of the rights of labour; when Zweifel tried to enforce heavy-handed discipline in conditions of hardship and short rations the Temnes angrily demanded repatriation, and Zweifel could only re-establish discipline by shooting several leaders.[40] This atrocious affair was successfully hushed up by the Company, despite much indignation in the Colonial Office, and Zweifel and his superiors went unpunished; but it ended the Company's attempt to develop a major trade in rubber.

Beyond the forest belt, the Company's trade progressed even more slowly. In 1885, only five out of the twenty-one stations originally opened on the Benue by David McIntosh were still active. By 1889 the Company was trading at twelve places in this river, but at only seven did they have 'stations' ashore. Some comprised only a dwelling-house and an iron store, and most did only a minor trade in 'wild' products like ivory, rubber and benniseed.[41] Hausa traders in ivory were said to be so little attracted by the Company's offerings of Manchester cloth that they preferred to carry their tusks north to Kano, so that if they reached the Company at all it was usually by an extremely circuitous route to Nupe.[42] Hopes were pinned on reports of the mineral resources of the Bauchi plateau, and messengers were sent to try to persuade the Emir to divert consignments of tin from northern markets to the Benue; but internal revolts and Tiv hostility made this route unsafe, and full exploitation of mineral resources had to await the establishment of formal colonial rule.[43]

In general (agents reported) non-Muslims lacked the confidence to venture afield in search of marketable products,[44] while the

[40] Flint, *Goldie*, pp. 167–9; cf. C.O. 267/370, Rowe to Knutsford, 130, 19 May 1887 and enclosures.

[41] F.O. 403/131 (Macdonald Report) pp. 57–9, 72–89. See also the informative book by his secretary, A. F. Mockler-Ferryman, *Up the Niger*. Narrative of Major Claude Macdonald's mission to the Niger and Benue Rivers, West Africa (1892) p. 66.

[42] F.O. 403/131, pp. 87–8.

[43] U.A.C. Library, 'New Products' book – Watson, 15 September 1886; Zweifel, 10 April 1887; Wallace, 21 August 1887; McIntosh, 1 January 1888; cf. Mockler-Ferryman, pp. 83, 75; F.O. 403/131, p. 11.

[44] U.A.C., 'New Products' book; Zweifel, 24 April 1887; McIntosh, 21 July 1887.

local Emirs remained suspicious. In Adamawa, the Emir maintained the traditional position that 'the river belongs to Allah, but the land belongs to me'; and refused to deal with Europeans without written authority from Sokoto. In September 1889 the Company did induce the Sultan to write and direct that they should be allowed to land and build houses; 'there is no need of humbugging one who is on the water', 'Umar declared.[45] But the Emirs – Sanda (c. 1872–91) and Zubeir (1891–1901) – preoccupied with internal resistance movements, were less trustful; only in 1893 did Zubeir sign a treaty with the Company, and he would not allow them to erect buildings at Yola until three years later.[46] Powerless to override such opposition, the Company could only use its admitted superiority upon the rivers to try and prevent foreign rivals from establishing themselves in the area and so challenging the basis of their monopoly.

On the Niger itself, the Company's position above the confluence was based on half a dozen factories somewhat uneasily established within the Emirate of Bida and smaller Nupe emirates. Its treaty with Etsu Maliki of 19 March 1885 conferred no political sovereignty but only the rights to regulate the trade of foreigners, and to mine. In 1889 Maliki succinctly defined the attitude which he had consistently taken in his dealings with the Company:

> Respecting the affairs of foreigners it is in your hands. Respecting the affairs of my country it is in my hands, with both buying and selling – both to heathens and Muslims my country is open to trade, excepting to thieves and hypocrites.[47]

As Macdonald noted in the same year, the Company possessed 'very little *de facto* jurisdiction outside their factory gate'.[48] This lack of any clear legal standing underlined the diplomatic importance of Thomsons' treaties with Sokoto and Gwandu. But the Company did control the waterway, and so the import of firearms; this provided a bond of mutual self-interest with Maliki, who

[45] U.A.C. Library; R.N.C. correspondence; R.N.C. to Sultan of Sokoto, 6 December 1888; Sultan to Emir, 3 September 1889.

[46] Mockler-Ferryman, pp. 90–5, 115.

[47] U.A.C. Library, R.N.C. correspondence, Maliki to R.N.C., 24 February 1889.

[48] F.O. 403/131, p. 20.

needed arms to assert his authority over independent-minded and discontented subjects, and to pursue an expansionist policy towards the south-east.[49] However, if the opportunity of doing business with others appeared, Maliki was always liable to opt for free trade; and once foreigners were established in Nupe they would not only breach the Company's monopoly but could question the diplomatic premises on which the British representatives at Berlin had retained the right to regulate trade in their own hands.[50] In 1887 this danger materialised with the arrival of a German, Jacob Hoenigsberg, who stirred up the independent traders to put pressure on Maliki; before he was deported by the Company his presence had enabled Maliki to negotiate an increase in his stipend from £400 to £2,000 a year,[51] and had also revealed the Company's precarious position to foreigners. The Auswärtige Amt took up his grievance, obliged the Foreign Office to ensure that Goldie respected the Berlin Act and the Anglo-German agreement of June 1885, and so reminded the British government that they could not escape ultimate responsibility for their expanding empire.[52]

Clearly, the Niger Company did not have the resources to engage in great programmes of political expansion; nor, as Professor Flint's notable study shows, had it any immediate intention of doing so. The impressive array of political and judicial functions conferred on its officials after the grant of the Charter were designed for the explicit purpose of regulating the activities of persons foreign to the Niger (whether African or European). African states as strong as the emirates had necessarily to be politically respected – a necessity later turned into a virtue by theorists of Indirect Rule. The Company's priorities were to protect its existing monopolies, to prevent the presence of foreigners from precipitating conflict and disorder, and to raise sufficient revenue in customs duties to finance the whole operation.

In fact, its operations in the North were not economically viable. The outposts in Nupe and on the Benue, and the armed constabulary of 400 men, were still financed largely by the profits of trade

---

[49] Michael Mason, 'The Nupe Kingdoms in the Nineteenth Century. A Political History' (Ph.D. Thesis, University of Birmingham, 1970).

[50] Cf. *Prelude*, p. 336; Flint, *Goldie*, 68–70.

[51] F.O. 403/131, p. 21.

[52] Flint, *Goldie*, pp. 114–19.

in palm produce conducted below Lokoja, where the Company's operations cut into the commercial hinterland of the Oil Rivers Protectorate. This had become a serious subject of conflict and contention with the Liverpool, Glasgow and Bristol merchants who had developed the commerce of this area during the nineteenth century, and also with their African suppliers in the coastal trading-states who claimed that the Company was poaching within their own established domain. Eight of the nine leading delta houses were at this time in the process of combining to form the African Association (which was finally incorporated on 3 June 1889);[53] in the summer of 1887 Goldie began to negotiate with them for a commercial merger. By ending these conflicts and broadening his own financial base, he hoped to create a consortium strong enough to justify the extension of chartered government to the whole area claimed for British sovereignty between Lagos and Kamerun.[54]

Initially, these negotiations proceeded with the knowledge and approval of the Foreign Office. In its own sphere the Niger Company had so far provided the expected political umbrella effectively enough; and although the government had had plenty of altercations with Goldie, he had not, apart from the Hoenigsberg case, made many demands for diplomatic assistance, and none for taxpayers' money. If other interested parties were willing to acquiesce, an extension of the charter to the delta might save the government much trouble.

But by the summer of 1888 this premise seemed highly questionable. Besides the protests which might be anticipated from the Company's German rivals, strong opposition was developing from the powerful West African shipping interest led by A. L. Jones, who was in process of building up his own international shipping ring. Jones knew that an extended Niger Company would be able to dictate freight charges and might ultimately start its own shipping line; besides bringing direct pressure on the Government he played on the apprehensions of some Liverpool merchants to weaken and divide the African Association.[55] The Foreign Office,

[53] See the typescript 'History of the United Africa Company', by J. J. Rankin (U.A.C. Library) pp. 73 ff.
[54] For these negotiations, see Flint, *Goldie*, pp. 98–111.
[55] Flint, *Goldie*, pp. 107–11.

probably hoping to frighten the waverers by presenting an alternative which would mean higher taxes and closer administrative supervision, now suggested that the Colony of Lagos might consider taking over the whole Oil Rivers protectorate. Predictably, the Colonial Office were extremely reluctant to consider extending their responsibilities;[56] but this action brought Goldie's schemes to the notice of African and European traders in Lagos, whom Goldie had always tried to exclude from the Niger. On 11 May 1888 a meeting of leading Lagosians protested strongly against any extension of the monopolistic system from which many of them had suffered, and called instead for the annexation of the whole protectorate to Lagos. Governor Moloney, underlining the strength of local opinion, suggested that Lagos might at least absorb the western Niger delta, and so secure control of the Forcados estuary. (Until the improvement of the Lagos harbour entrance, this was where ocean-going steamers discharged their cargo into smaller vessels plying along the Lagos Lagoon.)[57] Although the senior members of the Colonial office refused to consider this, Moloney's case was supported by R. L. Antrobus, a conscientious younger official who was exercising a growing influence on West African policy.[58]

Reluctantly therefore the Foreign Office realised that Goldie's convenient scheme for extended Company government would be opposed by foreign merchants (and possibly their governments), by the domestic shipping interest, and by the commercial community of Lagos. By October 1888 they were also beginning to understand that there might also be opposition from intelligent and sophisticated African chiefs within the Oil Rivers Protectorate. The responsibilities they had acquired for the embryo empire in Nigeria were too complex to be quietly disposed of. In December 1888 Salisbury appointed Major Claude Macdonald as Commissioner to 'inquire into certain questions affecting Imperial and Colonial interests on the West coast of Africa, and into the position of the Royal Niger Company'.[59] These broad

[56] C.O. 147/62, F.O. to C.O., Conf., 2 November 1887, and Minutes; cf. Flint, *Goldie*, pp. 104 ff.

[57] C.O. 147/64, Moloney to Knutsford, 172, 7 June; 185, 16 June 1888; C.O. 147/66, Moloney to Knutsford, Conf., 9 October 1888.

[58] C.O. 147/68, Minutes on F.O. to C.O., 28 July 1888.

[59] Flint, *Goldie*, p. 129; cf. F.O. 84/1940, Salisbury to Macdonald, 17 January 1889.

terms of reference showed that, while the Foreign Office accepted Goldie's thesis that the problems of the delta and of the Niger were connected, they were not prepared to accept his inferences of an extended Charter.

CREEPING IMPERIALISM IN THE OIL RIVERS

When the Gladstone Cabinet authorised the wholesale signature of protectorate treaties in the region of the Oil Rivers, they had been chiefly concerned to secure a legal basis on which to resist possible French 'encroachments'. These treaties represented no desire on the part of Liberal Ministers to rule over Africans, any more than the assent expressed by the African signatories reflected a conscious desire to invite such rule. The British representatives at Berlin had demonstrated the limits of their interest by success-fully working to exempt such protectorates from the obligation placed upon occupying powers to establish a measure of effective authority. They were still content that authority should be exer-cised by co-operative African rulers, and had positively shrunk away from any obligation to intervene in internal African affairs – in particular avoiding any moral obligation to deal with the delicate problem of domestic slavery.

The attitude of the Consulate, and of some of the British traders whose interests it represented, was rather different. Even before 1884 Consul Hewett had been pressing for permission to act against the monopolies of coastal middlemen; and article VI of the standard treaty form used in 1884, which stipulated that trade should be open to all 'in every part of the territories' of the African signatories, could provide justification for such action. True, some of the shrewdest and most successful of the trading chiefs had rejected this article; but a Consul really intent on coercing them could find pretexts all the same. Initially however the new Oil Rivers Protectorate was merely a slightly strengthened version of the old Consulate, and its influence depended on the existence of willing collaborators among the rulers of the delta. In Bonny, for example, the 1880s saw a fierce struggle between the highly anglicised George Pepple, who was committed to policies of modernisation through the encouragement of Christianity and attacks on traditional religion, and his more traditionalist oppo-nents. When George Pepple was deposed in 1883 for exceeding his royal prerogatives. Hewett worked for his restoration; when

this was accepted by the chiefs in January 1887 the alliance between the Consulate and the modernising Christian party was
finally confirmed.[60] As often before, the Consulate had secured
its aims by more or less indirect forms of pressure. But now that
they were committed to uphold Britain's ultimate sovereignty,
the Consulate would not always be able to remain even so far in
the background; agents of energetic temperament were increasingly able to impose their own solutions without effective regulation from Whitehall.

The principal target for this creeping frontier imperialism was
Jaja, founder and ruler of the prosperous trading-state of Opobo.
Modern Nigerian historiography tends to depict Jaja as a sort of
proto-nationalist: the late Professor Anene even propounded the
'fascinating hypothesis' that by building on his connections with
the Aro oracle he might have himself achieved the political unification of eastern Nigeria.[61] What the records show more clearly
is an intelligent and audacious entrepreneur who, having risen
from servile origins through skill and enterprise in trade, was
proving equally adept at directing the policies of a trading state
with an annual revenue estimated at £30,000. With remarkable
shrewdness for a man who had not travelled outside the Delta,
Jaja tried to promote innovations on a much more selective basis
than George Pepple, encouraging those foreign merchants who
were prepared to pursue their interests under his authority: wel-
coming schools, without permitting a missionary offensive by
African Christians bent on overthrowing traditional religion as
the basis of the state.[62] Ultimately Jaja hoped to become independent of European intermediaries, so that power in his state would
be reserved to those who accepted its values; but he was no xeno-
phobe. He tried to increase his independence of foreign merchants
by shipping oil directly to Liverpool; but when he discovered that
this tied up his working capital for too long he readily worked

[60] For an account of George's deposition and restoration from traditional Bonny sources, see Adadonye Fombo, 'Short Outline History of
Bonny', typescript in University of Ibadan Library, ff. 62–4, see also
Ayandele, *Missionary Impact*, pp. 93–7; Anene, *Southern Nigeria*, pp. 76–7,
94.

[61] Anene, *Southern Nigeria*, p. 55; cf. K. O. Dike, *Trade and Politics in the
Niger Delta* (Oxford 1956) Chap. 10.

[62] See the perceptive discussion in Ayandele, *Missionary Impact*, Chap.
3.

with the Glasgow firm of Miller Brothers against the demands of
the African Association's 'ring'.[63] Europeans of widely different
background found Jaja tough, realistic, but essentially reasonable,
amenable to compromise on any issues except those which touched
his fundamental rights and interests as a ruler and a man.

Formally, the Consulate came into conflict with Jaja over his
claim to exercise sovereign rights over those inland markets, especially Ohambela and Essene, which were the source of his
wealth; but more profoundly, because they feared his power
might become too great to be readily controlled. Hewett, a fussy
hypochondriac, fretted over Jaja's success, possibly 'finding in this
Nigger King a man of superior natural abilities to his own';[64] in
1883, after a long dispute over Jaja's attempt to exclude British
traders from the Qua Ibo river, Hewett had hinted at deposition.
But he concluded weakly 'I must leave it to Your Lordship to deal
with Jaja in regard to this matter'; and since it was hardly realistic
to expect Lord Granville to act so energetically, nothing was
done.[65] Jaja remained strong enough not only to insist on the
deletion of the 'free trade' clause from the protectorate treaty he
signed in 1884, but to secure a written admission from Hewett
that 'the Queen does not want to take your country *or your
markets.*'[66]

Hitherto part of Jaja's strength was that the six British firms
trading at Opobo, recognising that the bird in their hands was a
succulent one, were content to pay the duties and accept the
limitations which he set upon their commerce. But when palm-oil
prices began to collapse in 1884 five of these firms, members of
the African Association, combined to try and force down the prices
and duties which Jaja's monopoly enabled him to charge. Jaja
resisted by coming to a separate arrangement with the sixth
merchant house, Miller Brothers of Glasgow, and by intensifying
his attempts to trade directly with Britain; only then did the members of the ring retaliate by complaining to the Consulate about
the level of duties and by claiming the right to deal directly with

[63] C. de Cardi, in Mary Kingsley, *West African Studies* (1st ed., 1899)
pp. 541–2.

[64] C. de Cardi, loc. cit., p. 546.

[65] P.P. 1888, LXXIV, C.5365, p. 17; Hewett to Granville, 5 February
1883.

[66] F.O. 403/86 (Confidential Print No. 5871) No. 1, Hewett to Jaja,
1 July 1884 (Emphasis added).

Jaja's inland markets. These were methods of bringing pressure on a successful middleman, not an attack on middlemen as such; as Dr Gertzel has shown, the associated merchants were not anxious to face the problems of dealing regularly at the markets themselves, and did not do so after Jaja's fall. 'It was the Consul, not the traders, who wished to see the middleman abolished.'[67]

Jaja's tactics thus provided Hewett with an opportunity to resume his harassing campaign; he sanctimoniously declared, 'Her Majesty's Government having decided that they will allow no monopolies in their territories, I must decide that the European agents were in their rights in going to the markets in question.'[68] Leaving aside the hypocrisy of propounding such a doctrine as the Niger Company prepared to receive its charter, not all British subjects in the delta found free trade principles applicable. Miller Brothers clearly did not; and neither, in general, did senior naval officers on the coast. One commanding Admiral had already pointed out that 'the "middlemen" . . . have a clear and decided use . . . The so-called "monopolies" I look upon as being dues fairly leviable for the security of the traders;'[69] another, finding Hewett 'strongly imbued with one idea, *viz*, that Jaja was at the bottom of . . . all the difficulties that have arisen', now tried to cool his renewed ardour for deportation.[70] The Consulate had been led by dislike of Jaja's independent attitude to strike false moral attitudes in support of the commercial interests of the Liverpool firms. As a later business historian noted,

> Jaja was always willing to do business with other firms on the same terms as with Alexander Miller, Brother & Co., and Mr. George Miller . . . was far too reasonable a man to demand a permanent monopoly of Jaja's custom.[71]

[67] Cherry Gertzel, 'Commercial Organisation on the Niger Coast, 1852–1891' in Leverhulme Foundation, *Historians in Tropical Africa* (Salisbury, 1962) pp. 301–3, cf. de Cardi, loc. cit., pp. 548–9; F.O. 403/86, pp. 5–6.

[68] F.O. 403/86, encl. in No. 14. 'Decisions of her Majesty's Consul on Matters of Complaint brought before him by the European Agents and Jaja', March 1886.

[69] Richards to Lister, 5 December 1884, quoted Anene, *Southern Nigeria*, p. 85.

[70] F.O. 403/86, No. 11, Hunt-Grubbe to Admiralty, 15 March 1886.

[71] J. J. Rankin's typescript, 'History of the United Africa Company', U.A.C. Library.

But the responsible officials in the Foreign Office had been converted to Hewett's anti-middleman thesis, and wrongly believed

> . . . that Jaja is determined to use his exceptional power and influence among the native tribes to oppose the extension of European trade, and to keep traders within such limits as the middlemen of the coast may choose to impose . . . he is acting in such a manner as to make the exercise of the British Protectorate difficult unless he is sharply dealt with.[72]

They persuaded the new Foreign Secretary to issue a portentous warning that 'It is not to be permitted that any chief who may happen to occupy a territory on the coast should obstruct British policy in order to benefit himself';[73] and they had already sent out, as Hewett's assistant and deputy, a vigorous young man of similarly astringent views.

Harry Johnston was, like Jaja, a rising man within his own society. His origins – in a comfortable, pious, business family in the London suburbs – were by no means servile; but by choosing a career in the service of British imperial expansion Johnston moved into social circles where, even after his talents had brought him unusual recognition, he never felt entirely secure. Although his intellectual versatility was outstanding, his education had been irregular and plebeian; long after his most spectacular social successes he felt a need to retell and embellish them, as if to convince himself they had been real.[74] Johnston was no racist bully; his relationships with Africans were (by comparison with most European contemporaries) sympathetic, enlightened and humane; and when he became Vice-Consul in the Oil Rivers at the age of 27 he accepted the official doctrine that there was no need to force the pace of political expansion. 'So long as we keep other Europeans nations out, we need not be in a hurry to go in.'[75] Where

[72] F.O. 403/86, No. 9, Lister to Admiralty, 2 March 1886.

[73] Ibid., p. 25, Rosebery to Ja Ja, June 1886.

[74] In his autobiographical novel *The Gay-Dombeys* (1919) as well as in *The Story of My Life* (1923) Johnston revisits some of the summits of his social climbing (notably his visit to Lord Salisbury at Hatfield over thirty years earlier) as though he can still hardly credit his success. Compare a revealing letter written to his father in 1886; Alex. Johnston, *The Life and Letters of Sir Harry Johnston* (1929) p. 125.

[75] Johnston to Anderson, Pte., 13 November 1886; quoted by Roland Oliver, *Sir Harry Johnston and the Scramble for Africa* (1957) p. 101.

Johnston was ahead of official orthodoxy was in his vision of the possible future development of 'new India' in tropical Africa. When he was eventually able to visit Jaja's markets between Opobo and the Cross River, Johnston revived the rhetoric he had last used when urging the Gladstone government to occupy Mount Kilimanjaro. The people were 'industrious, very friendly' (though 'easily terrorized by a swaggering bully like Jaja'); the country 'admirably cultivated'; the roads broad and clean; the livestock flourishing. 'Here is the country where white men may hope to settle and enjoy good health, and it is from lands like these that runaway slaves and upstart Kings like Jaja are trying to keep us from penetrating, lest their ill-gotten gains as middlemen may be diminished.'[76]

But it rested with British representatives on the spot to secure – or to fumble – these attractive opportunities by authoritatively asserting the rights of the stronger. Jaja's independent behaviour was setting unacceptable limits upon Consular power; as even his friend de Cardi recognised, Hewett's hesitations had produced conditions where 'some decisive measures were necessary to uphold the dignity of the Consular office'.[77] So, from his arrival in West Africa, Johnston embraced the 'conventional wisdom' handed on by Hewett and the Foreign Office – that Jaja's behaviour presented a critical case of a middleman obstructing direct contact between enterprising Europeans and 'the industrious thrifty tribes of the interior', and that his overthrow would open the road to great commercial expansion under a light umbrella of British rule. 'I am convinced that few countries in Africa may be so easily and economically governed', Johnston wrote after a few days on the coast. 'A force of 100 armed Houssas and one gun-boat would be amply sufficient to keep the boldest chief in awe, and the "comey" and taxes and presents now paid to middlemen might be diverted to meet the cost of this police force.'[78]

But Johnston's hostility to Jaja was not just a matter of free trade principles. During 1886 the Consulate was much occupied with affairs in Bonny; in January 1887, after Johnston had taken

[76] P. P. 1888, LXXIV, pp. 52–3, Johnston to Salisbury, August 1887. Cf. Johnston to Fitzmaurice, 10 July 1884, quoted Oliver, *Johnston*, pp. 66–8.
[77] de Cardi, loc. cit., p. 546.
[78] F.O. 493/86, No. 7, Johnston to Salisbury, 15 January 1886.

over from Hewett, George Pepple was finally restored as King.
One factor which aided the re-establishment of unity within
Bonny was the 'cold war' with Jaja, which had continued since
1873; in 1886, according to traditions collected by Mr. Fombo,
Jaja had 'planned a coup d'etat on all Bonny inland markets and
a rapid invasion of the capital'.[79] It may be that Bonny trading
magnates accepted George's return because he seemed to enjoy
the favour of the Consulate; they expected British assistance in
regaining access to the lost markets, which they regarded as 'the
joint and common property of all Bonny and Opobo-Bonny citizens'.[80] As one condition of George's restoration the chiefs promised 'to support the King substantially and heartily in any scheme
which he may lay before us for re-opening the roads to the interior
oil markets so as to bring back good trade to Bonny.'[81]

Johnston on his side was well aware of the connection between
Bonny and Opobo. In backing George Pepple he not only made
himself available to advice and pressure from one party to the
dispute, but adopted a policy of supporting Christian Anglophils
which might resolve British difficulties in Opobo also. He therefore resolved to compel Jaja to accept (white) Primitive Methodist
missionaries, as he had reluctantly agreed in the Treaty of 1884,
as an earnest of still wider changes to come. Somewhat incon-
gruously, for a man who made much parade of having abandoned
the religious doctrines of his youth, Johnston believed that
Christianity would not only end cruel and bloody practices which
were legitimate under indigenous systems of ethics, but would
prepare the road for 'the white man's advent'.[82] Johnston knew
that traditional religion (or 'juju') provided sanctions for Jaja's
authority at the disputed markets; such obstacles could perhaps
be removed only by a complete and ostentatious revolution at
the seat of authority.

On 27 July 1887 Acting-Consul Johnston arrived by warship
at Opobo and took up residence with Thomas Wright, agent for
Messrs. Harrison, one of the firms in dispute with Jaja. It seems
clear that he had decided to compel Jaja to surrender on the

---

[79] Fombo typescript, f. 57–8.
[80] F.O. 403/86, No. 112, encl. 5; Bonny chiefs to Ja Ja, 22 July 1887.
[81] Fombo typescripts, f. 254–5, Agreement of Bonny chiefs, 19 January
1887.
[82] Ayandele, *Missionary Impact*, pp. 101–10.

crucial issue of his claim to exclude foreigners from the markets, and to force the issue before the deputation which Jaja had sent to appeal to Lord Salisbury in London had an opportunity to be heard. For that deputation had a persuasive case; Captain Hand, a senior naval officer who joined Johnston with a second warship on 3 August, was 'impressed with the justice of Jaja's complaints against the British government'.[83] On 5 August, Johnston keyed himself up for a decisive confrontation; Jaja was summoned before an assembly of traders and chiefs and compelled to agree, under protest, not only to punish any of his subjects who molested British traders at his markets, but formally to 'break Juju' and release his officials from the ban on trade with white men.

But Johnston suspected that this was only a tactical retreat and that Jaja was still placing hopes on his deputation to London. After a melancholy day of 'feverish attacks and palpitations', and a discouraging journey to Ohambela with the emissaries who formally executed the breaking of the 'juju', Johnston recorded his conviction 'that this country will never be really opened to the full tide of commerce and civilisation till Jaja has been removed from his position as King.'[84] These apprehensions were soon confirmed, when the Ohambela chiefs derisively declared that white men were free to trade – but only in foodstuffs and in slaves! The conflict escalated as predicted. Johnston forebade all trade between Jaja and British subjects (effectively striking at Miller Brothers) and began to make his own treaties with Ibo chiefs within Jaja's sphere of influence; Jaja retaliated by blocking the creeks with booms protected by armed guards. On 11 September Johnston telegraphed for permission to deport Jaja to the Gold Coast. By 19 September, having received no reply from London and only counsels of restraint from Captain Hand, Johnston was again screwed up to high nervous tension; summoning Jaja to a new meeting, he demanded that he should immediately embark on H.M.S. *Goshawk* for Accra, where the British government would hold a 'searching inquiry' into his conduct. Jaja, recognising that he could not fight the British government, accepted this ultima-

[83] Johnston's diary, 4 August 1887. Microfilm in University of Ibadan Library.

[84] F.O. 403/86, No. 47, Johnston to Salisbury, 12 August 1887; cf. No. 48, Ja Ja to Salisbury, 12 August 1887; Johnston's diary, 5–10 August 1887.

tum; authority in Opobo was provisionally transferred to a Governing Council on which British merchants outnumbered the African members.[85]

Why did Johnston judge it necessary to take such drastic and unauthorised action? One argument he used was that Jaja planned 'to sell his country to France' and had actually sent an emissary to that country. The only apparent foundation for this was a rumour originating with Johnston's Bonny allies, with little evidence to support it,[86] but Johnston doubtless knew that it was an argument which would commend respect in London. More plausibly, Johnston feared that Jaja might repeat his tactics of 1869 and execute another physical displacement of authority. By moving inland to his Ibo homeland Jaja 'would have had all the Bonny and Opobo commerce at his mercy'; he might 'with his cannon, rifles and war canoes, his 4,000 fighting men and his own personal courage and tactical skill become a mighty conqueror among the peaceful, timid, Ibo people at the back of Opobo.'[87] But underlying Johnston's specific fears was a conviction that the confrontation would decisively affect Britain's future authority with the protectorate; the issue, in Humpty-Dumpty's phrase, was 'who is to be master.'? The question of Ohambela, Johnston wrote on 20 August, involved more than the opening of Ibo country to direct British enterprise. His Bonny allies were watching closely: at present they recognised

> the inevitable march of events which is causing Africa to be opened up to the white man's enterprise; but if they see Jaja's ... clever stratagems ... crowned with success, they will themselves see the advisability of their following his example and of maintaining their position and their profits as the middlemen ... It is no exaggeration to say that, from Benin to Old Calabar, all the native chiefs are watching with interest the long struggle between the traders and the Trader-King of Opobo. As either side is victorious they will rule their conduct accordingly.[88]

[85] F.O. 403/86, Nos. 80, 94, 95, 111, 116, Johnston to Salisbury, 20 August; 6 September; 11 September; 24 September; 4 October 1887.

[86] F.O. 403/86, No. 95, Johnston to Salisbury, 11 September; pp. 95–6, King and Chiefs of Bonny to Ja Ja and Chiefs of Opobo, 22 July 1887.

[87] Ibid., No. 111, Johnston to Salisbury, 24 September 1887.

[88] Ibid., No. 80, Johnston to Salisbury, 20 August 1887. Like most of Johnston's reports, this was printed in full in the Parliamentary Paper C.5365 of April 1888.

Such language, destined for early publication, amounted to an assertion that the future of Christianity, civilisation and British commerce in West Africa now depended on the British government's readiness to use its own power more actively.

The Foreign Office officials, with Hewett available to advise them, were generally sympathetic to Johnston's approach; Lister welcomed the blockade as likely to teach 'a severe lesson' to 'a false and cruel king'. The moral judgements of the Secretary of State were more restrained. If Jaja was *de facto* ruler of Ohambela he was acting within his rights – and, Salisbury added, '*de facto* dominion is the only thing of which we can take notice, for none of us are learned enough to determine the legitimacy according to the Native Laws of a Guinea king.'[89] He therefore looked to the experience of naval officers to restrain Johnston and to establish what was the just course of action. But, as Salisbury would have to recognise many times over, it is difficult to keep to the rules of justice while engaging in the practice of imperialism.

It is sometimes implied that, had Salisbury not been on holiday in France during September, Jaja's fate might have been different. This ignores the extent to which the initiatives in such matters had passed to 'men on the spot' who were prepared to act as resolutely and irregularly as Johnston. If Salisbury had been available to receive the Opobo deputation on 13 September, he might have shown more patience than his Under-Secretary in listening to Chief Cookey Gam's 'disjointed and incoherent utterances',[90] but he would have hardly have been converted to the Opobo case; had he been in the office to receive Johnston's request to deport Jaja he would have replied more expeditiously and cautiously, but it is very unlikely that he would have taken the responsibility of imposing a categorical veto. And once Johnston had acted and Jaja was abroad the *Goshawk*, Salisbury knew that, even if his action was not defensible 'according to European notions of good faith', it was not reversible. Since Britain's position in the delta depended on the assumption that the resources of an empire lay behind the precarious façade of consular rule, Salisbury recognised that 'we shall do more harm by dropping than supporting

---

[89] Memo by Salisbury, 9 September 1887, quoted by W. N. Geary, *Nigeria under British Rule* (1927) pp. 280–1.

[90] F.O. 403/86, No. 62, F.O. to Johnston, 30 September 1887.

Johnston.'[91] Salisbury understood the logic of empire, though he despised its rhetoric; and that logic precluded Jaja's return.

For the peoples of southern Nigeria Johnston's coup had been a portent of things to come – a sign of the power which could be wielded by resolute agents of the British government. Despite Johnston's ostentatious collaboration with the African Association, it was not the aims of the merchants that had changed – they were soon back at Opobo, trading through middlemen as before. It was the Consulate, gradually metamorphosing into a formal protectorate administration, which had revealed new capacities for political intervention ashore. 'I don't know which are worse for a peaceably minded Foreign Office – Colonies or Consuls,' Salisbury grumbled;[92] what he did know was that in changing African conditions, neither could easily be prevented from extending their power.

Yet in this transitional period, such bold strokes were exceptional; the British still preferred to govern through the co-operation of African *élites,* and Africans thus retained some freedom to decide how far collaboration seemed compatible with their own essential interests and values. Some, like George Pepple, were already irrevocably committed to the British system; others judged it expedient to compromise. The terms of such compromises, and the statecraft of those who negotiated them, could decisively affect the relative advantages of different Nigerian peoples within the coming colonial order.[93]

An example of an African people manoeuvring with greater success during this proto-colonial period is provided by the Itsekiri. During four centuries experience of trading with Europe from

[91] Minutes by Salisbury, quoted in Oliver, *Johnston,* pp. 118, 133 (F.O. 84/1828).

[92] Sal. P. D32, Salisbury to Holland, 4 October 1887.

[93] A. J. H. Latham, *Old Calabar, 1600–1891* (Oxford, 1973) describes another state where the growth of the oil trade during the nineteenth century created tensions, and demands for British intervention from elements within and without the traditional social structure. Once the British government, prompted by fear of foreign intrusion, included Old Calabar within the protectorate of 1884 Johnston and Hewett proceeded, here too, to intervene more drastically than those who promoted their advent had intended.

their home on the coast of the western delta this small people had built up a strong middleman organisation throughout the oil-producing country of the Urhobo, their land-locked neighbours.[94] Though numbering only a few thousand the Itsekiri were proudly attached to their culture; in 1875 their leader Olomu refused to allow Bishop Crowther to establish a mission, and when they gave Hewett his protectorate treaty on 16 July 1884 the Itsekiri not only refused, like Jaja, to agree to free trade under Article VI but also insisted on deleting Article VII, which would have guaranteed freedom to Christian missionaries. Their chief spokesman was Nana, recently elected to succeed his father Olomu as 'Governor of the River'. This was not the traditional chieftancy or Olu-ship, to which no election had been possible for many years, but an office which had evolved in response to the needs of external trade; its holder was responsible, among other things, for the collection of 'comey' and the supervision of credit, whether granted by Europeans to Itsekiri brokers or by the latter to their Urhobo suppliers. Olumu and Nana, having achieved election to office through acknowledged skill in their commercial and diplomatic dealings with both Europeans and Urhobo, fortified their position by maintaining strong forces of both war and trade canoes.[95]

But Nana's position among the Itsekiri, though strong, was not unquestioned; in particular, his succession to his father's position was regarded as unconstitutional by members of a rival lineage. The immediate effect of Hewett's endorsement of his election was to strengthen Nana's position; in the long run it made him dangerously dependent on continued consular favour. In 1886 Nana had a first warning of this when, in protest against the fall in oil prices, he imposed a ban on trade which lasted over six months; faced with a brusque ultimatum which reflected Hewett's growing sense of imperial power, Nana, unlike Jaja, gave way and re-opened trade.[96] This discreet concession won him a temporary return to British favour; a year later Johnston, fresh from deporting Jaja, formed favourable impressions of Nana's intelligence

[94] The following passage is based, unless otherwise stated, on two admirable books by Obaro Ikime: *Merchant Prince of the Niger Delta* (1968) and *Niger-Delta Rivalry: Itsekiri-Urhobo Relations and the European Presence, 1884–1936* (1969).

[95] Cf. P. C. Lloyd 'The Itsekiri in the Nineteenth Century' *JAH* IV (1963) pp. 221–3.

[96] Ikime, *Merchant Prince*, pp. 57–9.

and courtesy, of the order and cleanliness of his town.[97] A more substantial reward for his willingness to recognise the reality of consular power was that Hewett and Johnston supported Nana's claim to control Burutu and other Ijaw territories in the Forcados against counter-claims from the Royal Niger Company. Temporarily at least, discretion served Itsekiri interests better than defiance.

MACDONALD'S HALFWAY HOUSE

A serious difficulty for Africans who, like Nana, wished to come to honourable terms with the insurgent British authorities was the unpredictability of British behaviour. In 1862 a thoughtful official in Whitehall, commenting on 'the disparity between our power and our knowledge', had noted that his country risked resembling 'the kings in burlesques who with comical vigour dispatch one slave with a blow and cover the other with honours, long before they can know whether either deserves his fate.[98] Though the British government's supply of information had improved somewhat since then it was still far from adequate to ensure consistency in policy, especially when the appointment of new 'men on the spot' brought new appreciations and new prescriptions. In 1889 the Foreign Office showed, by commissioning Macdonald, that it wished not only to bring its knowledge up to date, but to introduce greater rationality and justice into the administrative arrangements it had been improvising in Nigeria since 1884. In general Macdonald fulfilled both purposes; although his major conclusions were by no means revolutionary they pointed in the right direction – away from any extension of chartered governments towards a better-organised and staffed administration in those districts where the Foreign Office could most readily provide it. But his conscientiously-detailed recommendations also involved some lesser shifts of policy – from which Nana, as it happened, was to be one of the sufferers.

Macdonald, a thoughtful and upright infantryman who had lately been acting as Consul-General in Zanzibar, made serious attempts to see that the development of British control (which he assumed to be inevitable and beneficial) was reconciled with the

[97] H. H. Johnston, *The Story of My Life* (Indianapolis, 1923) pp. 196–8.
[98] C.O. 147/1, Minute by T. F. Elliot on Freeman to Newcastle, 4 June 1861.

welfare and wishes of Africans; the care he took to ascertain and document the views of ruling *élites* in African states went far beyond the letter of his instructions. His conclusions about future administration, and the procedure by which he reached them, have been discussed by other writers[99] and may simply be summarised here. For the Niger Company's sphere Macdonald accepted the continuation of chartered government. Indeed he largely applauded the Company's record; he detailed their achievements, accepted most of their treaties as having been made in good faith, and concluded that 'for the majority of the complaints that have been laid before me, there are no grounds.'[100] The grievances expressed on behalf of 'merchants, traders and residents of Lagos' were discounted as inspired by former employees dismissed by the Company; and although Macdonald unenthusiastically endorsed a suggestion by Bishop Crowther that more encouragement should be given to Africans carrying on 'petty trade in common articles of native make, such as country-made cloths, beads, mats, shoes, sandals, pipes, lamps, calabashes and potash', he seems to have accepted some of the Company's prejudices against independent African traders.[101]

The basic reason for not questioning the position of the Niger Company, however, was simply that the Foreign Office could provide no alternative – as the sequel to the enquiry showed. Besides detailed reforms in the administration of justice, in methods of accounting, in the incidence of tariffs, Macdonald proposed to recognise the right of natives of the protectorate to trade more freely within the Company's sphere; these apparently limited changes, as Flint has shown, would collectively have had the effect of undermining Goldie's monopoly.[102] For this reason the Foreign Office did nothing to enforce them; if Goldie declared these changes unacceptable and again threatened to withdraw, the government could call his bluff only if it was prepared to take over the responsibilities that had been delegated to him. So long as the British imperial system needed to work through such agents, it could not dictate the manner in which they operated.

In the Oil Rivers, however, changes did follow. Macdonald's

[99] Flint, *Goldie*, Ch. 7; Anene, *Southern Nigeria*, pp. 121–34.
[100] F.O. 403/131, p. 95.
[101] Ibid., pp. 40–4; 83–5; 96.
[102] Ibid., pp. 95–97; Flint, *Goldie*, pp. 150–5.

soundings of African and European opinion in the delta led him
decisively to reject any idea of chartered government, whether
under the Niger Company or some new group to be formed by
the African Association. A separate colonial administration alone
would meet the wishes of the people and remove their fears of
monopoly; it would also simplify relations with foreign governments, and would be relatively easy to institute.[103] But faced with
official hesitancy on the grounds of expense, and of the slavery
question, Macdonald agreed that it was not necessary to begin
with the relatively costly governmental apparatus implied by a
Crown Colony; it would be possible to discharge the still indeterminate responsibilities of the British protectorate through a
fortified Consular administration. (But he thought the designa-
tion of the Consul should be changed, lest enthusiastic German
frontiersmen from Kamerun should regard his province as still an
area of independent African states.) During 1890 detailed proposals were prepared and costed. The Consul became a 'Commissioner and Consul-General', with increased administrative
responsibilities; the Vice-Consuls, increased in number to six, also
assumed new functions; an armed police force supplied with
launches gave the administration means of enforcing its decisions.
On 1 January 1891 Macdonald himself was appointed as head
of the reorganised protectorate, which for three years he governed
with vigour and fair-mindedness.

Essentially these changes were not necessitated by complaints
from foreign competitors; apart from minor problems on the
Kamerun frontier, these presented no major problem in the Oil
Rivers. It was difficulties and anomalies in the internal operation
of the system improvised in 1884 which had suggested the need
for more effective control – for 'a paternal government under the
direction of the Foreign Office'.[104] Thus the British took a vital
step towards converting their principal West African protectorate
into full colonial rule. They reluctantly accepted that, if their protectorate government was to discharge its responsibilities to
Africans and Europeans consistently and effectively, something
more was needed than the largely nominal control of foreign relations envisaged at Berlin. The Consulate must be better informed,

[103] F.O. 84/1940, Macdonald to Salisbury, 12 June 1889; F.O. 403/131,
pp. 98–102.
[104] F.O. 403/134, Memo by Lister, 1 July 1890.

better armed, better organised. Financial and political limitations meant that the new arrangements were something of a compromise, a halfway house; and the ultimate destination had not yet been very exactly defined. But the logic of Britain's position was becoming clearer, especially to her more far-sighted agents.

Harry Johnston, consulted in August 1890 while on leave from a new appointment in Mozambique, indicated some of the immediate implications. While still arguing that the theoretically desirable solution might be an ultimate takeover of the Oil Rivers by a reformed Niger Company, Johnston advocated a more radically active form of administration than any Company was likely to adopt. He envisaged a 'paternal government' which would accept a more direct responsibility for economic and social development by employing technically trained officials – two engineers, a 'scientific gardener' from Kew, a medical officer capable of carrying out scientific observations – and at the same time deliberately seek the 'gradual sapping of the power and influence of the native chiefs' and 'the substitution of European government for Negro rule'.[105] Such a deliberate approach to developmental imperialism was not immediately acceptable in London; but Macdonald's administration did indeed undertake a gradual tightening and extension of political control. To African eyes, its methods and behaviour must have seemed as unpredictable as ever. But gradually it became clear that the direction in which the British protectorate was moving was towards full colonial rule.

[105] F.O. 403/132, Memo by Johnston, 11 August 1890.

4 The Balance of Power on the Slave Coast

By 1885 the French in Senegambia and the British on the Niger were committed to asserting more or less exclusive control over regions of long-established interest, although the nature of their interests and the type of control currently being sought differed considerably. Between these two incipient empires lay West African territories whose future remained less clear. Here, not only the two main European rivals but also Germany, Portugal and Liberia had staked imperial claims by appropriating territorial footholds and claiming coastal protectorates. But the methods by which Europeans would penetrate the interior, and the lines along which they would divide it among themselves, still remained to be decided.

Next to the Oil Rivers, the most intensive development of an export economy had taken place in the area of the 'forest kingdoms' (not altogether accurately so called) formed by the Yoruba, Aja and Akan peoples. Here relatively large and complex African states with rich cultural traditions had, since the eighteenth century or earlier, been in quite close commercial and political contact – and in some cases in military conflict – with Europeans based among and sometimes closely identified with smaller states with a seaboard. These contacts had complicated the internal strains and problems of state-building, generally making them worse, particularly when an element of inter-European rivalry was added. During the later nineteenth century, as the Danes and the Dutch withdrew from political involvement on the Gold Coast, it had seemed that Britain might acquire a general paramountcy over the region without experiencing any urgent need to define it politically; between 1874 and 1886 Lagos was administered as part of the Gold Coast Colony and serious attempts were made to secure French and Portuguese approval for British fiscal control

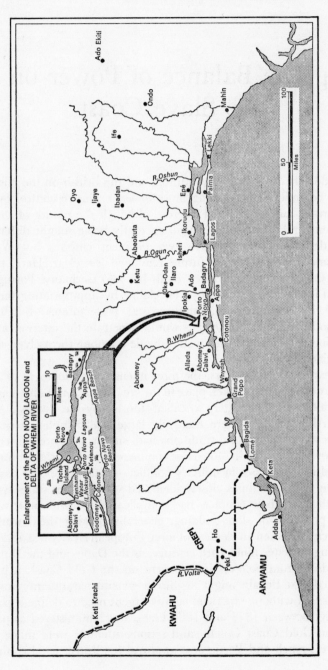

2 The Slave Coast

over the intervening coast. But the growing involvement of the French government in the politics of the area, encouraged by traders and missionaries, had prevented that solution; and in 1884 Germany had also staked political claims. The interior states were thus laid open to a scramble for political, fiscal and economic advantages by competing European imperialisms.

But the pause in governmental expansion after 1885 meant that the method, the timing, and to some extent the direction of foreign penetration still remained undecided. African states felt the pressure in different ways. Towards Asante and Dahomey, states which in the recent past had demonstrated a strong military capacity, the general tendency of Britain and France respectively was to work for their disintegration; but in neither case was this yet a very purposeful policy, and there were still those in London and Paris who believed that an adaptable 'strong native power' might offer the best channel for European penetration. Among the Yoruba states, where political disintegration was already far advanced through internally generated forces, the possible advantages of a restoration of old unities were gradually becoming more apparent to the British in Lagos.

BRITAIN AND THE YORUBA WARS

The Yoruba people possess one of the richest cultural traditions in Africa, and all sections of the nation take pride in this; even those expatriated to Sierra Leone by the hazards of the slave trade were noted for their solidarity in the new environment. But in their homeland this sense of unity has never in modern times found adequate political expression. After the disintegration of the old Oyo empire and the southern thrust of militant Islam in the early nineteenth century the area became torn by rivalries among sectional state-builders, and frequent wars.[1] It is difficult to measure the extent to which these sporadically protracted campaigns, waged by substantial forces of infantry armed with imported flintlocks, were destructive of life, or of trade. There was a loss of productive labour when soldiers were conscripted from the farms, but increasingly the fighting seems to have been done

[1] J. F. Ajayi and R. S. Smith, *Yoruba Warfare in the Nineteenth Century* (Cambridge, 1964) is the best discussion of these operations. See also the pioneer study by A. A. B. Aderibigbe, 'Expansion of the Lagos Protectorate, 1863–1900' (Ph.D. Thesis, University of London, 1959).

by professional warriors; and in some southerly states at least the effects on the production and transport of palm produce were more than offset by the employment of captive labour.[2] Moreover, war gave its own stimulus to trade by placing a premium on the import of firearms. Nevertheless, these conflicts often disrupted the normal activities of British traders and missionaries who hoped to use Lagos as a base for penetrating this attractive territory; and they also threatened to create openings for the infiltration of other European foreigners.

On the issues at stake in these conflicts, researches by Nigerian scholars are producing a rich literature, so rich that it is not yet easy to synthesise. Once the political authority of Oyo was eroded, the claims of potential successor-states became highly contentious; Yoruba approaches to government are legalistic, and presumptous or unconstitutional claims seem often to have caused as much resentment as actual oppression or exploitation. The state whose armies had done most to check the *jihad,* and which seemed most able to constitute a new centre of power was Ibadan, a cosmopolitan Yoruba city founded about 1829, which established a complex and flexible system of political supervision over a very extensive area in central and North-east Yorubaland. Since its rulers lacked the *charisma* of traditional authority their pretensions were resented by neighbours or subjects who felt they were being abused.[3]

The presence of the British colony of Lagos served to intensify rather than appease the conflicts. Christianity and commerce, which Victorians regarded as the foundation of peace and order, here had primarily divisive effects. The spread of Christian missions not only created new tensions within the various Yoruba states; in interstate conflicts individual missionaries tended to side with the rulers who patronised and protected their work, joining their African converts in claiming favours from the colonial

[2] A. G. Hopkins, 'Economic Imperialism in West Africa: Lagos, 1880–92', *Econ. H.R.*, 2nd series, xxi (1968) pp. 587–8. In ibid., xxv (1972) pp. 303–12; J. F. A. Ajayi and R. A. Austen make some rather peripheral criticisms of this article, and Hopkins usefully clarifies his argument in reply.

[3] B. Awe, 'The *Ajele* system: a Study of Ibadan Imperialism in the nineteenth century', *JHSN*, iii, i (1964). Also her thesis, 'The Rise of Ibadan as a Yoruba Power, 1851–93' (D.Phil., University of Oxford, 1964).

government. At the same time, the expanding trade in palm produce brought wealth, and so the capacity to buy arms, to certain
belligerents. Abeokuta and Ijebu in particular not only produced
much oil themselves but straddled the main trade routes to Ibadan
and beyond. Unlike the unfortunate Egbado, whose comparable
location merely made them a target for intervention by their
neighbours,[4] they possessed sufficient military power to regulate
the passage of supplies, and intervened against Ibadan in the Ijaye
war of 1860.

Yoruba belligerents looked for support among their kinsmen in
the cosmopolitan colonial port of Lagos – including not only those
who had migrated there directly to find trade of employment, but
also Christian repatriates from Sierra Leone and Brazil. Many who
had acquired status, wealth and influence within Lagosian society
remained ethnic patriots, and used these resources to further Ekiti,
Egba, or Ijebu interests. For others, ethnic loyalties competed with
wider visions of Yoruba or even African unity, and with genuine
Anglophilia. Men like James Johnson, a Sierra Leone-born
clergyman who in 1874 settled in Lagos as pastor of Breadfruit
Church, shared the faith of the missionary strategist Henry Venn
that Christian Britain would provide spiritual and technical resources from an emergent West Africa nation. Johnson was not
free from predetermined sympathies – with the Ijebus for his
mother's sake, the Ijeshas for his father's, the Egbas on account
of their initial response to Christianity – but he believed that all
might be reunited, under leadership from Lagos, in a future league
of independent Yoruba states.[5]

Not all Lagosians shared this confidence. Many Yorubas remembered the British annexation of Lagos in 1861 as an example
of arbitrary and perfidious tyranny, and many perceived similar
examples in subsequent British behaviour. To the colonial government, the Yoruba wars became a source of endless frustrations,
which not all bore patiently; officials longed for a decision, which
might permit Yorubaland to be opened to 'civilising' influences

---

[4] K. Folayan, 'Egbado and Yoruba-Aja Power Politics, 1832–94' (M.A.
thesis, University of Ibadan, 1967); see within, pp. 146–7.

[5] E. A. Ayandele, *Holy Johnson* (1970) pp. 203–8. Cf. J. F. Ajayi, '19th
century Origins of Nigerian Nationalism', *JHSN*, II (1961); H. S. Wilson,
Origins of West African Nationalism (1969).

under the patronage of some strong and benevolent 'native government'.[6] During the service at Lagos of John Glover (1863–72) the
conventional wisdom was to cast Ibadan in this role. Glover became prejudiced against the Egbas and Ijebus, accepting too
readily the charge that they were unproductive middlemen who
aimed to monopolise trade; his rejection had important reper-
cussions on the balance of forces within these states. At Abeokuta
the missionaries whose interests had been backed by returning
Sierra Leoneans were expelled in the *ifọle* of 1867; in Ijebu missionaries were excluded altogether.[7] Wiser British Governors
recognised the need for prudence; one rejected a proposal for the
payment of stipends to chiefs as 'opposed to the custom and public
opinion of the country known as Yoruba'. In view of past experience it 'would most probably be interpreted as a bid for jurisdiction . . . or as indirect acquisition of territory, or as the first
move towards actual possession'; and recipients of stipends 'viewed
in the light of traitors to the country, or as persons in whom no
confidence can be placed'.[8] Yet the very prudence and conciliatory restraint of such men helped to allay suspicion; and during
the 1880s many Lagosians believed, like James Johnson, that the
colonial government might safely be invoked as mediator or protector against external threats without jeopardising the essentials
of Yoruba independence.

Meanwhile, even restrained British policies affected the Yoruba
balance of power. Glover, forbidden to open the roads by force,
applied himself to developing a circuitous alternative route to
Ibadan, passing far to the east through Ondo.[9] Although this did
not supercede older and more direct routes it did have the effect
of stimulating trade, missionary activity, and political conscious-
ness among the Ekiti and Ijeshas of north-east Yorubaland, whose
territory could also be reached by this route. This group of small
coequal states began to combine to resist the often oppressive rule
which Ibadan had been extending in the area since about 1850
and to seek an opportunity to proclaim independence. In this they

[6] On the notion of 'strong native government', cf. *Prelude*, pp. 73–8.

[7] S. O. Biobaku, *The Egba and their Neighbours* (Oxford, 1957) Chap. 7;
E. A. Ayandele, *The Missionary Impact* . . . , pp. 54 ff.

[8] C.O. 147/60, Moloney to Holland, 334, 19 September 1887.

[9] S. A. Akintoye, 'The Ondo Road eastwards of Lagos, 1870–95',
JAH, x (1969) pp. 581–98.

were encouraged by their kinsmen among the Sierra Leonean Christians of Lagos, already linked in associations which, from the mid-1870s, addressed themselves more particularly to the problem of liberating their homeland.[10]

Their opportunity appeared when in 1877 Are Latosa, a high-handed and agressive Muslim who had become leader of the Ibadan military oligarchy, provoked a new war with the Egbas who were quickly joined by the Ijebus.[11] In May 1878 provocative behaviour by an Ibadan *ajele* set off risings in much of Ekiti and Ijesha country; an armed confederacy – the Ekitiparapo – was organised under a new generation of military leaders who had learned by observing the successes of Ibadan. With the intervention of Ilorin, and subsequent rebellions in subject areas (notably Ife in 1882) Ibadan had to face prolonged hostilities in many quarters. At the battlefield called Kiriji, on the borders of Ekiti, two entrenched camps which together may have contained as many as 100,000 men, women and children, fought one another from 1880 until 1886.[12] In Lagos the Ekitiparapo Society, besides supplying some skilled recruits to the embattled army, from 1881 organised supplies of modern breach-loading rifles; they were paid for partly by sales of palm products and cloth, partly by selling captured slaves for export through Dahomey, or for labour within Yorubaland.[13]

The economic effects of the war were severe, especially in the lands of Ibadan and of her reluctant ally the Alafin. Commercial connections with the coast were insecure (although that through Ijebu was reopened in 1883); returns from exports were diverted to purchasing arms, at inflated prices; food supplies were affected by the demands of the armies on the agricultural population for men and supplies and by the raids of their various enemies on the

[10] S. A. Akintoye, *Revolution and Power Politics in Yorubaland 1840–1893* (1971) Chaps. 2 and 3; also his article 'The Economic Background of the Ekitiparapo, 1878–93, *Odu*, IV (1968). J. A. Otonba Payne, *Table of Principal Events in Yoruba History* (Lagos, 1893) p. 37 shows the Ijesha, at 2095, as the third largest tribal group in the town of Lagos.

[11] B. Awe, 'The Rise of Ibadan . . .' Chap. 7 Also her article. 'The End of an Experiment; the Collapse of the Ibadan Empire 1877–1893', *JHSN*, III, 2 (1965) pp. 221–30.

[12] Akintoye, *Revolution* . . . , p. 116; Awe, 'The Rise of Ibadan . . . ,' pp. 277 ff.

[13] Akintoye, *Revolution* . . . , pp. 118–21, 149–51.

farms. Prices of consumer goods, especially imports like salt, rose sharply, and reports of general distress (possibly somewhat exaggerated) poured into Lagos.[14]

The effects on Lagos itself are hard to calculate; the quantity of oil exported never fell below the level of 1874, a peaceful year, and fluctuations were probably affected by world prices and by seasons of low rainfall at least as much as by war. There *was* a sharp drop in exports in 1878, but the previous year had been exceptionally good; the safest conclusion may be that the period of general hostilities up to 1886 saw a check in a rising trend of production, rather than any general and severe decline. Indeed Dr Hopkins suggests that declining world prices may have stimulated producers to try to recoup their losses by recruiting more slave labour, and that the needs of trade may thus actually have helped to prolong hostilities.[15] Nevertheless there were strong reasons why the Lagos Government should try to promote pacification; merchants, missionaries and leading Africans all wanted this (though not all on the same terms). And as early as 1882 it was clear that mediation by Lagos would have more prospect of success than any initiative from within Yorubaland.[16]

The official who understood this most clearly was Captain Cornelius Alfred Moloney (1848–1913), who administered the government of Lagos several times between 1879 and 1884 and returned as substantive Governor in 1886–90. Although a Sandhurst-trained soldier who had fought in Asante, Moloney was a man of peace, a Catholic who on his eventual transfer to the Caribbean was congratulated by the Secretary of the Aborigines Protection Society that 'all through the long term of your administration not a single shot was discharged with hostile intent, not a single native hut burnt down.' At the same gathering a young Lagosian called Herbert Macaulay, whose engineering studies Moloney had sponsored, declared that 'Sir Alfred was the best Governor Lagos had ever had, and his influence over the natives

[14] Hopkins, 'Economic Imperialism . . .' p. 590; E. A. Ayandele, *Holy Johnson* (London 1970) p. 208; Awe, 'The Rise of Ibadan . . .', pp.291-2.

[15] Hopkins, 'Economic Imperialism . . .', pp. 591-2. See also Appendix, Table 2.

[16] Cf. Akintoye, *Revolution* . . . , pp. 154 ff.

had been great, because they knew that his policy was inspired by justice, and a constant desire to aid them in every way.'[17] Similar admiration seems reflected in the name by which Moloney was known to Lagos Yoruba – Oba Abgǫrunsoke (or 'the king who holds his head up and aims high').[18]

Moloney's outstanding qualities – which included respect for the personality and opinions of Africans, appreciation of the autonomy of African cultures,[19] scientific interest in economic development – are better appreciated today than they were by the contemporary Colonial Office.[20] Believing that 'it is the bounden duty of every one to promote, as far as his lights may admit, the condition of the people among whom his lot may be cast,'[21] he devoted hard work and study to economic problems. Anxious to save the Yoruba economy from excessive dependence on palm oil, he looked to 'native agency' as the only means of developing a wider range of agricultural and mineral resources; he believed that a key role in this could be played by repatriates from the Americas, and did much to encourage and accelerate repatriation of Yorubas from Brazil.[22] It is true that he expected that the principle of international division of labour would leave West Africa as a primary producing economy, and was prepared to see Lancashire cotton goods, if improved in quality, drive out local cloth producers in order 'to let loose the native energy confined thereto

[17] *A West African Governor*. Report of the Proceedings at the Westminster Palace Hotel on Thursday 25 June 1891 on the occasion of a Breakfast given by the Committee of the Aborigines Protection Society to Sir Alfred Moloney K.C.M.G. (London 1891) pp. 7, 13.

[18] J. A. Otonba Payne, *Table of Principal Events* . . . , p. 7. I am grateful to Professor E. A. Ayandele for this translation.

[19] On 15 November 1889 he addressed the Manchester Geographical Society 'On the Melodies of the Volof, Mandingo, Ewe, Yoruba and Houssa People of West Africa.'

[20] 'He is a hard-working, conscientious and well-meaning man; but he writes grotesque despatches and has an exalted idea of himself. He is fond of running up the expenditure.' C.O. 147/62, Minute by Fairfield on Moloney, Pte, 24 March 1887.

[21] C. A. Moloney, *West African Fisheries. With Particular Reference to the Gold Coast Colony* (1883). There is an admirable account of Moloney's economic policies in Aderbigbe, 'Expansion of the Lagos Protectorate . . .', pp. 165–87.

[22] 'Cotton Interests, foreign and native, in Yoruba, and generally in West Africa', *Journal of the Manchester Geographical Society*, v (1889) (reprint) pp. 10–18.

for more extended agricultural pursuits';[23] these sentiments, which would today invite denunciation as crude neo-colonialism, were then widely acceptable as a progressive expression of contemporary economic liberalism.

Moloney encouraged Africans to develop their resources by various methods. While administering Lagos in 1882–3 he wrote to the press to emphasise the economic possibilities of wild rubber, giving detailed advice on methods of production; and again to warn that reckless depletion of forest resources by indiscriminate felling and burning was liable to affect the climate and water resources of Yorubaland.[24] He read an informative and well-documented paper to the International Fisheries Exhibition in London in 1883, arguing that the development of marine and freshwater fisheries would not only improve African diets, but could promote local industries producing fish oil and guano.[25] In 1887 Moloney published a substantial volume on the economic prospects of West African forestry, expressing the hope that it would contribute to the 'enlightenment and progress' of the people.[26] But his main emphasis was on agricultural development. He arranged for two young Africans, T. B. Dawodu and G. B. Leigh, to receive agricultural training in Jamaica and at Kew, later returning to work at the Botanical Station which was opened at Ebute Metta in 1887. Moloney (who himself carried out experiments in growing eucalyptus trees) attached great importance to this 'as a teaching centre and depot whence may be spread information on the utility, value and mode of culture of trees and plants, and eventually a distribution of seeds and plants for cultivation among the natives effected', and the Lagos station became the pattern for the earliest experiments in agricultural extension work in West Africa.[27]

[23] Ibid., p. 3.

[24] Letters to *Lagos Times*, 25 October 1882, 14 February 1883, reprinted in a pamphlet in Ibadan University Library; *The Eagle and Lagos Critic*, 31 March, 28 April 1883. For his influence on the development of rubber production, see R. Dumett, 'The Rubber Trade . . . .,' *JAH*, xii (1971).

[25] Moloney, *West African Fisheries* . . . , pp. 64–5.

[26] Moloney, Preface to *Sketch of the Forestry*.

[27] C.O. 147/63. Moloney to Knutsford, 91, 19 March 1888; C. A. Moloney, 'Notes on Yoruba and the Colony and Protectorate of Lagos', *J.R.G.S.*, XII (1890) p. 600; *A West African Governor* . . . , p. 11; Alfred Moloney, *Sketch of the Forestry of West Africa. With particular reference to its Present Principal Commercial Products* (1887 pp. 249 ff., 226 ff.

Clearly, all such projects for development were jeopardised by the Yoruba wars. In a long (and somewhat rambling) despatch of 12 May 1881 Moloney had attempted to modify the simplified 'middleman thesis' of his predecessors by expounding a view of Yoruba history which he had learned from 'local gentlemen of considerable experience', like James Johnson and Otouba Payne The balance of power between the constituent members of 'the Yoruba kingdom of old' (Oyo, Abeokuta, Ketu and Ijebu Ode) had been upset when Ibadan was able to use imported firearms to support a policy of military aggression and slave-trading; the hostility of Egbas and Ijebus was motivated by their aim of controlling imports of arms, not of monopolising trade. Moloney therefore proposed a British blockade of all imports of arms into Yoruba country, through Porto Novo, Benin and Nupe as well as through Lagos. This he hoped would induce the Yoruba states to put their 'national interest' before their sectional jealousies, and to send representatives to Lagos to negotiate, under British auspices, a peace settlement which would permit the development of their country under a more unified political system.[28]

Moloney's superior as Governor-in-Chief of the Gold Coast Settlements, Sir Samuel Rowe, was another old coaster and veteran of the Asante war. In Sierra Leone during the later 1870s Rowe had attempted to extend British influence and fiscal control by diplomatic intervention in the Northern Rivers; the consequent complications, with Africans and with the French, had brought him under official censure.[29] Rowe was determined not to get into similar trouble again, nor to allow Moloney precedence as a guide to African politics. Rowe not only doubted whether an arms blockade could be made effective, and whether it would deter the Yorubas from continuing their wars with bows and arrows, but developed moral scruples about 'the right of the Lagos Government to act in the way proposed so long as their own borders are not invaded or menaced'. Rowe saw no substitute for 'time and perseverance and an improved staff', and the Colonial Office could only welcome this recipe (or at least the first two ingredients). Kimberley, the Secretary of State, drew on his past experience

[28] P.P. 1887, LX, C.4957, Encl. 2 in No. 1, Moloney to Rowe, 12 May 1881.
[29] Cf. *Prelude*, pp. 216–23, 230–2, 247–9.

to veto any idea of again pursuing 'the will o' the wisp of preventing the importation of arms into West Africa'.[30]

Rowe's restraint did not apply only to the arms blockade. When in December 1882 James Johnson used his family connections in Ijebu to promote a diplomatic initiative through the party of influential Lagosians connected with ex-king Docemo, he refused Moloney's request for authority to support it by additional exppenditure on presents for chiefs, and warned him not to allow African officials like Payne to become involved 'in the political affairs of States beyond our borders'.[31] The new image which Rowe thus acquired in Lagos as 'the do-nothing Governor' was most welcome to the Colonial Office. Kimberley endorsed his refusal to 'approve any measures involving direct interference with the inland tribes', which were liable to involve 'dangerous complications' and unacceptably extended responsibilities; his successor Derby agreed 'that no encouragement should be given to any interference on the part of the native residents of Lagos with the affairs of the Chiefs in the interior'.[32]

When Rowe went into residence at Lagos in mid-1883, he did make some attempt to work with leading Lagosians like James Johnson, Robbin and the Willoughbys; he went so far as to suggest sending a British officer 'to visit among the tribes'. He wrote lengthy and opinionated appreciations of the Yoruba situation, which he interpreted by analogies with Sierra Leone; if Ibadan traders came more regularly to Lagos Rowe hoped that they (like the caravan traders he had known at Freetown) would be so tempted by the goods in the shops as to become converted to a policy of peaceful production for export.[33] But no very clear policy emerged from his wordy despatches; and without some indication that the Colonial Government might use its power to

[30] C.O. 147/44 and C.4957, Rowe to Kimberley, 79, 2 July 1881; Conf., 3 July 1881, with minutes by Kimberley, 30 August.

[31] C.4957, No. 3, Rowe to Derby, 7 February 1883, encl. Moloney, 26 December; No. 4, Rowe to Derby, 15 February 1883, encl. Moloney, 31 January. On the 'traditional' leaders of Lagos and their relations with the interior, see Patrick Cole, 'Modern and Traditional Elites in the Politics of Lagos' (Ph.D. thesis, Cambridge, 1970).

[32] Ibid., No. 2, Kimberley to Rowe, 26 August 1881; No. 5, Derby to Rowe, 28 March 1883.

[33] Ibid., No. 6, Rowe to Derby, 11 May 1883; No. 8, Rowe to Derby, 18 May 1883.

enforce a settlement, such peace missions as those which the Rev. J. B. Wood, a respected Anglican missionary, paid to the Kiriji battlefield in September 1884 and March 1885 had no success.[34]

By January 1886, when Moloney returned to Lagos as first Governor of the new separate Colony, there was a clear need for some more active policy. The trade depression, its effects added to those of continued hostilities, was producing a desire for peace among Lagosians which began to transcend sectional loyalties; already nearly two hundred leading Africans and Europeans had declared in a Memorial 'it is now time that the English Government should appoint an Ambassador and Plenipotentiary to settle the interior feuds.'[35] There was now also the danger of international rivalry to be reckoned with; German claims to Mahin beach in January 1885 had come as a nasty shock, and the French at Porto Novo were being drawn into supporting its ruler's dynastic claims in southern Egbado. Although Britain had averted the former danger by her boundary arrangement with Germany of June 1885, prolonged war in the interior might still offer temptations to foreign intruders. Moloney therefore began sending letters to the principal combatants urging an end to the war and hinting (to the Ekitiparapo) at the possibility of enforcing such an arms blockade as Rowe had refused to sanction in 1881.[36] In March, Moloney despatched two respected and able African clergymen, Samuel Johnson and Charles Phillips, with messages to, respectively, Ibadan and the Ekitiparapo, inviting them to state their peace terms and to offer such guarantees of good intention as might justify the Colonial Government in acting as mediator. Many belligerents were indeed ready to respond to this suggestion, when backed by such a respected figure as Moloney; active diplomacy by the two clergymen brought to Lagos messengers from Oyo, Ibadan, Ijebu, the Ekitiparapo and Ondo. By 4 June 1886 they had worked out, under Moloney's presidency, the terms of a peace settlement which recognised Ekiti's independence from Ibadan. In September two British Commissioners, escorted by an armed

[34] For attempted peace negotiations, see Akintoye, *Revolution* . . . , pp. 171–6.

[35] *The Eagle and Lagos Critic*, 11 April 1885.

[36] C.4957, pp. 51–2. Moloney to Kings of Ijesha and Ekitiparapo, 52 January 1886.

force of fifty Hausas with a seven-pounder gun, supervised the dispersal of the camps on the Kiriji battlefield – a critical point for the Ekiti, who claimed that only fear of Ibadan treachery if they broke camp first had prevented them from accepting Wood's peace proposals in 1884.[37]

This diplomatic success was only partial. It was not possible to implement the terms agreed between Ife and Modakeke, the local ally of Ibadan; not all Ijebu accepted the peace terms; no armistice was made on the Ilorin front; and the Egbas (who had recently not been very actively involved) were not included in the negotiation. On all these fronts hostilities continued, more or less half-heartedly, for the next seven years. But in Yorubaland as a whole there was a great reduction of fighting, and an immediate revival of trade. Most significantly the Lagos government had committed itself to a more active policy, directed to promoting unity in independence among the Yoruba states. 'A bundle of sticks tied together is stronger than such sticks scattered,' Moloney had exhorted the delegates – adding his sincere assurances that their independence and lands would be respected by the British.[38] As long as he remained at Lagos, Moloney became increasingly anxious to 'promote Yoruba unity' under British auspices.

> Yoruba represents racial and linguistic unity; [he wrote in 1887] the bulwark against the barbarous and devastating Dahomey on the west, and Mohammedan aggression from the north; its confederation . . . under the enlightenment of the Government, should prove of future benefit to the country and to this Colony.[39]

But the rope to bind the sticks together would have to be supplied by the British government; and with the development of rival French activity on the western frontiers of Yorubaland that rope began to be drawn more tightly than any of the participants in the 1886 peace conference could have foreseen.

[37] Ibid., pp. 69–70, Ekitiparapo to Moloney, 20 April 1886 and cf. p. 96. The peace negotiations, which may be followed in this Parliamentary Paper, are summarised in Akintoye, *Revolution* . . ., Chap. 6. The text of the Treaty is at C.4957, pp. 116–18.

[38] C.4957, pp. 95, 99; minutes of meetings of 21, 31 May.

[39] C.O. 879/26, C.P. African 334, No. 165, Moloney to Meade, Pte, 15 July 1887; cf. C.P. 879/27, C.P. African 345, No. 16 encl. Moloney to Onilado, 24 September 1887.

THE AJA UNDER PRESSURE

For much of the nineteenth century Europeans, worried perhaps by the example of Asante, tended to exaggerate the military strength of the Fon Kingdom of Abomey, and to underestimate its receptiveness to Westernising influences. During the reign of Gezo in particular, many British observers, misled by their own stereotype of 'African despotism', failed to realise that the power of the King, formidable though it was, was limited by an over-riding obligation to conform to the will of the ancestors. This obligation clearly gave real political power to priests and ministers authorised to interpret the ancestors' will;[40] a strong traditionalist party limited Gezo's capacity to act instantly upon his professed desire to reduce human sacrifice and to move from a slaving towards an agricultural economy, and may have caused his death in 1858. His successor Gelele was thus obliged to give absolute priority to the preservation of traditional values, of Dahomean independence, and of her territorial claims.[41] Thus, although he admitted missionaries to operate in Dahomey, it remained impossible for a true Fon to become a Christian; as the missionaries noted:

> from the moment when, in one way or another, an individual is regarded as being attached to a creole, a mulatto, or to one of these blacks who call themselves white because they live in the manner of the whites, there is no more opposition . . . Christians are considered as foreigners living among the blacks.[42]

Behind the front of monolithic unity, however, important Dahomean nobles who were themselves actively engaged in the production and sale of palm produce still favoured cautious attempts to co-operate with Europeans. But the movement of the terms of trade did not favour any rapid growth in their in-

[40] The latest contribution to the rich anthropological literature are W. J. Argyle, *The Fon of Dahomey* (Oxford, 1966) – esp. chap. 4; J. Lombard, 'The Kingdom of Dahomey' in C. D. Forde and P. M. Kaberry (ed.) *West African Kingdoms in the Nineteenth Century* (1967).

[41] David Ross, 'The Autonomous Kingdom of Dahomey, 1818–94' (Ph.D. Thesis, University of London, 1967) chaps. 2 and 3.

[42] Diary of Fr. Borghero, April 1864, quoted J. M. Todd, *African Mission* (1962), pp. 82–3.

fluence,[43] and they never secured the upper hand over the intransigent traditionalists, one of whose leaders was a certain Noughododhue of Whydah. Gelele himself, though Skertchly found him alert and vigorous in 1871, soon afterwards began to go blind, and the struggle for power became more intense. In 1870 during a blockade imposed by aggressive British naval officers, a Vi-Dahou or Crown Prince who favoured conciliation was overthrown by some sort of palace revolution and replaced by Gelele's son Kondo; the policy he adopted during the blockade and afterwards was that Dahomey should forego her commerce rather than allow European interference in mercantile litigation which lay within her own jurisdiction.[44] Under Kondo's direction, the military organisation of the Fon state was overhauled, so as to increase the strength of the standing forces and their capacity to control the palm-producing areas in which Europeans were chiefly interested.[45]

About the same time there was some revival of the older Dahomean policy of capturing slaves for export. New overseas demands developed from two main sources: first the Portuguese needed labour to work their new cocoa plantations of Sao Thome and Principe; then, from about 1889 Belgians began to recruit workers for the Matadi–Leopoldville railway on which the development of the Congo Free State was to depend.[46] Although

[43] On the role of Dahomean nobles in commerce, C. Coquery-Vidrovitch, 'De la traite des Esclaves à l'exportation de l'huile de palme et des palmistes au Dahomey' in Meillassoux, *Development of Indigenous Trade* . . . Madame Coquery estimates the total oil exports of all Dahomean ports at about 4000 tons in 1876, rising to 6616 tons in 1891; (this suggests that figures provided by French merchants in 1878 – *Prelude* p. 208 – were probably a little high). At European prices 4,000 tons of palm-oil in 1876 would be worth roughly the same as 6,616 tons in 1891 – about £140,000.

[44] Ross, 'Autonomous Kingdom . . .', pp. 204–6, 213–23; J. A. Skertchly, *Dahomey As It Is* (1874) pp. 122, 141f., 219. Catherine Coquery, 'Le Blocus de Whydah . . .', *CEA*, II, 7 (1962); cf. *Prelude*, pp. 201–7.

[45] On Fon military forces, see David Ross, 'Dahomey', in M. Crowder (ed.) *West African Resistance* (1971) pp. 146–56. For traditions of Kondo's association with the war party, M. J. and F. S. Herskovits, *Dahomean Narrative* (Evanston, 1958) pp. 375–6.

[46] In 1889 Captain Braconnier, a Belgian officer, paid approximately £16 each for about one hundred men whom he shipped as indentured labourers to the Congo. He would have bought more had not his money been stolen, apparently by Lagosian abolitionists. There is much correspondence about this episode in C.O. 147/71 and C. O. 147/73.

Europeans described these schemes as involving indentured labour, not slaves, this distinction was not appreciated in Dahomey, nor did it affect traditional methods of recruitment. From the early 1880s there were reports of Dahomean involvement in the Kiriji war in search of Yoruba captives, and there were major Dahomean invasions of Ketu in 1883 and 1885. This renewal of traditional military policies tended to strengthen Kondo's position against those chiefs (now led by his younger brother Topa or Dapeh) who were prepared to co-operate more closely with French merchants to develop the produce trade. According to some reports Gelele died about 1884; if so, Kondo lacked sufficient support in Abomey to reveal the fact and claim the succession, but he still exercised the dominant voice in Dahomean affairs.[47]

Until about 1887 the new Fon policies were pursued with the co-operation of Tofa, the French-protected ruler of Porto Novo. This state had been established during the eighteenth-century upheavals in what Professor Akinjogbin has – somewhat controversially – called the '*ebi* commonwealth' of the Aja people.[48] Though its Gun settlers had become ethnically distinct from the Fon its independence of Abomey had never been clearly established; according to some French sources Tofa included among his titles 'royal prince of Dahomey'.[49] Although in many matters Porto Novo operated as an independent polity, when the Fon needed to use its territories – during their campaigns against the Yoruba in the 1840s, for example – they treated it as a vassal state.[50]

By accepting the protectorate which the French finally proclaimed in April 1883 Tofa had played a large part in precipitating the European scramble for West Africa;[51] but his own purposes had always been clearly defined within the local African context. The first of these was undoubtedly, in the words of Tofa's

---

[47] See Ross, 'Autonomous Kingdom . . .', esp. pp. 229–45, 251–9; cf. C.O. 879/29, C.P. African 365, No. 10, Moloney to Knutsford, Conf., 14 December, 1888, and interview with Gbenbosi Honi, 10, 12 December.

[48] I. A. Akinjogbin, *Dahomey and its Neighbours, 1708–1818* (Cambridge 1967) Chap. 1.

[49] E.g. P. A. de Salinis, *Le protectorat français sur la Côte des Esclaves* (1908) p. 10.

[50] Ross, 'Autonomous Kingdom . . .', p. 44.

[51] *Prelude*, pp. 207–13, 294–301.

missionary friends, 'to have the backing of force that he needs in order to override the custom which would prevent his son from reigning after him'.[52] Tofa, whom local traditions recall as 'rancorous and vindictive, like all his ancestors [but] firm and tenacious, and endowed with remarkable gifts for organisation and adaptation',[53] had in 1864 been equally prepared to seek French or British support in order to contravene custom and succeed his father Soji. Having finally secured election in 1874 Tofa relentlessly opposed any challenges from the sons of Mepon (King 1864–72) – Mewounou (who was assassinated early in the reign) and Soigbe.[54] This dynastic opposition retained considerable strength in outlying districts of the kingdom; during his early years Tofa had to wage military campaigns against Soigbe's supporters, both in the rich palm lands of the Wheme valley, and in the marches of Yoruba country.[55]

Internally therefore Tofa relied heavily on the support of members of the trading communities, including representatives of French interests like the Corsican J. A. Colonna di Lecca, as well as those Brazilian repatriates who had been largely responsible for the commercial development of his father's time.[56] While most Brazilians were Catholics, some had taken the lead in establishing a Muslim community, and Tofa was careful to maintain close relations with both immigrant religions, besides observing the traditional rites of his state. He was as ready to invite the Tijani mosque to pray for the health of co-operative French officials as to request the presence of a French military detachment at a solemn Mass offered for the well-being of his state.[57] Since 1868 the Lyon-based *Société des Missions Africaines* had regarded Porto Novo rather than Whydah as its main base in the region; its

[52] 'Note sur Porto-Novo, émanant de la mission catholique', n.d., *Etudes Dahoméennes*, IX (1963) p. 21.

[53] A. Akindélé and C. Aguessy, *Contribution à l'etude de l'ancien royaume de Porto Novo* (Dakar, 1953) p. 81.

[54] *Prelude*, pp. 118–19; Akindélé and Aguessy, pp. 75–7, 81–5.

[55] According to Moloney the people of the Wheme valley considered themselves one with those of Ketenou; they had sought British protection in 1878 and 1884. C.O. 879/29, C.P. African 365, p. 5, Moloney to Knutsford, Conf., 14 December 1888.

[56] Akindélé and Aguessy, pp. 84, 90.

[57] ANSOM, Senegal IV/124/b, Beeckman to Thomas, 177, 6 May 1889; Dahomey I/1/b, Bayol to Etienne, 12 October 1889.

educated converts were among Tofa's warmest supporters, and its priests tended to regard co-operation with Tofa as the surest means of promoting the Gospel.[58] Their support reinforced the political alliance with France to which Tofa had been committed since 1883; for he undoubtedly regarded the French as allies rather than masters. Christian supporters encouraged Tofa to maintain the forms of sovereignty, sending letters (in Portuguese) to the French President on his own regally-headed pink writing paper. Although his attitudes struck some French officials as presumptuous, the first full-time French Resident, Colonel Dorat, knew that France could achieve little by relying solely on her garrison of twenty or so African troops and that it was necessary to treat relations with the 'least barbarous and best-organised' state of the region very seriously.[59]

But the relationship also imposed external obligations; Tofa expected French support in consolidating and extending his territorial control, especially on his eastern frontiers. In the first place this involved resistance to the British of Lagos, who since 1879 had occupied allegedly Porto Novo territories at Ketenou and Appa, which obstructed Tofa's access to the ocean and provided refuge for his dynastic opponents.[60] Such support was essentially diplomatic, though backed by new hoistings of the French flag when these could be safely undertaken by the tiny French garrison. From the proclamation of the French protectorate, relations with Lagos were acrimonious; voluminous complaints concerning petty but often gruesome disputes passed between the colonial authorities. Tofa threw a British 'protected subject', Jidonu, into a noisome gaol, where despite British representations he later died; Tofa's agents were accused of desecrating the grave of Thomas Tickel (who as representative at Badagry had vigorously promoted British interests) and of removing his head.[61] But the principal grievance remained British control over channels of navigation in the lagoon. Early in 1887 Lieutenant-Governor Bayol visited Porto Novo; he

[58] Ross, 'Autonomous Kingdom . . .', pp. 193–200; cf. J. M. Todd, *African Mission, passim.*

[59] AE, Afrique 83, Note by Dorat, 26 October 1886; Tofa to Grevy, 13 May 1886. See also Dorat's reports of 26 July and 23 August 1884, ix, pp. 36–45.

[60] Cf. *Prelude,* pp. 210–14, 293–302.

[61] C.O. 879/26, C.P. African 334, Nos. 36, 41; Evans to Stanhope, 38, 21 January; Conf. 6, 4 February 1887.

installed a new *Commandant particulier*, Dr Pereton, who, in order to prevent Tofa's claims from lapsing through default, challenged the right of the British representative at Ketenou, the Lagosian F. C. Green, to supervise canoe traffic in the lagoon.[62] On 26 March Pereton hoisted the French flag opposite Green's post in the Agege channel and installed a military guard which itself began to inspect passing canoes; this created alarm and uncertainty among the local people and heightened tension between the colonial authorities.[63] On 29 April, while Bayol was in Lagos, negotiating somewhat stiffly for a mutual withdrawal of flags and troops, a British Hausa was killed in an exchange of shots between colonial troops.[64]

It was not only against British control of the lagoon that Tofa sought French asistance. His anxiety to eliminate the dynastic threat from Soigbe involved action on his eastern frontier, which could easily be extended to support Tofa's expansionist ambitions in the Egbado districts of south-western Yorubaland, This area, which originally owed its importance to its command of the route from Old Oyo to Badagry, remained in contention between Egba and Aja throughout the nineteenth century. Although the Gun of Porto Novo never enjoyed a high military reputation, during campaigns against Abeokuta the Fon had supplied them with troops with which to raid southern Egbado, and allowed them to dispose of prisoners taken.[65] The development of palm oil trade brought the Porto Novans new incentives to contest Egba influence in Egbado market centres; and the sufferers from this rivalry began to seek support from the British at Lagos. After the first French appearance at Porto Novo in 1863 Glover had accepted the cession of the three Egbado markets of Badagry, Ado and Okeodan, although the home government authorised the retention only of Badagry. So when after 1874, Tofa used the Dahomean alliance to attack his enemies in the area, the Egbado responded firstly by supporting the claims of Soigbe to Tofa's throne, then

[62] Ibid., No. 58, Evans to Holland, 79, 24 March 1887; Bayol to Governor, 21 March 1887, *E.D.*, IX, pp. 79–83.

[63] African 334, No. 61, Evans to Holland, 82, 30 March 1887.

[64] Ibid., No. 83, Evans to Holland, 110, 1 May 1887. The French version of these events may be studied in AE Afrique 83, especially Bayol's report enclosed in Etienne to Flourens, 21 October 1887.

[65] Akindélé and Aguessy, *Contribution . . .*, p. 86.

after 1881 by urging their friends among the Lagos traders to obtain renewed British support.[66]

Tofa, and the merchants who had invested so heavily in his dynastic claims, replied by trying to involve his French protectors more deeply in Egbado affairs. In August 1883 Tofa tried to force a French flag on Ado; in February 1884 he used Dahomean troops to attack Soigbe's supporters in Okeodan;[67] in January 1885 the French Resident Dorat (who, Tofa claimed, had promised to restore the territorial integrity of his kingdom) appeared in person at Ado and Ipokia.[68] To the Egbado, this meant a renewed threat of domination by old enemies; to the merchants and government of Lagos, a danger that untaxed French spirits would invade their markets in Yorubaland. Lagos traders like Taiwo and officials like Tickel therefore encouraged the Egbado hopes of British support; Tofa's ambitions threatened to bring France into conflict with British interests over a still wider area.

From 1887, France ran growing risks of conflict with Dahomey also. Towards the end of the dry season Tofa invited Fon assistance in an attack on Jofin (or Wefin), an Egbado frontier town where one of his dynastic rivals (presumably Soigbe) was organising Yoruba support. After the campaign, Fon and Gun traditions agree that a bitter dispute developed over the disposal of prisoners; Porto Novo sources also complain that Dahomean troops violated lands of a leading Gun warrior called Gbenou.[69] It is significant that this quarrel closely followed Bayol's visit of March 1887, when he renewed and extended Dorat's promise to support Tofa's dynastic and territorial claims, both in Egbado and in the Wheme valley.[70] These assurances (and from November 1887 the presence in the lagoon of a small French pinnace, the *Eméraude*) evidently

[66] This and the following paragraph are based chiefly on K. Folayan 'Egbado and Yoruba-Aja power politics, 1832–94' (M.A. thesis, University of Ibadan, 1967).

[67] C.O. 879/29, C.P. African 365, p. 105, Gelele to Denton, 26 January 1889.

[68] Bayol to Thomas, 21 March 1887, *E.D.*, ix, pp. 79, 81; cf. C. W. Newbury, *The Western Slave Coast . . .*, pp. 109–10.

[69] Akindélé and Aguessy, *Contribution . . .*, pp. 85–8; cf. the versions in Gelele to H.M.G., 12 May (C.O. 147/71), Gelele to Carnot, 12 May 1889, and in Herskovits, *Dahomean Narrative*, pp. 381–4. This last Abomey tradition ruefully concludes 'the whites came here because Glele broke Wefi.'

[70] Bayol to Thomas, 21 March 1887, *E.D.*, ix, pp. 79–81.

emboldened Tofa to take a truculent line towards the Fon, which increasingly infuriated Kondo; apparently without the French realising it, their ally's relations with Dahomey steadily deteriorated until they exploded in conflict in March 1889.

But although it was largely Tofa's truculence which would lead the French into conflict with Dahomey, there already existed a serious latent dispute over the town of Cotonou, increasingly the principal port for the palm exports of the Aja country. If the French trade at Porto Novo was not to be left at the mercy of the British at the mouth of the Lagos lagoon, Cotonou represented the only really satisfactory alternative port of shipment. In 1868 and 1878 French traders had secured from the Fon authorities of the town treaties purporting to cede a tract of thirty-six square kilometres to the French state. These were accepted as valid in Paris, but never in Abomey; it seems clear that no responsible Fon official could have authorised such a cession of territory. Only after 1883, when armed parties of Frenchmen began to land at Cotonou on their way to Porto Novo, had the nature of this conflict become apparent;[71] and even then both sides still found it prudent to avoid forcing this issue. The French government understood the local situation well enough to appreciate that an attempt to exercise sovereignty at Cotonou would lead to reprisals by the Fon against French traders and missionaries at Whydah and other Dahomean ports (Godomey and Abomey Calavi). This could lead to a full-scale war with Dahomey; and although a few interested parties favoured this,[72] the political climate in Paris made it unthinkable. So the French continued to tolerate Fon control of Cotonou, and to pay them duties on the goods they landed there; some patriots found this humiliating, but it was better business than importing tobacco and liquor through Lagos.

On the Fon side, there was little eagerness to face the issue. Some notables profited from the increase in trading opportunities, and the customs duties made a useful contribution to the Fon treasury. But there must also have been some perception of the danger of French aggression; and it may have been in hope of providing a counterweight that the Whydah Brazilian Julio da

[71] Texts of both treaties in *E.D.*, IX, pp. 27–9; cf. *Prelude*, pp. 117–20, 208–10.

[72] E.g. AE Afrique 81, J. A. Colonna di Lecca to Portier, June 1885.

Souza (grandson of Gezo's confidant) attempted to involve the less formidable Portuguese. The government of King Luis I was using da Souza to recruit slaves in Dahomey for the plantations of Sao Thome; they were also desperately anxious to protect old political pretensions suddenly threatened by the new interest in Africa shown by other European powers. By the Constitutional Charter of 1826 the miserable little slaving fort at Whydah had been declared part of the kingdom of Portugal; the government placed a small military guard there in 1865, and refused to abandon their title during their negotiations with Britain in 1882–3.[73] Early in 1884 there had been signs of increasing interest in Dahomey by Portuguese sailors and Portuguese priests;[74] on 5 August 1885 a small Portuguese delegation signed what they declared to be a treaty of protection with Kondo in Abomey. 'The Portuguese protectorate of Dahomey', the Royal government now proudly proclaimed, 'is the lighted pathway that links the kingdom of darkness with Europe.'[75]

This was of course a grandiose illusion. The Portuguese lacked the strength either to contest the claims of France (from whom they were at this time having to accept an unfavourable frontier settlement in Guinea, in return for a worthless statement of vague support for Portuguese pretensions in southern Africa)[76] or to make good any real protectorate over the Fon. The Portuguese version of the treaty appeared to place the whole Dahomean coastline under Portuguese protection, and to provide for the abolition of human sacrifice; but apparently the Dahomeans understood only that Portugal would offer physical protection if other Europeans objected to an agreement which they simultaneously made to supply one hundred slaves a year as indentured labour for Sao Thome. Portugal's impotence was quickly revealed. On 21 August 1885 French agents at Cotonou carried out a long-cherished plan by blasting a channel through the coastal sandbar so that small boats could enter the lagoon from the ocean and sail directly up to Porto Novo. The Portuguese responded to this molestation

[73] R. J. Hammond, *Portugal and Africa* (1966) pp. 68–71; *Prelude*, p. 302.
[74] AE, Correspondence Politique Angleterre (Freetown) 71, Bareste to Ferry, 27 February 1884; Afrique 79, Planque to Ferry, 10 April 1884; O'Neill to Peyron, 10 April 1884.
[75] Decree of 1885, quoted by Hammond, *Portugal in Africa*, p. 102.
[76] Cf. above p. 81; Hammond, *Portugal and Africa*, pp. 103–4.

of Dahomean rights by sending a small party of troops under Julio de Souza (now appointed a Portuguese Lieutenant-Colonel) and hoisting their flag at Cotonou; the only result was that French troops landed nearby and encamped against them. Neither force exercised any control over the people of the town. In December the Portuguese government prudently ordered withdrawal of their garrison; the French troops remained.[77]

Auguste Cesar Rodriguez Sacramento, Governor of Sao Thome and probable sponsor of the whole crazy enterprise, visited Whydah in February 1886 in hope of persuading Glele to regularise Portugal's claims; but the King refused to invite him to Abomey and the Governor, as he stewed away in da Souza's house at Whydah, realised the fragility of the whole enterprise.[78] Meanwhile it became clear that Portugal's 'friend at court' had lost all credibility there; da Souza had already been summoned to Abomey and thrown into prison, from which he does not seem ever to have re-emerged. On 26 December 1887 the Lisbon government, having failed to obtain any confirmation in Abomey for their interpretation of the treaty, prudently issued a formal renunciation of this abortive protectorate and of the responsibilities it might be held to have implied.[79]

So the French, with their turbulent *protégé* at Porto Novo and their dubious claims at Cotonou, were left uneasily facing Dahomey. Despite the hawkish attitudes of some merchants and missionaries the government intended only to defend the interests of their citizens, and what they believed to be the proper treaty rights and prestige of the Republic. Even without those temporary constraints which precluded a forward African policy, they would have hesitated to become needlessly embroiled with a Dahomean state whose military power was still commonly exaggerated by Europeans. Yet it was not easy to protect French interests while remaining disengaged from Aja politics. Quite

[77] Ross, 'Autonomous Kingdom . . .', pp. 263–75.

[78] AE Afrique 83, M.M.C. to M.A.E., 23 March 1886, encl. Bayol, 20 March.

[79] C.O. 147/62, F.O. to C.O., 30 December 1887; P. Verger, *Les Afro-Americains* (Dakar, 1952) pp. 50–2 gives a convenient collection of contemporary French versions of this episode, drawn from e.g. E. Foà, *Le Dahomey* (1893) pp. 36ff.; A. le Herissé, *L'ancien Royaume du Dahomey* (1911) pp. 336ff. Ross, 'Autonomous Kingdom . . .', pp. 278–81, summarises French reports of Portuguese–Fon negotiations.

apart from the potentially dangerous dispute at Cotonou (where the new channel quickly became unnavigable), France's alliance with Tofa was not only drawing her inexorably towards conflict with Dahomey, but also tending to revive conflicts with the British at Lagos, which the diplomatists had tried to damp down.

THE COLONIAL OFFICE AND THE LAGOS FRONTIER

Despite the greatly intensified activity in West Africa for which its agents had been responsible, the British Colonial Office was still by no means a centre of imperialist fervour. By contemporary standards of bureaucratic efficiency it compared favourably with other British Ministries, and with the equivalent organisations of other governments. Mid-Victorian reforms had left the Office relatively well-equipped to ensure the regular despatch of correspondence with colonial governors at the measured pace which had been appropriate before the extension of telegraphic communications; public money was administered with due concern for economy and regularity, the claims of individuals and groups within the empire were handled in a spirit of impartial justice, even tempered with humanity. After 1877 its junior posts were filled by some of the ablest civil servants recruited through open competition (the best-known, though not the most typical, being Sydney Webb); but the office was still directed by urbane gentlemen of aristocratic connections, whose highest ambitions were that existing machinery should run smoothly.

Although Robert Herbert (first cousin to Lord Carnarvon), who was Permanent Under-Secretary from 1871 until 1892, had departed from the normal career of an aristocratic lawyer by becoming the first Prime Minister of Queensland during the 1860s, he was more at home in Whitehall than in colonial politics; his abilities, as Lord Kimberley put it, were 'more or less those of tact and managing men, than of supreme control where personal action and decision were required'[80] The 'great difficulty in committing himself to any long-range policy', which a recent scholar notes,[81] was particularly obvious in his dealings with a region of such perplexing obscurity and dubious viability as West Africa.

[80] Kimberley to Ripon, 23 December 1894, cit., B. L. Blakeley, *The Colonial Office, 1868–1892* (Durham N.C., 1972) pp. 36–7.
[81] Ibid., p. 37. This paragraph owes much to Dr. Blakeley's careful and perceptive study.

Robert Meade, his deputy in African matters and eventual successor, was urbanely competent in a similar style. With their former colleague Holland (whose lack of drive had long been noted in the Office) as political head, these senior officials intended to keep West African quarrels under strict control. While determined to administer existing colonies justly and economically, they resisted any tendencies by patriotic governors to extend the imperial frontiers, and remained anxious to dispose of consequent disputes with foreign powers by discreet diplomacy.

The indifference was partially offset by the more energetic attitude of Augustus Hemming, Principal Clerk in charge of the African Department since 1879, who as early as 1875 had advocated

> a policy of development and improvement, a policy of real and earnest efforts to raise the natives of our settlements from the slough of ignorance and barbarism in which they are sunk

and more specifically had wished to consolidate British territories in West Africa by exchanging the Gambia with France.[82] Hemming, always more ready than his superiors to back up governors who acted vigorously on their frontiers, regarded the behaviour of Tofa and his French protectors as 'scandalous'; he repeatedly suggested that to occupy new strategic positions on the creeks was 'the only way to convince the French we are in earnest and to prevent further aggressions'. In his belief that further diplomatic approaches to France would be effective only if combined with extended physical control, Hemming was apparently supported by Percy Anderson of the Foreign Office;[83] but his superiors preferred to allow Lagos to suffer pinpricks patiently rather than to retaliate, for they had little hope of any effective negotiations with France during the Boulangist crisis. Meade, at least, seems even to have feared that French politicians might be prepared to release the tensions of domestic nationalism by a colonial war. 'We have unfortunately given a pledge to Europe

---

[82] C.O. 87/108, Minute by Hemming, 14 October 1875, cit., *Prelude*, pp. 184–5.

[83] C.O. 147/58, Minutes by Hemming, 26 and 28 May on Evans to Holland, 101, 15 April 1887. There are several other minutes by Hemming to a similar effect in this volume and in C.O. 147/62.

by occupying Egypt, and we have the Suez Canal, New Hebrides, Newfoundland Fisheries, etc. We have not got a free hand', he noted gloomily; and again: 'We cannot go to war over this matter as we have other subjects in dispute of still greater importance, e.g. the New Hebrides, where we have still graver complaints as to French proceedings.'[84]

There were however limits to the restraint which an imperial government could hope to exercise over its colonial subjects and officials and to the humiliations which it could defend before its own public opinion. The death of the Hausa soldier in April 1887 marked a setback for attempts to control the situation by local discussion; when further attempted French occupations were reported early in June, shortly following news of French advances towards the Gambia, Lord Onslow, a Conservative peer recently appointed as Parliamentary Under-Secretary, supported Hemming's view that retaliatory occupations should precede further negotiations – 'if we do not do so we shall soon have nothing left.'[85] Holland agreed, fearing that otherwise the French 'will secure themselves all along the road from Kotonou to Porto Novo and greatly cripple Lagos'. Salisbury was angered by the opposition of the new Rouvier government to the agreement over the future of Egypt which Drummond Wolff had just concluded with Turkey; he accepted Holland's proposal to retaliate with unusual speed. 'The French', he grumbled, 'are seeking a counter-irritant for their internal pains, and we are performing the part of blister.'[86] After informal consultation between Salisbury and Onslow, the Foreign Office sanctioned the hoisting of the Union Jack on Toche island and on the north shore of Zuna creek.[87]

The Anglo–French rivalries thus unleashed were not restricted to the lagoon. Tofa took the opportunity to pursue his ambitions

[84] C.O. 147/62, Minute by Meade on F.O. to C.O., 4 April 1887; C.O. 147/58, Minute by Meade, 19 April, on Evans to Holland, Tel., 13 April 1887.

[85] C.O. 147/59, Minutes by Hemming and Onslow on Moloney's telegrams of 1 and 10 June 1887. For the Gambia situation, see below, pp. 226–30.

[86] Salisbury Papers, E. Holland to Salisbury, 3 June 1887; D.32, Salisbury to Holland, 3 June 1887.

[87] C.O. 879/26, C.P. African 334, Nos. 101, 103, C.O. to F.O., 14, 15 June; No. 106, F.O. to C.O., 18 June 1887; cf. C.O. 147/59, minutes by Onslow and Holland on Moloney, Tel., 10 June.

in southern Egbado by persuading the French to reoccupy Ado and Ipokia; and Moloney began to fear that French ambitions might extend as far as Abeokuta. He therefore sought permission to negotiate treaties of friendship and commerce with the Egbas, and with other Yoruba states, which were to include a clause precluding the signatories from accepting the protectorate of any other power. His primary aim was to 'guard against a repetition here of a diversion of trade and influence such as we now experience in the upper Gambia, effected by French activity and undermining'; but in the background lay his wider design of promoting the unification of Yorubaland under British leadership.[88]

This authority was granted, with Foreign Office approval;[89] but it was not intended to launch a new scramble, uncontrolled by diplomacy. Although Salisbury had hitherto tried to avoid the melancholy rituals involved in discussing recondite African questions with the Quai d'Orsay, his aim was always to dispose of them by negotiation. By October Anderson claimed to recognise a 'generally more amenable tone' in Paris, following an agreement on 24 October to shelve the conflicts in the New Hebrides by appointing a Joint Commission of naval officers.[90] The first step would be to induce the local administrators to reach some *modus vivendi* to guard against further collisions in the creeks, the second to define spheres within which the two countries might operate in future.[91] After renewed friction in November, when an armed French launch passed up to Porto Novo, the first stage was reached by a 'provisional convention', signed on 2 January 1888 by Moloney and the new French Resident, Victor Ballot, which regulated navigation in the creeks and excluded further flag-hoistings or occupations of territory.[92] Meanwhile the Colonial

[88] C.P. African 334, No. 105, Moloney to Holland, Tel., 17 June; No. 135, Moloney to Holland, 160, 13 June; No. 139, Moloney to Meade, Pte., 19 June 1887.

[89] Ibid., No. 148, C.O. to F.O., 27 June; No. 163A, F.O. to C.O., 6 August; No. 169A, Holland to Moloney, Conf., 17 August 1887.

[90] C.O. 147/62, Minute by Hemming, 31 October, on F.O. to C.O., 10 September 1887; for the New Hebrides incident, see S. H. Roberts, *The History of French Colonial Policy, 1870–1925* (1929) pp. 531–2.

[91] C.P. African 334, No. 89, F.O. to C.O., 8 June; No. 165, F.O. to C.O., 12 August 1887.

[92] C.O. 147/63, Moloney to Holland, 6, 2 January 1888. The text of the Convention is also printed in *E.D.*, IX, pp. 76–8.

Office began to consider possible bases for a definitive and rational frontier settlement.[93] This seemed to require more time; the British government's desire to comprehend as many West African disputes as possible in a single settlement suggested a need for caution in defining conditions for negotiation.[94] But in 1888 the process was accelerated by an alarming threat to the commercial hinterland of Lagos.

One essential pillar of Moloney's united Yorubaland was to be the Egba city-state of Abeokuta. This community had a complex political structure: the elected ruler, or *Alake,* was a chief arbitrator rather than an executive monarch, and policy decisions depended on the resolution of conflicting interests of influential chiefs and title-holders through the secret counsels of the *Ogboni* society. Long-standing rivalries and alliances within the traditional leadership became involved with wider issues affecting the community's future, which were insistently raised after the return of repatriates from Sierra Leone in the 1840s; the status of Christians, the priority to be attached to new commercial activities, the relations of Abeokuta with the British at Lagos. After 1867 there was a reaction against the more zealous Christian 'modernisers'; and though their position was temporarily protected through the influence of Ogundipe, a powerful military chief or *ologun,* Abeokuta's external relationships were again thrown open to question when he died on 15 August 1887.[95] Moloney tried to influence the leading chiefs – the Onlado (reputed head of the Ogboni), Sorunke (Balogun, and Jaguna of Igbein) and Ogundeyi (the Magaji) – to support a strong government which would collaborate with Lagos 'in promoting the unity of Yoruba';[96] but, as he suspected, Egbas hostile to the Lagos connection were tempted by the possibility of invoking French support.

French influence first arrived at Abeokuta in 1880, with the Fathers of the *Société des Missions Africaines*; their evangelistic methods had some success with Egbas who had found that Pro-

[93] C.O. 147/59, Minutes on Moloney to Meade, Pte., 15 July 1887.

[94] See below, pp. 230–5.

[95] S. O. Biobaku, *The Egba and their Neighbours, 1842–1872* (1957) pp. 83–8; Ayandele, *Missionary Impact,* pp. 45–8.

[96] C.O. 879/27, No. 16a, Moloney to Holland, 347, 4 October 1887, enclosing letters to Nlado, 24 September, to Sorunke, 29 September.

testants demanded too sharp a break with traditional religion, and their presence offered an alternative to political opponents of those Christian 'Saro' who favoured the British connection. As early as 1884 Father Planque, head of the mission in Lyon, reported that the Egbas would welcome French protection against Dahomey and the British. Certainly the Onlado was interested in re-establishing commercial links with Porto Novo which Mepon had broken under pressure from Glover in 1865;[97] he despatched messengers with a horse's tail, which Porto Novans interpreted as an offer of alliance. Dorat, the French Resident, hoped to respond by visiting Abeokuta, which he regarded as the key to the Niger; but his health did not permit the journey and he offended the Egbas by retaining the horse's tail (mistaking the emissaries' credentials for a personal gift).[98] In January 1886 the Minister of Marine, Admiral Aube, favoured accepting such an alliance in hope of using the Egbas against Dahomey, but the Foreign Ministry prudently ruled such a scheme to be premature, since it could still be easily frustrated by British hostility.[99] But for the Egbas the French option still seemed open.

Early in March 1888 Edouard Viard arrived by steamer at Lagos, prepared at last to carry out that journey to the Niger which he had proposed two years before.[100] On August 1886 he had appeared not in Porto Novo but in Saint-Louis (to the surprise of the colonial government), intending to travel to Timbuktu to avert a supposedly imminent British threat;[101] his abrasive personality led him into conflict with the French Commandant at Medina and by October he had reverted to the idea of approaching Timbuktu from down stream.[102] But Viard still retained

[97] Akindélé and Aguessy, *Contribution . . .*, pp. 76–7.

[98] Ayandele, *Missionary Impact*, p. 49, MAE Afrique 79, Planque to Ferry, 20 January 1884; Afrique 83, Note by Dorat, 26 October 1886; cf. ANSOM, Senegal III/17/b, Ballot to Thomas, 25 April 1888 (printed in *E.D.*, IX, pp. 86–7); Viard's journal, 30 March 1888.

[99] AE Afrique 83, Aube to Freycinet 15, January; Note by Desbuissons, 24 February; Freycinet to Aube, 10 March 1886.

[100] See above, pp. 56–7.

[101] ANSOM, Senegal III/17/a, Genouille to Aube, 28 August 1886; de la Porte to Freycinet, September 1886. *MAE*, Afrique 85, M.A.E. to M.M.C., 5 December 1886.

[102] ANSOM, Senegal III/17/a, Genouille to Aube, 12 October 1886; note by Revoil. Cf. Viard's waspish *Renseignements sur la Colonie du Sénégal*, May 1887, in *MAE*, Afrique 85.

enough credibility in Paris to receive, early in 1888, a subsidy of 8,000 francs from the Colonial Department, for the purpose of 'studying the creation of a commercial route linking Porto Novo to the middle Niger above Boussa', on condition that he confined himself to commercial aims and avoided British territory.[103] These instructions he consistently ignored. In Lagos he associated with French Catholic missionaries, and begged a lift to Porto Novo on one of G. L. Gaiser's steam launches by posing as a priest (although 'his free and easy manner on board and generous consumption of wine and spirits made Mr Fischer form the opinion that he was a curious clergyman'.[104] To politically naïve French missionaries Viard posed as a far-sighted patriotic strategist, explaining eloquently (and no doubt alcoholically)

> how that with the Soudan cut off from the French by the Niger on the South and Abyssinia on the North, they were bound to effect a passage by way of Abeokuta and on through, starting of course from their own territory of Porto Novo. . . .[105]

On 19 March Viard left Porto Novo with the open intention of exploring a route to Boussa on the Niger, where he optimistically claimed to have a rendezvous with Gallieni. His political ambitions at this point centred on Oyo (and ultimately on Gwandu) since British influence was assumed to be dominant in Abeokuta.[106] But experience of the complexity of Egba politics tempted him into intrigues which transformed his journey from a mere exhibition of Quixotry to a potentially dangerous international incident.

Viard's political enterprise began on 22 March in the central Egbado town of Ilaro; its chiefs, he claimed, granted the French exclusive rights of trade and exemption from customs duties, and were willing to proceed to accept a French protectorate.[107] Although these chiefs later denied that they had signed any treaty

[103] ANSOM, Senegal III/17/b, M.A.E. to M.M.C., 12 January 1888, and notes by Colonial Department.

[104] C.O. 879/28, C.P. African 355, No. 1, encl. 7, Note on Viard, May 1888.

[105] C.M.S. Archives, G3/A2/O5, Fairley to Wood, 3 September 1888 (quoting Fr. Brun's version of Viard's ideas).

[106] ANSOM, Senegal III/17/b, Viard to Freycinet, 15 March 1888.

[107] ANSOM, Senegal III/17/b, Viard's journal, encl. in Viard to Etienne, 10 July 1888. A text of the treaty from the Porto Novo archives is included as an appendix to Folayan, 'Egbado . . .'

it is possible that some of them did express interest in a closer association with France. Apart from any attraction in Viard's hints that France might tolerate a continuing trade in slaves, Ilaro chiefs may have been growing disillusioned with the policy of look- ing to Lagos for protection against Dahomey and Abeokuta. For some weeks previously an Ilaro spokesman, Tena-Eni-Olorunda, had been in Lagos, citing earlier French activities in hopes of inducing Moloney to intervene; but the Governor, with his hope of using a strong Egba state as one of the pillars of Yoruba unity, had refused to consider such requests without the approval of the Egba overlords.[108] Nevertheless it is scarcely credible that the Ilaro chiefs seriously intended to cut existing links with Lagos for the sake of Viard's vague promises, or indeed that they under- stood the meaning of the paper in French which he left with them.

From Ilaro Viard was escorted to Abeokuta on 28 March, where he lodged with Ogundeyi, who supervised relations with Ilaro. A few days later he moved quarters to the Catholic mission. Father Brun, while not taking Viard himself too seriously, saw in his presence an opportunity 'to work for France, and . . . at the same time for the good of the mission';[109] he evidently encouraged Viard to seek a political treaty, and incited support for this idea among Catholic adherents who were influential in the Ogboni. Viard's own diary refers only sketchily to his discussions with the Onlado, Ogundeyi, and Osonakun, the recently elected Alake; these began with recriminations on account of his own proceed- ings at Ilaro and of the failure of the Porto Novo authorities to respond to the Onlado's overture of 1884 (or to return his horse's tail). In response Viard held out expectations that a French alliance would offer relief from British harassment, greater toler- ance in questions of slave-dealing and the return of runaways, a railway from Porto Novo, a supply of funds and firearms, and – the point to which Ogundeyi apparently attached decisive im- portance – a promise of full and complete protection against Dahomean raids. On 11 April, Viard claimed, the Egba chiefs accepted his treaty; the first four articles conveyed definite trad- ing privileges to France, the eight remaining ones provided,

---

[108] C.O. 879/27, C.P. African 345, No. 115, Moloney to Holland, 109, 2 April 1888.
[109] ANSOM, Senegal III/17/b, Planque to M.M.C., 14 June 1888.

subject to the approval of the French government, for a French protectorate.[110]

It is doubtful whether this is a full and accurate version of events. Since no Egba understood French, the negotiation clearly depended on the initiative of the Catholic Fathers, whose influence was suspect to many Egbas; hence a good deal of secrecy and obscurity was maintained. Although Viard's journal implies that the treaty was discussed in the councils of the Ogboni, as was constitutionally proper, information reaching the C.M.S. mission suggested that decisions were taken largely by Ogundeyi, Sorunke and the Onlado, together with the new Alake, unknown to or against the opposition of many 'secondary chiefs'.[111] Subsequent discussion among the Egba therefore centred on the constitutional propriety as well as the political expediency of the treaty. The opposition, stimulated by the C.M.S., was led by Egba descendents resident in Lagos, notably the Legislative Councillor C. J. George; discreetly encouraged by Moloney, they protested by letters and deputations, and suggested that instead there should be a treaty precluding political agreements with foreign powers without British approval.[112] This pressure succeeded in producing repeated denials that any treaty had been signed with Viard; the chiefs displayed their continuing spirit of independence by refusing him permission to continue his journey to Oyo. But the Egba authorities were unwilling to ally too closely with the British either. Their experience of the occupation of Lagos, and of Glover's policy thereafter, had deeply impressed 'many lettered Egbas, who go about repeating that to enter into any engagements with the British government is to put in the small end of the wedge, which will end in cession of Abeokuta in England'.[113] According to Viard British prestige had further suffered from reports of the reverses

[110] Ibid., Viard to Etienne, 26 June, 10, 15 July 1888, enclosing extracts from his journal. A copy of his treaty is in AE Afrique 128.

[111] C.M.S. G3/A2/O5, Rev. J. B. Wood to Lang, 23 April 1888. See also Wood's reports of 15, 29 May, 11, 25 June (ibid); initially, he provided the Lagos government with most of its information.

[112] The immediate and hostile reactions in Lagos may be traced in Moloney's despatches in C.P. African 345, Nos, 121, 125, 128, 134, 135, 136; African 355, Nos. 1, 33.

[113] Report by J. O. George and others to 'Committee of Egba Children at Lagos', 19 May 1888; encl. in C.P. African 355, No. 1, Moloney to Knutsford, Conf., 12, 22 May 1888.

on the Nile.[114] Some Egbas clearly hoped at least to keep open
the French option. Hence it was in a euphoric mood that Viard
returned to Porto Novo on 20 April.

Victor Ballot, French Resident at Porto Novo since November
1887, did not receive him warmly. It was Ballot, a level-headed
civilian experienced in African administration, who had signed
the *modus vivendi* with Moloney on 2 January, and he was
anxious to operate it in the spirit as well as the letter. Before Viard
had left Porto Novo Ballot had emphasised that his instructions
prohibited any political activity likely to offend the British and
had expressly warned him not to visit Abeokuta, foreseeing just
such an embarrassing temptation as he had fallen into. To compound this offence Viard on his return boasted of his achievements
to Tofa, who in reply complained about Ballot's relative ineffec-
tiveness in promoting his political claims. Ballot, therefore, with
the approval of Governor of Senegal, shipped Viard back to
France.[115]

He received a mixed reception. Frenchmen already interested
in expansion on the Slave Coast applauded Viard's exploits. Fabre,
and some of his colleagues in the Marseille Chamber of Commerce, believed Viard had secured the key to 'one of the finest
countries in the world' and hoped his coup would be followed by
an occupation of Whydah. Father Planque and Colonel Dorat,
predictably, joined in the applause.[116] De La Porte and the Colonial
Department, while hedging over any commitment to defend the
Egbas against Dahomey, favoured ratification of the treaty. But
the Foreign Ministry verbally pointed out that this would arouse
justifiable hostility from the British, who were capable of doing
grave damage to the French position at Porto Novo if they chose;
in July they ruled that the political clauses should not be ratified,
although the future of the commercial clauses was left open.[117]
This lost opportunity was bitterly resented by the colonial 'hawks';

[114] ANSOM, Senegal III/17/b, Viard to Etienne, 10 July 1888.

[115] ANSOM, Senegal III/17/b, Governor to M.M.C., 22 May 1888,
encl. Ballot 25 April 1888 (partly printed in *E.D.*, IX, pp. 86–7), C.O.
879/28, C.P. African 355, No. 1, encl. 7; Note on Viard, May 1888.

[116] AE Afrique 128, Marseille C. of C. to M.A.E., 11 July 1888,
Planque to Goblet, 6 August 1888; Dorat to Goblet, 31 August 1888.

[117] ANSOM, Afrique VI/66/d, De La Porte to Goblet (Draft) July
1888; M.A.E. to M.M.C., 12 August 1888; C.O. 879/28, C.P. African
355, No. 19, Goblet to Egerton, 24 July 1888.

Etienne, when he became head of strengthened Colonial Department in March 1889, declared that 'it should not have been impossible, despite the arguments raised by the British government, to make them accept a *fait accompli*.[118] A little later, when placing Viard's services at the disposal of the Porto Novo administration, Etienne formally expressed appreciation of the explorer's services and regret that circumstances had prevented colonial interests from benefiting as much as might have been hoped.[119] But the Foreign Ministry's view of international priorities could still overrule such inflated ambitions.

In fact, the main effect of Viard's mission was to persuade the British Colonial Office to move slowly towards a more positive policy in Yorubaland. In Lagos, Viard's escapade had emphasised the danger of separation from a country with which there were strong commercial, religious and family connections; Africans as well as colonial officials and European merchants reacted sharply. Many of the Lagosians who served as liaison officers with the Yoruba states were convinced by this episode, as well as by long recent experience of internecine war, that it was time to place British paramountcy upon some more secure footing. This did not of course imply a conscious option for direct colonial rule, but for an extension of informal suzerainty along the lines which Moloney, whom they trusted, clearly favoured. On 28 May leading African and European residents joined in requesting that the government should:

> . . . delegate the protection of British interests to the principal authorities in each of the centres of population, binding them not to give over their country to any foreign Government, without seeking it ourselves, and at the same time give these authorities an annual stipend.[120]

Moloney had already begun to act along such lines, using the

[118] ANSOM, Afrique VI/66/d, Etienne to Spuller, 29 March 1889 (passage deleted from draft).

[119] ANSOM, Missions 80, Etienne to Viard, 26 July 1889; AE Afrique 125, Etienne to Bayol, 13 August 1889.

[120] C.O. 879/28, C.P. African 355, No. 4, enclosing Lagosians to Moloney, 28 May 1888.

authority granted to him a year before.[121] Knowing that Yoruba rulers would be careful to avoid any abatement of internal sovereignty, Moloney used his personal reputation to construct a protectorate which would genuinely confine its purpose to the exclusion of foreigners and the creation of an extensive, peaceful and secure trading hinterland from Lagos. During 1888 he bombarded the Colonial Office with treaties, projected or provisionally signed. One group of these, relating to lands bordering Dahomey, contained not only provisions for trade and friendship, but offers of cession; such offers came from a number of southern Egbado towns, from Ilaro again, from Taiwo's Isheri, and from Ketu – the Yoruba state most vulnerable to Dahomean attack. The chiefs of Igbessa made explicit what was doubtless the intention of all – they desired Britain's 'protecting friendship' against external threats, but not a 'direct enforcement of British law among them or the British flag, if it involved such enforcement'. In Moloney's mind, there was no incompatibility of aims here.[122] The second type of treaty followed the lines rejected by Abeokuta, providing for peace and friendship, the preferential treatment of British trade, and a promise to make no further treaty and cede no territory without British approval. The most important of these was signed by Adeyemi, Alafin of Oyo, with the Reverend Samuel Johnson on 23 July 1888. Viard had hoped to use the influence of the Catholic mission to advance French influence at Oyo; but the influence of this African clergyman of Oyo origin, and of his fellow Protestants, now ensured that Moloney's skilfully-drafted appeal for Yoruba unity would prevail.[123]

The Colonial Office, being now embarked on a course of negotiation with France, declined to ratify any of these treaties until

[121] See above p. 154.

[122] C.P. African 355, No. 2, Moloney to Knutsford, 151, 23 May (Igbessa); also Nos. 9, 29 (Ilaro); 31 (Otta); 32 (Isheri and Agboyi); 30 (Ketu).

[123] Ibid., No. 40, Moloney to Knutsford, 258, 21 August 1888. Samuel Johnson, *The History of the Yorubas* (1921) pp. 572–5, prints the text of the treaty and of Moloney to Adeyemi, 23 May. Johnson omits the Yoruba proverb, 'Igun merin ni aiye ini' ('There are four corners to the world') which Moloney introduced into this letter: he thus endorsed an Oyo view of their own pre-eminence among the Yoruba Kingdoms; cf. R. C. Law, 'The Heritage of Oduduwa . . .', *JAH*, xiv (1973) pp. 215ff.; See also African 355, Nos. 59, 60, Treaties with Ife, 22 May, Itebu, 29 May.

the boundary had been defined by the agreement of August 1889. Even then they would accept no offers of cession, still regarding the offers of trade and friendship and pledges of non-alienation contained in treaties of the second type as sufficient.[124] But they no longer tried to restrain Moloney from establishing such special relationships: Hemming's colleagues accepted his view of the crucial Oyo treaty:

> In view of the expense and trouble incurred by the Government of Lagos two years ago in the settlement of the long-continued war in the interior we have a strong and legitimate claim to exercise exclusive influence in Yorubaland, and this Treaty of Commerce and Friendship is a fair outcome of it . . .[125]

Yet experience elsewhere was already pointing to the conclusion that limited engagements of this sort offered only unstable interim solutions to the problems of West African colonial frontiers.[126] Although Moloney sincerely sought only a sphere of influence in which Britain provided the rope to bind the sticks together, the unifying force in a league of independent states, he had in fact laid the foundations of a protectorate which more martially-minded Governors would build on.

TOFA, FRANCE AND DAHOMEY, 1888–9

This intensification of European activity on the Slave Coast was apprehensively observed from Abomey. As Kondo's anger against the provocative insubordination of Tofa mounted, he and his supporters in the internal struggle for power seem to have explored the possibilities of finding a European ally. The French became increasingly worried by rumours that the Fon might respond favourably to overtures from German agents at Whydah, which were said to have support from the administration in Togo;[127]

---

[124] C.P. African 355, No. 20, C.O. to F.O., 18 August 1888; C.P. A rican, 365, No. 161, C.O. to F.O., 21 December 1889.

[125] C.O. 147/65, Minute by Hemming on Moloney 258, 21 August 1888.

[126] Cf. below pp. 175–6.

[127] E.g. Beckmann to Thomas, 6 March 1889 (*E.D.* IX, pp. 94–5); ANSOM, Senegal IV/124/a, Bertin to O.C. Troops, 29 March 1889; Fabre to Etienne, 13 May 1889; Senegal IV/124/b, Tautain to Thomas, 1 June 1889.

but there is little evidence that Kondo took these particularly seriously before his accession to the throne.[128] A more concrete development was the arrival in Lagos on 24 November 1888 of a Dahomean mission, allegedly led by Kondo's fourteen-year-old son Fasinu, which invited Moloney to send a mission to Abomey to discuss the cession of the country to Britain.

One thing which is certain about this mysterious episode is that Fasinu's offer cannot be taken at its face value. Moloney at once appreciated that it was a tactical manoeuvre, designed to secure British support against French pressure, and perhaps to develop alternative outlets for Dahomean palm produce through Lagos or Ketenou. Kondo clearly had no intention of allowing the British, any more than the Portuguese, to exercise real power within Dahomey. Moloney therefore temporised, emphasising that as a precondition for British friendship Dahomey must desist from slave-dealing, human sacrifice and attacks on the Yoruba. But he recommended that the offer 'should not at once be absolutely declined', since a positive response might further 'the influences of civilisation'; and bring some reprieve to the Yoruba. His argument was surprisingly well received in the Colonial Office – a sign that British attitudes towards this region of Africa were changing. Hemming regarded the overture as 'an opportunity of opening up Dahomey to the world and letting in light, which ought not to be lost'; Baron de Worms, the Parliamentary Under-Secretary, thought the prospect of eventually abolishing slavery and human sacrifices would be welcomed in Parliament and even by 'the outside masses in this country'; Meade, Herbert and Knutsford were more sceptical, but did not exclude the idea.[129] However,

[128] M. Kalous, 'Some Correspondence between the German Empire and Dahomey, 1882–1892', *CEA* viii, 32 (1968) pp. 635–41, prints a letter from Gelele to the German Commissioner in Togo, complaining about French support of Tofa, written on 12 May 1889 on the same lines as letters to the French and British of the same date (see below). The extract printed contains no specific request for German support, only a general invitation to 'see and judge and to know what the Europeans are doing in my country'.

[129] C.O. 879/28, C.P. African 355, No. 68, Moloney to Knutsford, Tel., 3 December 1888; C.O. 879/29 C.P. African 365, No. 10, Moloney to Knutsford, Conf., 14 December 1888; and enclosures; C.O. 147/67, Minutes on above (and photograph of Prince Fasinu). For further background to the Dahomean mission, see Ross 'Autonomous Kingdom...' pp. 294–8.

even now no British official wished to exercise power in Dahomey for its own sake, or dreamed of using Gelele as an ally against France. It was understood that the offer could only be considered if the coming negotiations led to French withdrawal from Porto Novo; when next year it became clear that this would not happen, the Colonial Office accepted with relief that 'the French may do what they like with Porto Novo and Dahomey.'[130]

By that time the notion had become obsolete. In April 1889 Fasinu returned to Lagos with a letter in Gelele's name. Despite a tempting invitation to 'send merchant traders to my country, as palm oil and palm kernels are plenty', its central request was for British support in removing Tofa and installing Soigbe as ruler of Porto Novo. Even had this not involved conflict with France, there would have been no prospect of the British government agreeing, and the Acting Governor's reply was sternly discouraging. In June further messages reached Lagos with new letters from Gelele; these disavowed Fasinu's proposals, renewed the attack on Tofa, and recited a list of grievances against the French.[131] For during the early months of 1889 Kondo's quarrel with the petty tyrant of Porto Novo had involved Dahomey in a direct confrontation with France in which, as she clearly recognised, she had no possibility of securing British support.

The smouldering hostility between Kondo and Tofa turned into armed conflict in the Wheme valley in mid-March 1889. Although Porto-Novan traditions speak of a full-scale Dahomean invasion, French enquiries suggested that the trouble originated with the rebellion of Porto Novo's client state of Dekamé, and that no more than a hundred Fon troops were involved; when a French officer travelled through the Wheme district in October he found that many villages had remained completely peaceful and untouched by Dahomean troops.[132] Nevertheless the Porto

[130] C.P. African 355, No. 75, C.O. to F.O. 12 December 1888. C.O. 147/71, Minute by Antrobus, 6 June 1889, on Denton to Knutsford, Tel., 5 June.

[131] C.P. African 365, Nos. 67, 72, 123, Denton to Knutsford, Conf., 4 April (encl. Gelele to Denton, 26 January 1889); Conf., 15 April (encl, Denton to Gelele, 12 April); Conf., 27 June (encl. two letters from Gelele. dated 12 May 1889). A further letter from Gelele to H.M.G. is in C.O. 147/71.

[132] Akindélé and Aguessy, *Contribution* . . ., p. 88; ANSOM, Senegal iv/124/a, Beckman to Thomas, 5, 6 April 1889; Senegal iv/124/b,

Novan army put up a miserable performance and by late March
the capital feared a full-scale Dahomean invasion. Tofa, fortified with liquor, distributed firearms through the town and called
on his French protectors for support; but the tiny garrison of thirty
tirailleurs inspired little confidence, and the Navy was reluctant
to risk landing reinforcements. The French Resident, Baron de
Beckmann, was absent at Whydah, and when he returned on 1
April he could not control the growing atmosphere of panic. Next
day he found himself almost alone in a deserted town; 400 members of the trading community had retreated to Lagos aboard the
steamers of G. L. Gaiser, while Tofa, with the bulk of his own
supporters, crossed the lagoon to seek protection in the British
outposts around Ketenou.[133]

When the Dahomean army failed to appear, the life of Porto
Novo gradually revived. A landing party of seventy French
marines eventually arrived on 6 April; a few days later Tofa
returned to his palace, and his subjects gradually followed him.
But France's prestige had been shaken, and the crisis in her relations with Dahomey intensified. Ever since 1885 Frenchmen interested in the Slave Coast had been pressing for action to clarify
their rights at Cotonou (sometimes demanding also the occupation of Whydah, to prevent Germany or Britain from taking over
the abortive Portuguese protectorate). In February 1888 the
Colonial Department ruled any such action premature 'in view
of the sentiments recently manifested by the Chamber of Deputies
in respect of colonial extension';[134] but the existing relationship
was clearly unstable. Beckmann's visit to Whydah and Cotonou in
March 1889 had been largely for the purpose of warning Fon officials on the coast of France's intention to clear up the question of
Cotonou. Their reactions showed clearly that Abomey, far from
accepting French demands, would never recognise the treaties of

[133] ANSOM, Senegal ɪv/124/a. Bertin to O.C. troops, 29 March 1889;
Admiral Brown de Colstoun to Krant, 29 April 1889; Beckmann to
Thomas, 5–12 April 1889. (A heavily-edited version of the latter despatch
is in *E.D.*, ɪx, pp. 95–100.)

[134] AE Afrique 125, S.S.E.C. to M.A.E., 11 January 1888; M.A.E. to
M.M.C., 29 January; M.M.C. to M.A.E., 17 February, 1888.

Beckmann to Thomas, 176, 29 April 1889; Dahomey ɪɪɪ/1, Angot to
Bayol, 1 November 1889. Cf. Gelele to H.M.G., 12 May 1889 (C.O.
147/71), 'I am not going to fight the Porto Novo itself for the sake of the
late old kings which are dead.'

1868 or 1878. The Dahomeans regarded Cotonou as inalienable Fon territory, and had grievances of their own against the French; the violation of Dahomean soil by a French shell fired during the British blockade of Whydah in 1876, the attempt to pierce an entry into the lagoon at Cotonou in 1885, became the first items in a litany which would become very familiar to French agents during the next three years.[135]

But the major Dahomean grievance now became France's protection of Tofa. On 12 May, the same date on which letters denouncing his behaviour were sent in Gelele's name to the British and German representatives on the coast, Kondo's scribes addressed two similar documents to the French Resident at Porto Novo and (through Fabre's agents) to the President of the French Republic. After reasserting the claim to Cotonou, and incorporating French actions during the recent panic in his litany of grievances, Gelele asserted that Porto Novo had always been considered as his territory 'because this town was founded or peopled by a branch of my family coming from Allada'. Both letters demanded that Tofa should be deposed in favour of Soigbe and despatched prisoner to Abomey; if this were not done within eight months the Dahomean army threatened to invade Porto Novo and cut down the palm trees on which its trade with France depended.[136] (Later in the year reports reached the French that Dahomean smiths had forged 10,000 new axes for this purpose.)

The demand to get rid of Tofa was sympathetically received by Frenchmen by no means disposed to appease Dahomey. Beckmann and Captain Tautain (an experienced and irascible officer sent from Senegal to replace him) agreed that Tofa's reckless provocation of Dahomey, followed by his cowardly flight, had made him an embarrassment to the French administration.

A section of the population is inflamed against king Tofa, whose conduct has been contemptible [Beckmann reported]. I think his position is seriously compromised; in any case he has lost all his authority and prestige.[138]

[135] Beckmann to Thomas, 6 March, 5 April 1888 (*E.D.*, ix, pp. 93–6).
[136] ANSOM, Senegal iv/124/b, Gelele to Tautain, 12 May; 'Gellelem' to President, 12 May 1889.
[137] ANSOM, Dahomey i/1/b, Bayol to Etienne, 12 October 1889.
[138] ANSOM, Senegal iv/124/a, Beckmann to Thomas, 6 April 1889.

A whole season's commerce had been ruined by his foolishness: 'we shall not be able to maintain him without provoking a revolution, and of course the pillage of the factories.' From Paris the former Resident Ballot wrote to urge getting rid of 'that imbecile' for the sake of restoring relations with Dahomey.[139] Tautain agreed that, so long as Dahomey was hostile, not a single palm kernal would reach Porto Novo; he favoured finding some early opportunity to deport Tofa to Gabon, and replace him by a more direct French administration with more extensive powers – 'to make decrees and bring them provisionally into force, to provide himself with a military escort when he sees fit, to close the school and suppress the subsidy to the mission until its courses are wholly French.'[140] (This reflected impatience with the Brazilian Creoles and their missionary patrons who were Tofa's main source of support.)[141] In Tautain's view, the deposition of Tofa would be no retreat but a necessary preliminary to a forward policy based on the discreet re-establishment of an alliance with Abeokuta, and an eventual military campaign against the Fon on the scale of the Anglo–Asante war of 1873–4.[142]

All the indications are that Etienne sympathised with Tautain's view of France's ultimate goals; but he was not prepared to countenance the abandonment of Tofa. References to his ignominious conduct and proposals for his deposition were deliberately suppressed from copies of the relevant reports, even when designed for internal departmental circulation; Gelele's letter of complaint to the President was conveniently misplaced.[143] Possibly this was due to a fear that a confession that France had backed a poor horse would encourage domestic critics of French involvement in West Africa; conceivably, it was due to recognition of Tofa's close

[139] ANSOM, Senegal IV/124/b, Beckmann to Thomas 176, 29 April 1889. Trade figures in D'Albeca to Bayol 138, 1 November 1889 (Dahomey I/2/d), suggest the damage to trade in 1889 was not irreparable.

[140] ANSOM, Senegal IV/124/b, Tautain to Thomas, Tel., 27 May, in Thomas to Etienne, 1058, 5 June 1889.

[141] ANSOM, Senegal IV/124/b, Petition of Brazilians to Brown de Colstoun, 9 April 1889; Senegal IV/124/a, Planque to Etienne, 28 April 1889.

[142] ANSOM, Senegal IV/124/b, Tautain to Thomas, 1 June 1889.

[143] See annotations on documents cited above in ANSOM, Senegal IV/124.

financial ties with the French merchants.[144] But the decisive factor was probably Etienne's appreciation that to denounce the treaty with Tofa would again remove the juridical basis for France's presence at Porto Novo, at the very moment when her rights were the subject of negotiations with the British. The immediate priority was to negotiate a viable eastern boundary which would give the protectorate room to breathe; to carry this through the French needed Tofa, just as he needed them.

As for Dahomey, Etienne accepted the need for patience; since his colleagues would clearly not accept a substantial military commitment, it was necessary to tolerate the humiliating ambiguities at Cotonou for a little longer. In consultation with the merchants[145] Etienne strengthened the French administration and gave it a little more autonomy; later in the year Bayol returned to make a further attempt to settle the problem by negotiation. But the confirmation of France's alliance with Tofa doomed his efforts to failure and ensured that ultimately Franco–Dahomean relations would have to be settled by force. During the summer of 1889, the future of the Slave Coast was one of the issues at stake in the Anglo–French negotiations in Paris; but the outcome was in essentials already determined by alignments which the two countries had established among their African neighbours. The logic of these pointed increasingly clearly towards British hegemony among the Yoruba and French hegemony among the Aja.

[144] In February the agent of Mante Frères (successors to Régis) provided the British government with a promissory note for £100 in Tofa's name as security for the good behaviour of his subjects, C.O. 147/72, Denton to Knutsford, 315, 7 October 1889.

[145] ANSOM, Senegal IV/124/b, Fabre to Etienne, 13 May, Etienne to Fabre, 22 May 1889.

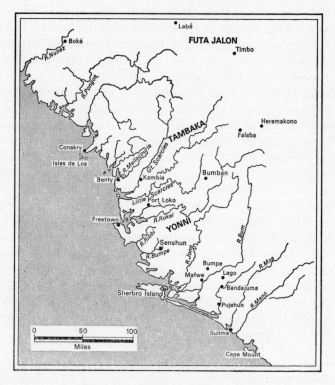

3 The Hinterland of Sierra Leone

5 Samori, France and Britain

The Colony of Sierra Leone had been founded with high hopes that it would exercise strong economic and cultural influences on the African continent. During the nineteenth century these hopes, greatly dimmed or extinguished among its British sponsors, were keut alive by the faith and enterprise of its own African citizens. But from the 1880s the conditions which limited the Creoles' contribution to African development, and so defined Sierra Leone's modest future role in the continent, became increasingly clear.

It was already long apparent that the founders had located their colony in a part of Africa not well endowed with natural resources or commercial opportunities; many enterprising Creoles preferred to seek their fortunes in other regions. The activities of the remainder fell within a limited area; many remained in Freetown, offering facilities to traders from the near or distant interior, while others moved to such nearby producing areas as the Rokel and Ribbi valleys, the coasts around the Sherbro estuary and the Gallinas, and the Northern Rivers.[1] But in 1882 an Anglo–French agreement (which both parties observed, although the French Chamber failed to ratify it) conceded to France that section of the Colony's commercial sphere which lay north of the Great Scarcies.[2] This did not immediately prejudice the livelihood of the British and Creole traders who operated there; until the 1890s France imposed only a general export duty of 5 per cent, whereas the tariff which the Sierra Leone government levied along the coast between the Great Scarcies and the Mano bore much more

[1] For a guide to their dispersion, see C. H. Fyfe, 'European and Creole Influence in the Hinterland of Sierra Leone before 1896', *SLS* n.s.6., 1956, pp. 113–23.

[2] *Prelude*, pp. 247–52, 289–94.

heavily on the trading staples of guns and powders, spirits and tobacco. Nevertheless, the French were now capable of obstructing any expansion of Freetown's commerce towards the south.

During the 1870s Sierra Leonean traders, attracted by growing European demand for palm kernels, had begun to penetrate a few miles inland from Sherbro estuary and to tap the produce of Mende country, which previously had little direct contact with outsiders. But their presence created new problems. Rulers of the small autonomous states which constituted Mendeland began to compete vigorously for direct access to the new commercial centres, and old rivalries were intensified by new possibilities of gain. As Creole traders clustered at Mafwe, head of navigation on the Bum river, for example, the states of Bumpe and Tikonko claimed rights of access which Gberri, the local ruler and an ally of the British, tried to deny.[3] Risks of violence were increased because many Mende chiefdoms, unable to absorb their whole populations in the commercial economy, still contained groups of mercenary soldiers or 'warboys', eager for employment in the only trade they knew. The traditional peace-keeping mechanisms of the Poro were strained, and those Mendes most interested in establishing settled relations with the Colony began to express some willingness to accept 'the white man's peace'.[4]

Falling prices for African products brought further complications to this region also, especially during the depression of the mid–1880s. The volume of produce exported through the Sierra Leone customs, while fluctuating as usual, remained more stable than prices (except in the case of groundnuts, diverted to French ports or ruined in the fields by the arrival of jiggers);[5] but there were fewer returns to be divided among producers, middlemen, merchants, the toll-collectors of the various chiefs, and the customs men of the Colony. Freetown merchants sought drastic solutions; early in 1885 the richer European and African residents formed a Sierra Leone Association, to initiate public discussion of the mounting economic crisis in the colony and to press for remedial action. Its President was Ernst Vohsen, German Consul,

---

[3] C.O. 879/24, C.P. African 318a, No. 23, Rowe to Granville, 85, 13 March 1886.

[4] C.O. 879/24, C.P. African 322, No. 5, Report by Peel, encl. in Rowe to Granville, 205, 18 June 1886.

[5] See Appendix, Table III.

local manager of Verminck's Senegal Company, and later a prominent member of the colonial movement in his own country; the Vice-President was a Sierra Leonean lawyer, J. B. M'Carthy.[6] On 3 March 1885 Philip Lemberg, a Silesian long established in Freetown who was one of the Association's leading members, presented a comprehensive list of demands for government action to a meeting in the Court Hall.[7]

Meanwhile companies like Paterson Zochonis of Manchester were active in Britain; they enlisted the support of the Manchester Chamber of Commerce and tried to stir up Parliamentary interest through M.P.s like Holland and C. H. Hopwood.[8] During the sessions 1882–9, no fewer than ten Parliamentary Papers were published, containing 800 foolscap pages of detailed reports about 'disturbances' in the neighbourhood of Sierra Leone; this would be a striking measure of public interest, if there were any means of ascertaining who read them. But how were these discontents to be allayed? Lacking any clear understanding of their cause, the Manchester merchants asked the Colonial Office to send back Sir Samuel Rowe.

As Governor from 1876 to 1881, Rowe had often prodded the Colonial Office into moving faster than it would have chosen towards the extension of British jurisdiction, and his vigorous resistance to France in the Northern Rivers had made him more popular in Freetown than in Whitehall. But by 1885 Rowe, now fifty years old and beginning to tire, had learned to give the Colonial Office what they wanted. Broadly this meant meticulous care in handling the financial crises which had periodically beset Sierra Leone since Governor Hennessy had 'reformed' the tariff in 1872, and a frontier policy which would give an impression of purposeful activity but entail a minimum of political and financial commitment. From Whitehall, Rowe's Lagos reputation as 'the do-nothing Governor' seemed a positive asset. His reappointment to Freetown in February 1885 was not intended to launch the expansionist policy which the traders favoured; rather, it was a

[6] On the Association see J. D. Hargreaves, *A Life of Sir Samuel Lewis* (1958) Chap. 4; Fyfe, *History*, pp. 451–65 *passim*.

[7] P. Lemberg, *The Commerce of Sierra Leone* (Freetown, 1885).

[8] C. H. Hopwood, (1829–1904), a libertarian lawyer, was Liberal M.P. for Stockport, 1874–85, for Middleton, 1892–5. He was extremely zealous in scrutinising acts of the government in Sierra Leone.

substitute for any such policy. The Colonial Office rightly expected Rowe to display great diplomatic activity on the frontier, work hard on the colonial finances, and accept no new responsibilities without instructions.

Much of Rowe's remaining energies were expended in scrutinising the monthly trends of the customs statistics: his governorship was dominated by the impossible aim of balancing the annual budget despite the extreme instability of produce prices, and the existence in Guinea of alternative channels for any item of trade that might be taxed too highly.[9] Rowe hoped to achieve this by restoring sufficient political tranquillity to encourage regular commerce between Freetown and its hinterland. He pursued this optimistic aim within a limited area. While regretting the loss of those Northern Rivers where he had formerly pursued such an active policy, he accepted French dominance there as a fact. In February 1886 a French naval officer, accustomed to regard Rowe as an arch-francophobe, was surprised to find him avowing in a patently sincere speech in French 'ses sympathies toutes françaises, ses regrets de n'avoir pas toujours réussi dans les négociations entamés.'[10] Although at the time of his return his old *protégé* Bokkari of Moriah was still resisting the French from bases in the British sphere, Rowe did not justify French suspicions by supporting him;[11] nor did he pursue the idea that the French might yet abandon the Mellacourie in exchange for the Gambia. His hopes now centred on relations with the numerous independent rulers of the Temne and the Loko, the Sherbro and the Mende; he did not speak of protectorates, but sought an informal and inexpensive overlordship, such as Maclean had once enjoyed on the Gold Coast, over a belt of territory extending about thirty miles inland.[12] Within this area Rowe intended to concentrate on the Sherbro hinterland, whose resources were being less fully tapped by Freetown traders, and could in any case not easily be diverted to French ports.

Assisted by three 'Special Service Officers' Rowe laboured to

[9] For his work on this problem, see C.O. 879/24, C.P. African 323, Correspondence relating to the Financial Condition of Sierra Leone . . .

[10] ANSOM, Senegal iii/12/b, Report by Raffenel of mission in *Rivières du Sud*, 20 January–1 March 1886.

[11] Cf. *Prelude*, pp. 217–22, 247, 291–2.

[12] C.O. 879/24, C.P. African 318, Rowe to Stanley, 106, 1 July 1885.

consolidate this sphere of influence, and to settle the conflicts of its peoples by patient mediatory diplomacy and exhortation. In countless interminable palavers, perspiring white men extolled the benefits to be obtained through peaceful trade, formally exchanged small presents and effusive letters, delivered stipends of a few pounds to co-operative rulers while threatening to withhold them from the bellicose. They preached good liberal doctrines of the harmony of interests; but not all African rulers saw their interests as harmonising. Those who enjoyed government favour, or occupied strategic positions on the waterside, remained reluctant to share these privileges with others; those who remained disadvantaged, often suffering most from falling prices, looked to war as the only means of redressing the balance or employing their surplus population. Rowe's successes were at best precarious and temporary. In November 1885, for example, an armed force of Temnes from the troubled chiefdoms of Yonni, denied a direct outlet to the coast, invaded British territory at Songo. Next February, after being incessantly harangued for twenty-six days by fussy Major Augustus Festing, Yonni leaders could stand it no longer and agreed to keep the peace.[13] But there was no central authority to head the Yonni, who still felt disadvantaged by comparison with their neighbours; in October 1887 their raid on Senehun moved the Colonial Office to authorise a specially-organised military expedition under Colonel Sir Francis de Winton. Pacific diplomacy thus proved ineffective, and not particularly cheap.

Even the Colonial Office began to recognise that this particular brand of half-measures would not do. John Anderson, a future Permanent Under-Secretary, toyed with the old dream of withdrawal, only to reject it. It was not only that there would be a storm of indignation against any Minister who would thus sacrifice 'British interests'; Freetown harbour was now regarded as a naval coaling station of Imperial importance, and work had already begun to strengthen its defences. Given the necessity of consolidation, the Colonial Office gradually and reluctantly accepted the case, somewhat discursively argued by Rowe, that the financial problem was insoluble without a more active policy of exercising jurisdiction and a measure of police control over the

[13] C.O. 879/24, C.P. African 322, Rowe to Granville, 206, 18 June 1886, enclosing Festing's reports.

areas whose produce provided its revenues. In September 1886
Anderson used the word protectorate;[14] and after talks with Rowe
in London, the tentative lines of a new policy were authorised in
a despatch of 8 March 1887.[15] Holland disliked the idea not only
of new annexations, but of a formal protectorate – there was no
threat of intrusion by European rivals, and he may have doubted
whether the states of the region were sufficiently well-ordered
entities to provide adequate foundations for a system of remote
British overrule; but he did approve a modified form of proposals
which Rowe had made for consolidating the British sphere of influence, even though they involved increased expenditure. A road
was to be cleared joining the heads of navigation on the rivers
from the Great Scarcies to the Mano, thus enclosing a belt of
territory extending about thirty miles inland. This area was to be
supervised by two Travelling Commissioners and patrolled by
Colonial Police, augmented for the purpose by 100 extra men.
'This proposal', the Colonial Office warned, 'involves no responsibility for the defence of the tribes in the districts concerned
against attack from tribes outside, and avoids all interference with
the internal economy and institutions of the people'. Despite this
caution the measures authorised (though not immediately effected)
represented a decisive extension of British responsibility on another
colonial frontier; a step towards a protectorate in fact if not in
name.

SAMORI'S CONTACTS WITH THE BRITISH, 1885–7

The physical horizon's of Rowe's policy were limited by his preoccupation with speedy fiscal returns. 'It is from the Sherbro district that the increased revenue of the Settlement must come so
long as the northern limits . . . do not extend beyond Scarcies,' he
believed.[16] But many Sierra Leoneans had invested considerable
emotional capital in the prospect of connecting Freetown to
established networks of interior trade. Indeed the Colony had

[14] C.O. 879/24, C.P. African 323, No. 33, Minute by Anderson, 4
September 1886. For background on the defence question (as on many
other matters treated in this chapter), see C. H. Fyfe, *A History of Sierra
Leone*, pp. 438–9; cf. within pp. 185–6.

[15] Ibid., No. 56, Herbert to Rowe, 8 March 1887.

[16] Ibid., No. 46, Rowe to C.O., 21 December 1886; cf. Africa 322, No.
3, Rowe to Granville, 122, 26 April 1886; G. H. Garrett, 'Sierra Leone
and the Interior . . .', *Proceedings RGS*, ns. 14 (1892) p. 436.

always done some profitable business with the *dyulas* who came down through Futa Jalon and Falaba to exchange their gold, ivory, hides and other products for imported goods. In Freetown, the shrewd and experienced Government Interpreter T. G. Lawson acted as their patron and 'landlord'; his figures showed that in 1884 a record number of 11,000 traders reached Freetown from beyond Falaba, 3400 more during the first quarter of 1883.[17] In general Rowe wished to encourage this caravan trade; it was he who in April 1879 had first sent messengers to Samori, as part of a general approach to Muslim rulers in the Western Sudan.[18] But he set only limited hopes upon such overtures, believing (on the whole realistically) that 'the produce which comes to the coast from the districts beyond 100 or 150 miles inland is of little importance compared with that that comes from districts nearer to us.'[19] This was particularly true from the fiscal point of view; many traders simply transhipped their hides and rubber to the Mellacourie, where tobacco could be bought more cheaply, and those who remained in Freetown bought textiles rather than spirits, and so contributed little to the colonial revenue.[20] Rowe therefore showed only limited interest when messengers from Samori began to reach Freetown around the time of his return to the colony.

Since his clashes with the French, Samori had grasped the importance of securing a supply of foreign weapons that would be beyond their control. Early in 1884 Langama-Fali (known to the British as Impha Allieu), recently appointed to command a new Western army of some 5000 men,[21] defeated the Houbous, a group of Fula dissidents from Futa Jalon who under their leader Abal had been impeding the route to Freetown, and then attacked the important staging-post of Falaba. It was these successes which explained the increase in long-range caravans reaching Freetown in early 1884. These *dyulas* brought to Lawson clear and consistent reports of Samori's intentions; while his essential purpose was to wage a *jihad*, his immediate aim was 'to clear the whole of the

[17] Sierra Leone Archives GILB, cf. J. D. Hargreaves, 'The Evolution of the Native Affairs Department', *SLS*, n.s.3 (1954) pp. 168–84.

[18] *Prelude*, p. 244.

[19] C.O. 879/24, C.P. African 318, No. 4, Rowe to Derby, 106, 1 July 1885.

[20] C.O. 879/24 C.P. African 323, No. 49, Hay to Stanhope, 13 December 1886.

[21] Person, *Samori*, II, pp. 1033ff.

interior road from molestation to travellers and that the road will
be so free that a single woman can walk from the Interior to the
waterside without being injured . . .'[22] 'It is gratifying', wrote
Lawson, 'to see strangers passing in the streets with ivory on their
shoulders going to the merchants' shops seeking where they can
obtain the best prices; this had been stopped for a long time.'[23]
But Samori's victories and the prospect of further advances towards the sea also brought problems for the colony. His agents
intervened in the troubled politics of the Mellacourie on behalf
of Bokkari, Rowe's old *protégé*; and they also put new pressure
upon Temne, Loko and Limba chiefdoms which fell within the
colony's sphere of commercial and diplomatic influence. Samori's
messengers moved towards the coast, lugubriously bearing limbs
of the late Abal, and called upon rulers not only to open the roads
but to build mosques and embrace Islam.[24] 'There is a great
shaking just now among the countries below Falaba,' Lawson
reported; 'the motto of the war coming down is very good in
itself but the proceedings should be closely watched by the Government.'[25]

Since Samori's aim was to secure a stable relationship with
Freetown, he was amenable to British sensitivities. In response to
friendly messages from Governor Havelock[26] he sent as envoy a
rich Kankan *dyula* called Dauda Kaba, who reached Freetown in
January 1885, just before Rowe's return. Besides concluding business arrangements for the purchase of arms, Dauda sought an
interview with the acting Governor, and asked that Samori might
receive one of the silver medals presented to chiefs in special
British favour. Such a medal was duly ordered by the Colonial
Office;[27] but Rowe, preoccupied by problems closer at hand, was
in no hurry to present it. Instead he sent Sanoko Madi (the same
messenger as in 1879) to warn Samori to keep away from the
Temne and Limba countries and to invite him to send another

[22] G.I.L.B., Lawson memo, 4 March 1884; Person, *Samori*, II, pp. 453–
73.
[23] G.I.L.B., Lawson to J. W. Lewis, 17 March 1884.
[24] Ibid., Lawson memos, 19 April, 22 April, 1 August 1884.
[25] Ibid., Lawson memos, 27 October, 3 October, 1884.
[26] Ibid., Lawson memo, 3 October 1884.
[27] Ibid., Lawson to Lewis, 4 February 1885, C.O. 879/24, C.P. African
318, No. 1, Pinkett to Derby, 32, 3 February 1885; No. 2, Derby to
Rowe, 6 March 1885. Person, *Samori*, II, p. 467, II, p. 616.

emissary. In August Nalifa Modu, a confidant of Samori, reached Freetown. He announced that Samori, out of respect for Rowe, would desist from his intention of invading Temne and Limba chiefdoms; that his own domains were 'free to all traders and travellers'; and that (according to an oral message) 'he wishes the Governor to ask the Queen to take the whole of his country under her protection.'[28]

Rowe's response to this last suggestion was extremely cool; he did not report it to London for nearly a year, and in his reply to the Sofas concentrated on warnings to respect 'the Queen's garden'.

'I want peace' [he warned Langama-Fali] 'so that the people may be able to plant and reap their crops without fear; I want a clear road, so that people may pass up and down to trade without being robbed, I want you all to know that Port Lokkoh and Mabelly are the waterside towns of this place to which strangers should pass when they are coming to trade with my people here. You say yourself and the Alimamy wish to be friends with my Queen – I am glad to hear it and shall always be glad to do all I can to help you, but I must tell you that the great Queen of England only extends her friendship to such persons as deserve it, and if your Alimamy and yourself wish to enjoy this friendship you must do your best to prove yourselves worthy of it by keeping the country in your charge quiet and doing your best to keep all the roads in your country free for trade . . .'[29]

The offer of a protectorate, Rowe assumed, was essentially formal:

'of the same character as the statement of the polite Spaniard who says that his house is entirely at the disposition of his visitor, and on a par with that of Native Chiefs who say that their country and everything in it belongs to the Queen to do whatever she likes with it. Such a statement does not in any way

[28] C.P. African 318, No. 6, Rowe to Stanley, 158, 31 August 1885; No. 11, Rowe to Granville, 19 June 1886, and enclosure 2, message delivered by Nalifa Modu, 25 August 1885. S.L.A. Minute Paper 1400/1885, Impha Allieu to Rowe, translated, 10 August 1885.

[29] Sierra Leone Archives, Minute Paper 1400/85, Rowe to Impha Allieu, Aborigines 45, 4 September 1885.

necessarily imply that Her Majesty or her representative may touch a single article without permission.[30]

While accepting generally that it would be useful if Samori's power in the interior could be maintained, and if possible 'exercised under English influence', Rowe had no confidence that Samori could prevent or greatly delay the French conquest; he did not want to become too closely involved with a potential loser, or to jeopardise relations with old associates on his account.[31]

Prudent though it was, Rowe's analysis not only underestimated Samori's military capacity but failed to foresee (as Lawson shortly did)[32] the possible short-term value of a treaty, even in the weaker form of an undertaking by Samori not to alienate his territories without British consent. Although the French government were bent on controlling the upper basin of the Niger, since Combes's debacle they had accepted the need to play the game by rules which gave high value to treaties with African states. In 1885 the Quai d'Orsay would have felt bound to examine any British treaty seriously – not out of respect for Samori's sovereignty, but because refusal to do so would expose to critical British scrutiny their own titles to control such states as Futa Jalon. Paradoxically, the very scepticism which most European officials felt about the real significance of treaties made by African rulers helped preserve some significance for such documents. Hence, even though Rowe's assessment of Samori's intentions was probably realistic, August 1885 seems a missed opportunity in the frontier policy of Sierra Leone.

Samori however was not discouraged. As French pressure on his territories increased he redoubled his expression of friendship and intensified his purchases of arms. When the caravan routes to Freetown were impeded, as at Tambaca in the upper Scarcies, Langama-Fali's troops moved to re-open them in the interests of both parties.[33] Lawson saw that routine dealings with the Sofas were sympathetically handled, and every desultory gesture of friendship which Rowe could be persuaded to make was effusively

[30] C.P. African 318, No. 11, Rowe to Granville, 208, 19 June 1886.
[31] Ibid., No. 7, Rowe to Stanley, 187, 12 October 1885.
[32] G.I.L.B.; Lawson memo, 2 November 1885 and 8 October 1886.
[33] G.I.L.B.; Lawson Memo, 4 January 1886. Lawson's quarterly returns of caravans show a marked fall between mid-1885 and November 1886.

reciprocated by Samori's scribes. 'What white men can do so for us but the English?' Samori's declared when some Sofa officers taken prisoner in Moriah were returned to him, 'protecting all our people and everywhere, especially Governor Rowe. He was the first Governor that sent me a letter with a present about six years ago, and it is he I take to be my friend.'[34] In November 1886 Samori's kinsman Lansana Touré brought Rowe assurances (which he repeated on a further visit three months later) that the Alimami had not ceded his country to France, 'that he desires to be no intimate friend to any other European nation but the English', and that he would welcome a visit from Major Festing of the Colonial Secretariat.[35]

This affection for Rowe was unrequited; the Governor was less influenced by Samori's blandishments than by fears that reports of his forced conversions would incite a violent reaction among the colony's animist neighbours, and so ruin the trade of the producing area. During 1887 a long period of residence in Gambia (still under the Government of Sierra Leone) reinforced his Islamophobia. Rowe now compared Samori's Sofas to the 'allied class' of militant Muslims represented by Foday Kabba–

> haughty, idle slave-holders, keeping their women in stern subjection and seclusion, jealous of the approach of the white man to their districts and insulting him whenever they dare, making their religious belief an excuse for the plunder and subjection of comparatively peaceful industrious, simple-living pagan tribes.

Complaining that Britain had missed opportunities to form a 'buffer' of 'Soninke' states around her Gambia settlements, Rowe urged the Colonial Office:

> to recognise the importance at Sierra Leone of surrounding her colony by tribes who are amenable to her influence, and who will, if properly used, form a useful barrier against the approaching Mohammedan hordes.[36]

[34] C.O. 879/24, C.P. African 318, No. 22, encl. statement by Santiigi Moroba, 3 November 1886, cf. above p. 177.

[35] Ibid., No. 24, Hay to Stanhope, 444, 19 November 1886; Memo by Lawson, 18 November; statement by Allanssanah Tooray, 18 February 1887; cf. Person, *Samori*, II, pp. 472–3.

[36] Ibid., No. 58, Rowe to Holland 9, 12 June 1887. Cf. the view of Rowe in Person, *Samori*, I, p. 16. Cf. within pp. 228–9.

Among the Africans and Europeans of Freetown, very different ideas on the colony's future were being expressed. At first, most members of the Sierra Leone Association showed Rowe's belief that the solution of the crisis would have to be found within the adjacent producing areas; but they soon began to express disappointment with his methods, which seemed both costly and ineffective. On 6 August 1885 the eminent Creole lawyer and Legislative Councillor Samuel Lewis made a powerful though essentially negative critique of government policy at a meeting in the West African Hotel; this was continued two weeks later in an evening of lively but somewhat imprecise discussion of the relative merits of annexation and protectorate as methods of controlling adjacent districts. Some participants were aware that the arrival of Samori's messengers had injected a new element into the situation, but most were uncertain of the proper response. Lewis, like Vohsen, seemed to regard Samori chiefly as a menace to the 'coast-tribes' and hoped this might make them more willing to accept British control; but he added, somewhat vaguely, that the government should also 'endeavour to perpetuate relations with him for the ultimate object we have of uninterrupted access to the interior for British merchandise'.[37]

Among Lewis's audience was a Negro intellectual who for twenty years had been arguing that West African Islam represented a civilising and organising force which African Christians should welcome as a partner in the opening-up of Africa. There could have been no more convincing manifestation of this vision of Edward Blyden than the appearance of Samori's messengers; 'providentially', Blyden declared, 'a force has been brought to the doors of the Settlement for the purpose apparently of being utilized for the great object before this country.'[38] Soon afterwards, in a letter sympathetically received by the Colonial Office, Blyden called for a dramatic new policy by which Britain would annex 'the comparatively unimportant population who are pagan and illiterate, inhabiting the Koranko, Limba, Loko and Timmanee countries'; offset the French drive to create 'a Catholic Muham-

---

[37] Sierra Leone Association: Paper by Samuel Lewis (Freetown, 1885) esp. pp. 10, 34, 36–7. This pamphlet is reprinted in C.O. 879/24, C.P. African 318a, encl. in No. 6.

[38] Ibid., pp. 20–4.

madan empire from Algiers to Futah Jallo'; and by collaboration with Samori open a field for settlement by the 'millions of practical Negro agriculturalists and mechanics' anxious to emigrate from the U.S.A.[39] During the coming years, although the Sierra Leone Association itself soon broke up, some Sierra Leoneans became increasingly attracted by such ambitious projects.[40]

Pro-Muslim doctrines now gained ground in the section of the secretariat charged with frontier policy. Old T. G. Lawson, who remained Government Interpreter until December 1888, saw his first priority as maintaining confidence in the Temne areas he knew so well, and was initially cautious about the idea favoured by 'many of our leading men . . . of placing agents among them [the Sofas]'.[41] But during 1886 he repeatedly brought Samori's power to the Governor's attention, emphasising 'how very necessary it is that some definite relation should exist between the British Government and himself'.[42] His collaborator and successor, Ernest Parkes, was a young Creole intellectual who felt the appeal of Blyden's views more directly. And similar attitudes gained ground with the European officer who supervised their work, Major Festing. By June 1886 this vain and garrulous man – formerly a paymaster in the Indian Army, now an intemperate Islamophil who affected Muslim dress – was also warning Rowe not to underestimate Samori's importance.[43] Although no friend of the Creole *élite*, once set loose in the Muslim north Festing was to outdo the most idealistic disciples of Blyden.

The problem of how the Colonial government could hold the balance between the Sofas and those who might feel threatened by them had now been raised in relation to Suluku, Limba chief of Biriwa, whose mountain capital of Bumban lay on the vital

[39] C.O. 267/362, Blyden to Rowe, 22 October 1885 (encl. in Rowe 32, 21 January 1886).

[40] E.g. Lewis in a Centenary Oration of 21 June 1887, regretting the Colony's failure to maintain regular contact with 'the far interior countries vast and rich'. *Memorial of the Celebration of the Jubilee of Her Majesty's Reign and of the Centenary of Sierra Leone* (1887) pp. 85–8.

[41] Sierra Leone Archives, Minute Papers 1400/85 [?], Lawson to Rowe, 20 August 1885.

[42] C.O. 879/25, C.P. African 332, Despatch . . . enclosing Information regarding the different districts and tribes of Sierra Leone and its Vicinity, Chap. 16.

[43] C.O. 879/24, C.P. African 318, p. 15, Festing to Rowe, 15 June 1886.

trade routes from Falaba. His country was beyond the range of Creole traders, but within the periphery of the Colony's system of diplomacy and treaties.[44] Islam had been advancing among the Limbas for decades and Suluku's position depended on his success in balancing the interests of his Muslim subjects against other groups within the state; the arrival of Sofa forces on his territory in 1885, demanding his conversion to Islam, not only led to a strain on his food supplies, but presented a serious internal threat. Suluku and the other Limba chiefs are more in fear of the Mohammedan children born in their country . . . who are seen as co-operating with the Sofas, for many have joined them openly,' the colony's messengers reported.[45]

In November 1886 Suluku sought to involve Sierra Leone more directly; faced by excessive requisitions for rice to supply Samori's campaign against Tiéba, he sent messengers asking for a mediatory visit by Festing, reputed to be 'the friend of those people of the east'.[46] The Colonial Office, advised by Rowe in London, hoped that Festing might combine the mission with the visit simultaneously requested by Samori; but by the time this decision was taken and the necessary expenditure authorised, there was only time for Festing to go to Bumban, and the mission to Samori was deferred until after the rains.[47] Festing eventually spent the period 27 March to 8 April in Bumban; keeping his Muslim sympathies under control, he used the well-known eloquence to reconcile the local Sofa commanders with Suluku.[48] But it seems probable that Festing was already dreaming of the great blow which he might strike for the economic and political interests of the British Empire by applying his gifts of persuasion to Samori himself.

[44] In 1869 Winwood Reade discovered that Chief Sankelle had a treaty entitling him to an annual stipend which had not been paid for twenty years; though contact was then resumed it appears soon to have been lost again.

[45] Ruth Finnegan and D. J. Murray, 'Limba Chiefs' in M. Crowder and O. Ikime (ed.) *West African Chiefs* (Ife, 1970) pp. 409–13. G.I.L.B. Report by Momodu Wakka and Weeks, 2 December 1886.

[46] C.O. 879/24, C.P. African 318, No. 26, Hay to Stanhope, 459, 4 December 1886; No. 29, 12, 8 January 1887; Person, *Samori*, II, p. 620.

[47] Ibid., No. 38, Memo by Rowe, 24 February 1887; No. 39, C.O. to F.O., 28 February 1887; encl. Memo by Rowe, 21 February; No. 42, Holland to Hay, Tel., 3 March 1887.

[48] His report was belatedly published in P.P. (1892) LVI, C.6687.

SAMORI BETWEEN FRANCE AND BRITAIN

The possibility that the fate of Samori's state might be a matter of serious concern to the British Empire first began to be accepted in Whitehall during 1886, when General Brackenbury, head of the War Office Intelligence Branch, began to compare Rowe's reports with unofficial or semi-official items gleaned from French newspapers. What worried Brackenbury was the vulnerability of Freetown, 'the most important coaling station and harbour refuge between the British Isles and the Cape of Good Hope'. Although the Commission on Imperial Defence which Lord Carnarvon chaired between 1879 and 1882 had recommended fortification of the harbour, the work was still hardly begun, and was in any case directed towards defence from seaborne attack. On the landward side the colony seemed as vulnerable as the Gold Coast forts had been earlier in the century and Samori's military capacity was probably greater than that of Asante. But it was not only a disastrous humiliation at African hands that was at risk; the newspaper reports raised the grim possibility that in case of war the French might try to use Samori's forces to overrun or neutralise Freetown harbour.

The reports of course deliberately exaggerated the concessions which Samori had made to France in the Treaty of Kenieba on 28 March 1886; there was no French protectorate, and no possibility that Samori would agree to act as a French client.[49] When the Foreign Office tried to verify the press reports, the Quai d'Orsay deliberately hedged, hoping that Gallieni might still supply the judicial basis for formally claiming a protectorate. On 12 October 1886 they communicated an evasive note, affirming that agreement had been established in principle between Samori and Colonel Frey, and misleadingly implying that this assured France of a protectorate over Samori's dominions on the left bank of the Niger.[50]

The War Office concluded that 'there is no doubt . . . that a treaty has been concluded between Samodu and the French

---

[49] Cf. above pp. 62–3.
[50] C.O. 879/24, C.P. African 318, No. 17, Egerton to Iddesleigh, 12 October 1886, enclosing French Note; cf. B. O. Oloruntimehim, 'Franco-Samori relations, 1886–1889; Diplomacy as War', *JHSN*, VI (1971) pp. 75–7.

Government'; as a long-term response they favoured negotiations with the French government for a partition of influence in the region, perhaps along the line of the eleventh parallel (which would of course have partitioned Samori's empire). But the political climate in France was still unfavourable, and in any case negotiations of this sort would need careful preparation if gains and concessions were to be balanced in all the disputed territories of West Africa. More immediately Brackenbury recommended:

> that we should establish the most friendly relations with Samadu, and that at the same time we should endeavour to create a barrier to his further progress towards the coast, by forming a confederation of the friendly tribes, such as was formed on the Gold Coast by Sir Charles McCarthy as a barrier against the Ashantee power.[51]

This somewhat ambivalent prescription largely reflected Rowe's own attitudes; but the War Office intervention underlined the expediency of sending the mission which Samori had just requested through Lansana Touré. However, partly because the Foreign Office failed to despatch the papers with sufficient urgency, the Colonial Office began to arrange this only in February 1887, and there was time only for Festing to pay his mediatory visit to the Limbas before the summer's rains. The mission to Samori was thus deferred. It seems that Rowe himself would have enjoyed the excitement and prestige of leading it;[52] had he done so he would have leaned towards the policy of 'creating a barrier' rather than that of alliance. But for much of 1887 both Rowe and Festing were occupied in the Gambia; and when there was an opportunity to take up Samori's invitation, the Colonial Office decided that, as requested, Festing should go.

During the year which the British had lost Samori's new zeal to enforce the stricter observance of Islam, and his related decision to move his main armies against Tiéba, had led him to agree to a French protectorate, in the Treaty signed with Péroz at Bisandugu on 25 March 1887.[53] The French Foreign Office decided to

[51] C.P. African 318, No. 28, F.O. to C.O., 22 January 1887, encl. W.O. to F.O., 17 December 1886. Cf. C.O. 879/26, C.P. African 334, No. 121, Note by Brackenbury, 27 January 1887.

[52] C.P. African 318, Nos. 39, 61, Rowe to C.O. (London), 21 February; to Holland (Bathurst), 8 September 1887.

[53] See above pp. 75–7.

keep this document secret until they had completed a system of Treaties which would exclude any possibility of British penetration of the upper Niger basin.[54] but again there were leakages. In June the Gambettist paper *La Republique française* published an unofficial text, and in July a statement by Gallieni claimed that the reference to Samori's *future* conquests might authorise the extension of French protection to Temne and Loko country. When these papers became rather belatedly known to Whitehall in November 1887, concern to keep French influence away from the neighbourhood of Freetown was redoubled.[55] Since no protectorate had been formally notified, the Colonial Office decided to expedite the mission of equiry, which Samori had continued to request. Festing had indeed been zealously preparing for this since his return from Bumban in May; but his preparations had been delayed by the Gambia campaign and by hesitations on the part of Rowe, of whom Festing had become intensely jealous and resentful. 'He is passé and useless any more . . . I am sick and tired of working with such a dawdler,' Festing wrote of his former patron. He was in no mood to be fettered by over-scrupulous obedience to Rowe's ponderous and pessimistic instructions.[56]

When he finally began his journey on 16 January 1888, Festing was feeling the physical and mental strain of three years arduous service in the claustrophic atmosphere of colonial Sierra Leone. But he was fortified through the trying experiences to come, not only by pride at having been directly appointed by the Colonial Office as Her Majesty's Commissioner, but by a strong sense of Divine favour in the personal mission to unite the moral forces of West African Islam with Protestant Britain. Scornful of the Creoles with their 'coating of European varnish',[57] Festing shared the contemporary European prejudices that Africans improved in direct proportion to their distance from the coast. The Temnes

[54] AE Afrique 122, De la Porte to Flourens, 3 April 1888.

[55] C.P. African 318, No. 63, W.O. to C.O., 10 November 1887; Nos. 64, 67, Holland to Rowe, Tels, 12, 16 November; C.O. 276/369, Minutes by Hemming, 11 November, Holland, 12 November.

[56] This diary, on which the following paragraphs are largely based, is printed in C.O. 879/29, C.P. African (West) 366. Entry for 12 January. (Cf. 1 March, etc.) Rowe's instructions to Festing are enclosed in C.P. African 318, Nos. 84 and 86.

[57] *Diary*, Entry for 10 June.

(who made difficulties over providing carriers at Porto Loko) were
'a despicably dilatory lot; they want the white man to help them
all they can, and render none in return. The chiefs are only so in
name; they have no power.'[58] The Lokos were no better; the
Limbas, a slight improvement. But the dominant conviction which
spurred Festing on was that Samori's empire remained a thriving
concern; that reports of his submission to the French were incredible and untrue; and that the future of West Africa lay in a close
alliance between the British empire and this strong native power.
Early meetings with Samori would confirm Festing's initial assumption that 'he is a Napoleon'.[59] When faced in the Sulima
district with evidence of resistance to the exactions which Samori
was imposing to support his campaign against Tiéba, Festing
solemnly treated the spokesmen to a splendid Whig interpretation
of English history.

> Told them all publicly that I wanted to see a united people,
> loyal to their Almami, whom they should acknowledge as their
> lawful ruler, and sink all tribal differences. Gave them history
> of the Heptarchy, etc., and of conquest of Scotland, Wales and
> Ireland, and how we are all one people now.[60]

Festing's plans for collaboration with Samori went considerably
beyond his instructions. While waiting to leave Freetown he had
lodged with T. J. Alldridge, a trader in the area since 1871 and
currently agent for the long-established London trading house of
F. & A. Swanzy. Festing's friendship with Alldridge was close
enough for Rowe to harbour suspicions of financial irregularity,
which Festing indignantly rejected.[61] But Festing did have a sub-
sidiary mission in Swanzy's interest about which he kept Alldridge
informed by very regular correspondence; he was seeking a concession of rights to establish trading stations and to build a railway
within Samori's empire. Andrew Swanzy, who had sponsored
Winwood Reade's journey to the upper Niger in 1869, had died
in 1880, leaving the business in the hands of his son (Francis
Swanzy the younger), William Cleaver and F. J. Crocker. I found
no evidence that they directly instigated this scheme and a phrase

[58] *Diary*, Entry for 21 January.
[59] Ibid., p. 120; Festing to Alldridge, 13 June 1888.
[60] *Diary*. Entry for 23 February.
[61] *Diary*, Entry for 12, 17, 18 January.

in one of Festing's letters[62] suggests that it originated in his own mind; he clearly hoped that the house of Swanzy might eventually secure an Imperial Charter, and join the Niger company in extending British influence into the Muslim interior. This advance of empire was to be achieved in genuine partnership with the Sudanese 'Napoleon'; Festing was undoubtedly sincere when he told Samori that 'we did not want his land, only the trade of his country, and that were he to offer me the whole of his territory, Her Majesty would not accept one single inch.'[63]

Despite his dogged courage, Festing's mission ended in frustration and eventual tragedy. During the early stages of his journey Samori's agents, while expressing general pleasure at Festing's appearance, hesitated to authorise him to proceed to their sovereign; though warmly welcomed in Bisandugu on 24 March, he was not authorised to proceed to Samori's military headquarters outside Sikasso until 21 April. Arriving there on 19 May, Festing was kept waiting for a further six weeks, his health and morale draining away as Samori engaged in intermittent but always inconclusive negotiations.[64]

Samori was in fact facing an acute internal crisis. As he attempted to tighten his theocratic rule he encountered increasing resistance from many provinces, and his empire was beginning to be shaken by widespread revolts. As the needs of the campaign against Tiéba imposed intensified requisitions upon the conquered provinces for tribute, conscripts and supplies, Samori's attempts to convert the laws and institutions of his state towards a theocratic

[62]A heavily-edited version of Festing's letters to Alldridge appears in C.P. African (West) 366. In that of 13 June, which gives the fullest detail of this project, Festing states, 'Long before the mighty Lemberg moved in the matter, I have felt convinced that a railway from Freetown to the navigable head of the Niger, Siguiri... in conjunction with a steamboat on its waters would be the finest thing for the opening up of this country, and for Freetown...' Philip Lemberg held a public meeting in Freetown in mid-1888 to arouse interest in a railway scheme for which he had tried to obtain a subsidy in 1886. This idea however seems to have originated with Blyden and seems to have been suggested to Lemberg by the Creole printer T. J. Sawyerr. (Lemberg, *The Commerce of Sierra Leone*; cf. O. Omusini, Railway projects and British Attitudes towards the Development of West Africa, JHSN, V, 1971, p. 501; Fyfe, *History*, p. 529.)

[63] *Diary*, entry of 20 May.

[64] These are described in the *Diary*, and analysed in Person, *Samori*, II, pp. 625–9.

model encountered deep-seated resistance. The basic units of Mandinka society, the *kafu*, felt their traditional identity threatened; and the loyalty of many of them was undermined by the presence of a French garrison at Siguiri. 'They have expelled your ruling *marabouts* (*Karamogho*), saying that the white men permit paganism and alcohol,' Samori's wife reported to him in mid-1888.[65] By the beginning of the rains of 1888 many provinces were in open revolt and communications were cut, not only between the central provinces and the supply ports of the coast, but between Bisandugu and Samori's army besieging Sikasso.[66]

Festing's belated arrival thus came at an embarrasing moment. Samori had been technically committed to French protection since March 1887, and he could not safely break the Treaty of Bisandugu (disappointing though it had proved) while the centre of his empire lay exposed to French attack. Hence Festing, though he continued to believe against the evidence that Samori was uncommitted to the French, could not secure his signature to the twenty-two articles of 'peace, friendship and alliance' which he had prepared. Apart from such difficulties as those involved in promising free access for Christian missionaries to his increasingly theocratic empire, it was impossible for Samori to undertake not to cede his territory or enter into treaties without British approval, or truthfully to assert that apart from 'a treaty of peace only' he had no such agreements with the French. Eventually, on 3 July, Samori formally declared his intention 'of signing the treaty agreed on between Major Festing and myself, so soon as the Bambara war is over'.[67] Since he had already granted Festing concessions for the construction of a railway and the establishment of a trading station at Falaba,[68] the Major set out for home with a certain residual euphoria, hoping that once placed in Swanzy's hands these would provide a basis for opening up the country. But his health had been undermined; on 17 August, Festing died in

[65] Tradition cited in Person, *Samori*, II, p. 1109, n.l. On the Islamisation of the empire, cf. above pp. 75–7.

[66] Person, *Samori*, II, pp. 1049ff., for a comprehensive study of 'The Great Revolt'.

[67] The draft of the treaty and Festing's formal report are in C.P. African 318, No. 126.

[68] The signed originals of these concessions are in C.O. 267/371, Hay to Knutsford, Conf. 25, 31 October 1888. Samori also offered a site at Bisandugu; Festing judged this impracticable.

Sankaran without having to face the inevitable censure of the
Colonial Office for having changed his mission from a simple
reconnaissance into an empire-building venture.[69]

It is not too difficult to understand Samori's purposes during
this tragical-comical episode. The initial welcome which Festing
thought he detected was in the hope that he might be bringing
material assistance; Samori's message to Bisandugu on 1 April
was that 'he does not want the white man to proceed to him unless
he brings guns and powder.'[70] On reflection Samori realised that
the prolonged presence of a European in his camp during the siege
of Sikasso would be of psychological advantage (though Festing,
like Binger before him, was shrewd enough to see the danger of
identifying himself too closely with Samori's cause.)[71] Still obsessed
by his feud with Tiéba, Samori declared that for the sake of
victory 'he would give up all . . . and he added, whoever would
help him to do so, to him, whether black or white, he would give
his country.'[72] But Festing's long-winded eloquence offered no
hope of immediate aid; and without this Samori, though by now
he must have abandoned any hopes of assistance from Gallieni,
would take steps which might justify the French in attacking his
rear.[73] The prospect of closer commercial relations with Sierra
Leone, now clearly designated as the main source of modern
weapons for the re-equipment of his army, could be safely and
advantageously accepted; but Samori would not recover freedom
of political manoeuvre until he had re-established his authority
over his own rebellious subjects.

By September he was making progress in this direction, at the
price of having reluctantly abandoned the siege of Sikasso. Moving

[69] C.O. 267/371, Minute by Hemming, 5 November, on Maltby to
Knutsford, 292, 13 October 1888.

[70] *Diary*, 1 April.

[71] C.P. African 318, p. 169, Festing to Governor, 1 July 1888; cf.
Person, *Samori*, II, p. 769.

[72] C.P. African 366, p. 119, Festing to Alldridge, 13 June 1888.

[73] C.P. African 318, p. 168, Festing to Governor, 1 July: 'the real
reason . . . for his declining to sign now is that he is afraid the French,
when they hear he has done so, will at once attack him in his most vital
part, Busandu [sc. Bisandugu], etc., when he is away. *Nothing* will persuade
him to the contrary.' Cf. above, Chap. 2, pp. 77–8, for Gallieni's growing
hostility.

his operational headquarters to Nyako, south-east of Kankan, Samori took vigorous and sometimes sanguinary measures to suppress the rebels. But he still needed reassurance against hostile action from the French. Samori's relations with Gallieni had come to be marked by intense actual distrust and suspicion; but in October 1888 Gallieni was succeeded as Commander in the Sudan by his own nominee, Major Louis Archinard of the Marine Artillery.

This ambitious and unscrupulous soldier had none of Gallieni's intellectual subtleties, nor the talent for devious diplomacy which went with them. He regarded it as his personal mission to liberate the Western Sudan from Muslim tyrannies by military force, and so to open the area to the rough but eventually civilising power of French imperialism. His temperament and prejudices ran counter to any serious thought of real collaboration with Muslim states, even in the semi-academic spirit in which Gallieni sometimes discussed that idea. But until his forces in the Sudan had been built up, and assured of political support in Paris, simple tactical commonsense suggested dealing with opponents one at a time. Gallieni, whose prior concern had been to ensure a French monopoly of the upper basin of the Niger, had been prepared to accept a stable relationship with Ahmadu while working to undermine Samori's power; but Archinard had inherited from Borgnis-Desbordes (now in the powerful post of military adviser to the Colonial Department) a distrust of the Tokolors, and an ambition to push French power further down the Niger towards Timbuktu. It thus seemed that the military exploits which would hasten his coveted promotion to the rank of Lieutenant-Colonel could best be performed at Ahmadu's expense; on 18 February 1889 he showed his hand by a sudden unprovoked attack on the outlying Tokolor fortress of Koundian.[74]

Archinard, a believer in rough wooing where Africans were concerned, initially adopted a haughty and minatory attitude[75] towards Samori. But Samori returned a soft answer, and indeed seems to have taken the initiative by offering to cede to France his remaining territories on the left bank of the Niger. The exact nature of this offer seems ambiguous – possibly Samori simply intended to convey to France lands where his rebellious subjects

[74] See Kanya-Forstner, *Conquest* . . . , pp. 174ff.
[75] For samples, see Méniaud, *Pionniers*, II, Chap. 5.

seemed hopelessly out of control – but Archinard found the approach encouraging. A temporary understanding with Samori could secure the French rear during the coming operations against Ahmadu, debar the Tokolors from any hope of aid from Sierra Leone, and stifle any attempt to organise an African coalition against France. Archinard therefore allowed Samori to resume trade in guns and horses along the northern routes under French control, and then drafted a new treaty which accepted the offered territories, confirmed France's protectorate over the rest of the empire, and so – Archinard hoped – finally excluded all danger of British intrusion into the Niger basin. For a time, Archinard seems to have been seduced by the vision of making Samori a compliant collaborator. 'I hope soon to be able to report that the treaty with Samori will be so modified as to give us the whole left bank of the Niger,' he telegraphed to Saint-Louis on 13 January. 'I concede nothing in return; Samori's embarrassments have made him afraid. There will be no need to construct new posts; a rich country is saved from ruin and brought under our close authority as far as Sierra Leone and Liberia.'[76] Archinard's text was taken by Lieutenant Bonnardot to Nyako, where Samori signed it on 21 February 1889, though with important verbal reservations. These excluded from the treaty those rulers on the left bank who had willingly accepted Samori's alliance or overlordship, and insisted that Samori maintain the vital right to trade with Sierra Leone.[77]

This curious liaison could not last. Samori was a proud and impetuous man, and his difficulties were not serious enough to turn him into the sort of compliant collaborator which alone would satisfy Archinard. He was angry when French officers continued to interfere in territories which he regarded as his own, and probably worried by the French attack on Koundian; within two months of signing the treaty he refused to meet Archinard at Siguiri, as originally arranged, or to receive a French Resident. When Archinard then led a fighting patrol down the left bank to occupy Kouroussa and clashed with some of Samori's allies on the way, Samori denounced the Treaty of Nyako by returning the document to the French (though he retained the earlier treaties of 1886 and 1887). Each party had quickly lost faith in the other's

[76] Quoted from ANSOM, Senegal IV/93 in Person, *Samori*, II, p. 1119.
[77] Person, *Samori*, II, pp. 1072–5. The text of the treaty may be found in E. Rouard de Card, *Les Traités* . . . , pp. 231–2.

goodwill. But since each had more urgent preoccupations the uneasy truce between them remained in force for a further two years, until Archinard felt strong enough to resort to arms against both Ahmadu and Samori at once.[78]

Samori's political skill, helped by a measure of good fortune, enabled him to use this truce to re-establish control of the bulk of his empire by the beginning of 1890. Among the forces working towards this end was the growing perception, which Samori shared with some of his African neighbours, of the menace to African independence inherent in the development of French military policy. Ibrahima Suri of Futa Jalon, who had resented the invasion of his territory by Plat and Audéoud, was reported to favour some sort of coalition. Tiéba, who after the raising of the siege of Sikasso had taken advantage of the rebellion to invade Samori's empire, did not press his attack; and Archinard's attempts to reassure him about French intentions did not reverse his growing suspicions of his former allies. The Tokolors, who in November 1888 had also invaded Samori's territories under Ahmadu's half-brother Madani, were warned of Archinard's hostile intentions by Aguibou; after the attacks on Koundian they began to negotiate for a rapprochment with Samori.[80]

Relieved from some of the hostility of his African neighbours, Samori concentrated on re-establishing his control in the heartlands of his empire, combining fierce military repression with a greater readiness to respect indigenous customs and abate his proselytising zeal. A young Sofa general, called Bilali, took command in the western provinces at a new capital called Heremakono ('await good fortune') near Falaba, with a primary responsibility for reopening and protecting the trade route to Sierra Leone. For now Samori had realised even more fully than before the primordial importance of obtaining a regular supply of modern precision firearms, and on an increasing scale. On the one hand this meant attempting, with remarkable success, to turn the productive ingenuity of the smiths and jewellers of the empire from the manu-

[78] Ibid., pp. 1075–84.

[79] Cf. Archinard's letters of January 1889 quoted in Méniaud, *Pionniers*, II, p. 136.

[80] B. O. Oloruntimehin, 'Anti-French Coalition of African States and Groups in the Western Sudan 1889–1893', *Odu*, 3 (1970) is more impressed than I by the progress towards a common front.

facture of flintlocks to modern rifles modelled on the Gras or the Kropatschek repeater; on the other, mobilising a larger economic surplus which the *dyulas* could exchange at Freetown for increased supplies of these weapons and the ammunition to supply them. Between 1890 and 1893, Person estimates that Samori obtained some 6,000 modern weapons through French and British merchants operating in Freetown.[81]

The new situation involved a shift in the emphasis of Samori's policy towards the immediate hinterland of Sierra Leone. It was now a matter of most vital urgency to secure the co-operation of the colonial government in permitting and encouraging the arms trade. There was no longer the same emphasis on the conquest or conversion of Temnes, Lokos or Limbas; Samori was not merely ready to respect 'the Queen's garden', but anxious that the Queen should cultivate it by establishing some sort of effective common frontier with him. Instead of regarding relations with Freetown as subordinated to his obligations to the French, he continually tried to revive discussions from the point where Festing had left them at Sikasso.

British policy, however, remained governed by Salisbury's determination to control West African boundary disputes through negotiations with France. The Colonial Office, though often angered by the sacrifices of local interests which this policy might require, accepted its objectives as reasonable, and were not prepared to risk international conflicts for the sake of Blydenesque dreams of alliance with Samori. They had authorised Festing's mission in order to test the *unofficial* reports that he had accepted French protection; as soon as the Foreign Office forwarded an *official* communication of the Treaty of Bisandugu on 12 April 1888 they were psychologically disposed to accept it, even though formal comment was deferred pending a report from Festing.[82] The same attitude was taken towards French claims to have established a protectorate over Futa Jalon, although Freetown had been in diplomatic and commercial contact with this state for over a century, and was indeed still paying an annual stipend to

[81] Person, *Samori*, II, pp. 1084–1109, for the re-establishment of the empire; pp. 905–12; 919–38; 1194–9, for the organisation of his arms supply.

[82] C.O. 267/372, Minute by Hemming, 14 April, on F.O. to C.O., 12 April 1888.

its rulers. 'I believe the French treaties to be, in almost all cases . . . unfairly obtained,' wrote Hemming, 'but how can we contest them?'[83]

The inexpediency of attempting to do so was at this very time underlined by the news of Viard's treaty with the Egbas.[84] The French refusal to ratify this coup (confirmed in writing on 24 July)[85] emphasised the common interest of the two powers in establishing working conventions to supplement the Berlin provisions for notification of protectorates. Both governments still found it safest to accept at their face value treaties produced by their rivals, even if they felt the basis to be suspect. For to establish the real intentions, even the real status, of the African signatories would entail complex and contentious investigations which neither country was well-equipped to undertake. During the winter of 1888 therefore the British government prepared to negotiate with France for a comprehensive settlement of West African boundaries questions, knowing that this would involve accepting serious limitations on the future expansion of Sierra Leone.[86]

Freetown could not resist the logic of this. Although many residents there – Europeans and Creoles, officials and unofficials – were still tempted by the dream of a frontier on the upper Niger, they could not hope to overturn the priorities decided in London in light of the needs of sound finance and prudent imperial strategy. In any case the tenuous links which Lawson and Festing had established with Samori had been effectively broken as a consequence of the revolts in his empire, and not until the beginning of 1890 was Bilali in a position to renew them. It would have been rash in the extreme to risk reprisals by seeking the alliance of this possibly crumbling empire when there was an urgent need to establish British authority nearer Freetown, among peoples who themselves feared Samori's power.

By the time of Rowe's death at Madeira in August 1888 officials in London as well as Freetown were tiring of the attempt to improvise a sphere of influence by intermittent military and diplo-

---

[83] C.O. 267/370, Minutes by Hemming, 13 May, on Rowe to Knutsford, Conf. 3, 13 April 1888; Meade, 24 March, on Rowe, 49, 25 February.

[84] Cf. above pp. 156–61.

[85] C.O. 879/28, C.P. African 355, No. 19, Goblet to Egerton, 24 July 1888.

[86] See Chap. 6, below.

matic activity. De Winton's expedition had dealt with the Yonni problem, and enhanced the power of certain African rulers temporarily well-disposed towards the colony. But there were still ceaseless complaints of insecurity from the Palma Trading Company at Sulima, and from the numerous European and Creole traders dispersed through the Sherbro region.[87] The colony's good relations with Momo Kai Kai and Momo Ja, trading chiefs in the Pujehun area, brought conflicts with their rivals further inland, notably with the military chief Makaia, who diverted trade from British factories. In 1888 Rowe had wanted De Winton to invade this area after his Yonni campaign, but War Office refused to sanction the use of Imperial troops; things seemed to get worse until January 1889, when a spirited operation by Captain R. E. Copland Crawford destroyed Makaia's stockaded town of Lago, and so (despite some alarm in the Colonial Office)[88] permitted the establishment of a police headquarters at Bandajuma.

In the northern rivers, the absence of any controlling authority embarrassed the French in Guinea almost as much as the British. The family of Alimami Bokkari, whose claim to Moriah chiefdom the French had denied ever since their installation at Benty in 1865, continued to enjoy strong support both in the French 'sphere of influence' and among Temnes and Susus from the valleys of the two Scarcies rivers. Bands of warriors, organised by Alimami Sattan Lahai of Rowula in the Scarcies, skirmished at will across the Anglo–French demarcation line of 1882. (In 1886 one of the leading Temne warriors, Kebalai, became ruler of the small Kasse chiefdom under the name of Bai Bureh.)[89] French officials blamed intriguers in Freetown for the manifest weakness of their authority. This was illustrated in a particularly humiliating way in November 1888 when Fourichon, Commandant at Benty, tried to establish a new customs post in a part of Samu chiefdom still under

[87] There is an interesting list in C.O. 879/27, C.P. African 350, No. 63, encl., C. H. Moseley 15 March 1888. He names the four large Sherbro houses as Fisher & Randall, C.F.A.O., S.B.A. Macfoy and Paterson Zochonis.

[88] C.O. 267/372, Minute by Herbert on Hay to Knutsford, Tel. 5 December 1888. 'With our present troubles in South Africa, this is an uncommonly inconvenient moment for beginning a little war with Mackiah.' Operations may be followed in C.P. African 346, 350, 361, or less fully in P.P. (1889) LVI, C. 5740.

[89] Denzer in M. Crowder (ed.) *West African Resistance*, pp. 246–7.

the influence of Creole traders; encouraged by the latter the Susu
authorities detained and robbed the Commandant and sent him
ignominiously home by way of Freetown.[90] When the 'great revolt'
undermined Samori's influence in these rivers (which had always
been exercised on Bokkari's side) the opportunities for European
involvement increased. In the upper Scarcies valleys a Susu warrior called Karimu tried to fill the vacuum left by Samori's withdrawal by organising a military hegemony of his own; the French
established relations with him and encouraged him to raid Limba,
Loko and Temne chiefdoms within the British sphere.[91]

The first step towards bringing this turbulent frontier under
control was to strengthen and implement the proposals for which
Rowe had won the reluctant approval of the Colonial Office in
1887.[92] In November 1888 his successor, J. S. Hay, produced
an amplified version of the scheme. He mapped out in detail the
proposed frontier road to link the heads of navigation, and obtained
a further reinforcement of the police force, whose duties were to
suppress armed robbery and murder and to prevent the passage
of overland slave caravans. 'This scheme is considerably larger
than that approved of in March 1887,' Knutsford admitted, 'but
I see no other chance of securing peace and order, and consequent increase of trade and revenue.'[93] Since there were still inhi-
bitions restraining the extension of British legal responsibilities,
the form of treaty which was authorised simply bound its African
signatories not to cede or sell their lands without British consent;
but the Colonial Office was beginning to appreciate that such im-
provisations could not hold up for long. Rowe had already pointed
out their inadequacy in the Gambian context, and Hemming
admitted that 'such Treaties could not be pressed against any
Power which might induce the Chiefs to break their engagement
and cede their territories'.[94] Some safeguard against French intrusion was provided by the Anglo–French frontier delimitation of

[90] ANSOM, Senegal iv/19/b, Thomas to M.M.C., 2083, 7 December
1888.
[91] Cf. A. Arcin, *Histoire de la Guinée française* (Paris, 1911) pp. 484–5.
[92] See above pp. 175–6.
[93] C.O. 267/372, Hay to Knutsford, 340, 7 November 1888; Minute
by Knutsford, 27 February 1889.
[94] C.O. 267/372, Hay to Knutsford, Conf. 26, 5 November 1888, and
minute by Hemming, 16 December, cf. C.O. 879/29, C.P. African 348,
No. 7, Rowe to Holland 131, 22 October 1887.

1889, but this did not solve the problem of Karimu, nor deal with territories in the north and east. Real security for British interests could come only through that sort of effective occupation which the government was still reluctant to accept.

So, once Treasury approval was obtained, the machinery of a protectorate took shape, without the name. The Frontier Police force was organised;[95] two former traders with long experience in the area, G. H. Garrett and T. J. Alldridge, were appointed as Travelling Commissioners; and J. C. E. Parkes was entrusted within the Secretariat, 'with the conduct of all matters connected with native affairs'.[96] By early 1890 these new arrangements were in force. Almost despite themselves, the British Government had created another machine capable of generating imperialism on the frontier. And it was manned in part by men still influenced by the dream of alliance with Samori.

[95] N. Etheridge, 'The Sierra Leone Frontier Police', M.Litt. thesis, University of Aberdeen, 1967.

[96] C.O. 267/372, Hay to Knutsford, 373, 19 November 1888, cf. J. D. Hargreaves, 'The Evolution of the Native Affairs Department . . .', *S.L.S.*, ns., III pp. 177 ff.

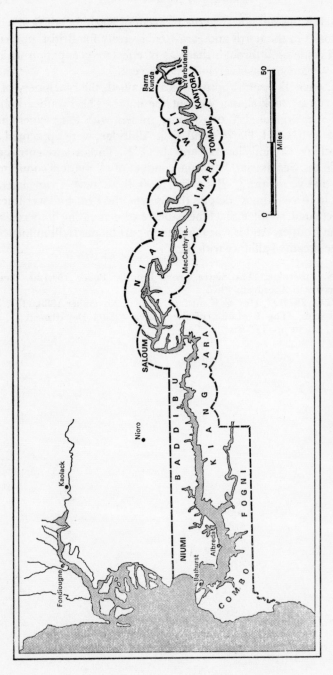

4 The Boundaries of the Gambia, 1889

6 The Best Diplomacy Can Do

IMPERIALIST DOCTRINE AND IMPERIALIST PRACTICE

Wherever European governments extended their authority in West Africa during the years 1885–9, some effective driving force can be identified within the frontiers of existing colonial societies, and related either to the widening horizons of merchants or missionaries or to the bureaucratic zeal of local colonial officials. The objectives often still seemed of purely parochial importance; places like Ipokia or Bandajuma had no significance for Europeans. Nevertheless, an increasing number of 'men on the spot' were being moved – like Binger and Archinard, Goldie and Johnston – by some sort of 'imperialist' purpose: that is, by explicit beliefs that extended authority within Africa would increase the wealth, power and greatness, even the moral stature, of their own nation. The practice of imperialism was turning some practitioners into articulate spokesmen for imperialist doctrines.

But the emerging 'ideological consensus' did not yet command general assent in Europe; on the contrary, some of the examples studied suggest that the arguments for specific advances often needed to be exaggerated if they were to be accepted. Many common generalisations about the effect of received ideas of pseudo-scientific racialism or vulgar Darwinism on European attitudes to Africa lack chronological precision. Although the exact dating of intellectual change is always difficult, it is doubtful how strongly those actually shaping policy in the 1880s were influenced by beliefs of this sort. Expressions of racial superiority and examples of discrimination can be traced in almost any period; Richard Burton had bolstered his prejudices with dubious scientific argument in the 1860s. But only in the last decade of the century did British administrators embark on systematic de-Africanisation or Frenchmen make serious attempts to abridge the rights of black citizens in Senegal; only then did many of the stock arguments by which white men justified their rule of black men pass into the 'conventional wisdom' of European politics. Curiously and sadly, the first systematic attempt to replace West Africans by Europeans in the name of high principles was made by young Anglican missionaries, who came out to Nigeria in the later 1880s full of zeal to evangelise the world in their own generation, and began by degrading African clergymen whom they judged unfit for such a task.[1] In government, men of Salisbury's generation usually took more tolerant views of Africans' rights – though whether out of humanity or indifference it is sometimes difficult to say. Up to 1889 only a small minority of really influential European figures – and probably a smaller minority of the electorates – seem to have been sufficiently impressed by a sense of national or racial mission to question the conventional wisdom that most political commitments would in the short run prove unrewarding, if not actively hazardous.

What *did* become more widespread during the 1880s were generalised expectations that economic benefits might eventually be obtained from Africa, and apprehensive fears of being denied access to these through the intervention of foreigners. Lacking any conviction of African incapacity, Europeans could still try to meet these fears by improvising systems of supervision which left substantial powers to African collaborators. Treaty-making provides one of the dominant themes of the present volume; and those treaties which formally transferred sovereign control to a protectorate authority could still leave large areas open to African initiative. Not only the Sultan of Sokoto and the Yoruba *obas* but Samori and Nana retained enough independence to negotiate with Europeans, not simply manoeuvre beneath their yoke.

But even they had received warnings of troubles ahead. This volume is entitled 'The Loaded Pause': by 1889 another Churchillian title, 'The Gathering Storm', might be equally appropriate. In the Western Sudan the storm clouds represented by French military forces were already dense, and Archinard's attack on

[1] Many accounts of this episode now exist; see, e.g., J. F. A. Ajayi, *Christian Missions in Nigeria* (1965) pp. 250–5. I intend to discuss the growth and application to West Africa of imperialist ideologies in a later volume.

Koundian was an ominous clap of thunder. In British spheres only the deportation of Jaja had a comparable effect; but there were many manifestations of a less spectacular but more widespread perception in Whitehall that the full protection of endangered interests might require commitments more extensive than originally intended. Thus by 1887 the Colonial Office acknowledged that, while treaties precluding the cession of territory or other sovereign rights to European foreigners might still work with the Yoruba states, they were becoming obsolete in the less highly structured environments of the Gambia and Sierra Leone.[2] The inner logic of frontier relationship was extending European commitments with little need for prior ideological justification. Once the immediate economic stringency of the mid-1880s abated, the principal restraint inhibiting such advances was concern lest they might prejudice more vital relationships elsewhere in the world.

THE INTERNATIONAL CONTEXT

The union in September 1885 of the two Bulgarian states ended the brief period during which Europe seemed sufficiently stable for leading statesmen to engage in colonial diversions. The rest of the decade was full of uncertainties. In Bulgaria itself affairs gradually settled down, as repeated interventions failed to impose Russian control upon the new state; the international dispute was finally liquidated in March 1888. But it had shown how dissatisfied nationalities in eastern Europe could provoke uncovenanted conflicts between Russia and Austria–Hungary, and it had destroyed the Three Emperors' League. Bismarck's diplomatic versatility had not made Germany immune from the risk of involvement in a great European war between Teutons and Slavs. This, as many of Boulanger's rash supporters argued, might offer France an opportunity to do something about Alsace. If such a crisis was possible, neither France nor Germany could afford the luxury of heavy commitments in Africa.

The British, who certainly did not intend to become involved in a continental war, also had their freedom of action restricted by involvement in the related problems of Turkey's residual empire in the Eastern Mediterranean. Their hands were tied primarily by their occupation of Egypt. In May 1887 Salisbury tried

[2] See, respectively, above pp. 161–3, below pp. 228–30, above pp. 198–9.

to relieve the attendant diplomatic embarrassments and yet retain a privileged position by negotiating terms for a future withdrawal in Drummond Wolff's Convention with the Sultan. The French government (against the preference of many diplomatists for an attempt to restore collaboration with Britain in the Mediterranean and elsewhere)[3] joined Russia in compelling the Sultan to abandon this. Instead of reducing pressure on her interests, Britain was warned that a Franco–Russian alliance might be more easily achieved in an imperial than in a continental context; her need for German support in the Mediterranean was re-emphasised, and Salisbury had to align himself a little more closely with Germany's Austrian and Italian allies. For Britain also, substantial new commitments in West Africa (as distinct from limited gestures, like her advances around Porto Novo in June 1887)[4] could only complicate the defence of major Imperial interests.

Uncertainties created by the ferment of suppressed nationalities or by the incoherence of the French political life thus made the later 1880s an uneasy period in Europe. In July 1888 another unpredictable element was added by the accession as German Emperor of Wilhelm II – a young man of strong but unstabilised opinions who soon appeared anxious to exercise his latent constitutional powers and uneasy about the special relationship with Russia which Bismarck had preserved through the secret Reinsurance Treaty of 1887. Until major international alignments were re-stabilised, European statesmen could only regard the increasing volume of African business which arrived on their desks as distracting. During the five years after the fall of Ferry no figure of Cabinet rank in any country was prepared to claim priority for such questions; even Rouvier, champion of the growing aspirations of Marseille, was occupied with more important matters.

Against this background, diplomatists were increasingly attracted by the prospect of a large-scale settlement of inter-European disputes, which would leave them free to settle their future African policies in their own time. Since frontiers in Africa inevitably generated friction it was desirable to have as few international boundaries as were compatible with established interests,

---

[3] P. Cambon to Spuller, 11 March 1889, P. Cambon, *Correspondence*, I (1940) pp. 331–3.
[4] Cf. above p. 153.

and to define them clearly. The most effective way to achieve this would be through comprehensive agreements involving both the exchange of isolated colonial enclaves, and the definition of spheres within which the major European governments would be left free to regulate their relations with African states. Such schemes might be favoured by convinced imperialists who aimed to develop compact and powerful colonies – thus Faidherbe's plans for Senegambia had been the starting-point for the abortive Anglo–French negotiations of the 1870s.[5] But much of the operational impetus would come in practice from less imaginative bureaucrats, concerned with administrative tidiness and the convenience of removing petty frontier conflicts from the 'dreary dribble'[6] of diplomatic correspondence.

The latter aim could however be achieved by more modest schemes. Boldly-conceived exchanges would offer the best prospects for Imperial development (and though the point was rarely mentioned, would reduce the number of arbitrary boundaries driven through the lands of kindred African peoples); but they would also affect more vested interests, of Africans as well as Europeans. The British in particular had learned in 1876 that proposals to cede territory could excite latent sentiments of Imperial patriotism, which could be marshalled into a formidable political opposition. Despite the absence during the 1880s of strongly organised movements of popular imperialism, there were politicians in every country ready to declare that national prestige or honour would be damaged by the surrender of established colonies or existing rights. Convinced Imperialists, like Harry Johnston, could contemplate such sacrifices for the sake of future African empires; the diffuse chauvinism which was still more common actually impeded such plans. Strong governments with clear objectives might still have been able to negotiate a comprehensive and rational partition of influence in West Africa during these years; the best diplomacy could in fact achieve during 1888–9 were piecemeal delimitations which ossified the pattern of fragmentation already sketched out along the West African coastline.

[5] Cf. *Prelude*, esp. Chap. 3.

[6] A phrase later used by Rosebery of the Lagos frontier. Rosebery Papers (National Library of Scotland), Letter book 88, to Kimberley, 15 September 1894.

THE GERMANS AND THEIR NEIGHBOURS IN
WEST AFRICA

The prospects of a comprehensive repartition had been greatly
reduced by Germany's emergence as a third West African power.
Although she lacked a major territorial base to compare with
those of France on the upper, and of Britain on the lower Niger,
both the limited commitments which Bismarck had accepted
proved capable of developing serious 'frontier imperialisms'.
Woermann's hopes that Kamerun would prove 'one of the most
important points of entry to the heavily populated hinterland of
the Niger region'[7] proved premature; it has been seen that
attempts by Flegel and Staudinger to pre-empt positions in Adamawa by pressing up the Benue from the south failed, through the
opposition of the Niger Company and the lack of serious government support.[8] But once a German administration was established
in the Duala area, the logic of its presence carried its influence
into areas where it was liable to conflict with French or British
interests.

Immediately, the aims of the Germans in Kamerun were confined to attempts to break the monopolies of the coastal trading-
states (on whose treaties their original claim to a protectorate was
based), to divert as much trade in palm produce as possible from
the British sphere around Old Calabar, and eventually to obtain
access to the Bamenda grasslands to the north. These were tasks
beyond the unaided resources of the traders, to whom Bismarck
had hoped to transfer administrative and financial responsibility.
The Hamburg merchants did form a *Syndikat für Westafrika*
under Woermann's chairmanship, but their aim was to claim a
privileged position as advisers to the government, not to assume
governing responsibility themselves.[9] In fact, early attempts to
extend German control of trading operations in the Duala area
aroused fierce opposition from trading-chiefs who in July 1884
had believed that Germany would safeguard their trading monopolies;[10] in December 1884 Imperial troops and warships were

[7] Woermann to Bismarck, 17 August 1884, cit. H. P. Jaeck in H.
Stoecker (ed.) *Kamerun unter Deutscher Kolonialherrschaft*, Vol. I, p. 77n.
[8] Cf. above pp. 98–104.
[9] Wehler, *Bismarck und der Imperialismus*, pp. 320–1.
[10] Wünsche der Kamerun Leute', 12 July 1884, in H. R. Rudin,
Germans in the Cameroons, 1884–1914 (New Haven 1938) p. 423.

brought in to put down insurrections against King Bell, who had come to seem little more than a German client. To explain this, some historians have emphasised the intrigues of the British and their romantic Polish agent Rogozinski, who during the winter of 1884–5 signed treaties which temporarily extended the sphere of British influence around Victoria and Ambas Bay.[11] But Germany's difficulties were not ended by the Anglo–German frontier agreement of April 1885, nor even by the agreement for the final withdrawal of the Baptist mission, negotiated in 1887.[12] The basic reason for African resistance was the identification of their German 'protectors' with the interests of German merchants.[13]

Unable to transfer responsibility to these merchants, the Imperial Government had little choice but to support their developing demands – at least in so far as these were directed against Africans, rather than France or Britain.[14] Increasingly, this meant sponsoring attempts to penetrate the hinterland of the Duala traders, and to press further inland. In November 1887 two patriotic young officers, Kund and Tappenbeck, began to probe in the direction of Yaounde, from the southern port of Kribi; in December 1888 Zintgraff set out for the Bamenda grasslands, where he proposed to organise a German paramountcy around Chief Galega of Bali-Nyonga, and pressed on to the Benue at Ibi. These were still lightly-armed explorations – military forces capable of subduing inland peoples were not available until 1892 – but they clearly illustrated the expansive tendencies of the German protectorate.[15] And once the Germans had consolidated their contact with the middle Benue, the possibility of penetrating the Niger Company's sphere through Adamawa was bound to re-emerge.

The impetus for all these advances developed within the colony

[11] Cf. J. A. Betley, 'Stefan Szolc Rogozinski and the Anglo–German Rivalry in the Cameroons', *JHSN*, v (1969); Wehler, pp. 318–20.

[12] Cf. above p. 44–5.

[13] Jaeck in Stoecker, *Kamerun* . . . , I , 71–7, also Vol. II (1968), pp. 181 ff., A. Rüger, 'Die Duala und die Kolonialmacht, 1884–1914'.

[14] Cf. Stoecker, I, p. 72.

[15] Elizabeth Chilver, 'Paramountcy and Protection in the Cameroons; the Bali and the Germans, 1889–1913' in *Britain and Germany in Africa, 1884–1907*, pp. 481–5; R. Kaeselitz, 'Kolonialeroberung und Widerstandskampf in Sud Kamerun, 1884–1907' in Stoecker, *Kamerun* . . . , II, pp. 13ff.

itself. Kamerun does not seem to have been the object of wide-spread interest in Germany, at least not until the economic depression began to lift in the later 1890s. Yet German investors, planters, traders, missionaries, officials and soldiers had gradually begun to acquire interests in a country which was originally the concern of a few Hamburg merchants. It would still be hyperbole to talk of 'the whole German people' being involved in a colony which was never of more than marginal interest to the German economy, but German interests in Kamerun did increasingly demand special attention within the context of German national policy. Far from handing over control to the merchants, in 1889 Bismarck had to establish a distinct colonial directorate within the Auswärtiges Amt.[16]

Missionaries from Bremen had worked on the coastline to the east of the lower Volta since 1884, and a number of merchants had followed them there.[17] The effective political units among the Ewe of this coast were tiny city-states, in each of which power was further diffused amongst the leading families engaged in foreign trade. Such a structure offered many openings for foreign intrigue. Governors of the Gold Coast had long been worried by the ease with which merchants who resented the heavy customs duties charged upon imported spirits could obtain facilities to supply the Gold Coast hinterland through independent Ewe ports. Their ultimate ambition was to exercise fiscal control over the whole Slave Coast as far as Lagos; meanwhile they acted against new centres of 'smuggling' piecemeal. In 1879 Governor Ussher had occupied Denu and Afflao, thus increasing British control east of the Volta; by 1882 his successor, Rowe, was planning a further advance. In the first place this would affect Bagida and Beh Beach (or Lome). These were the towns from which British, African and German merchants currently supplied the Gold Coast hinterland with dutiable goods.[18] But there were regions that Rowe's search

[16] For a thorough analysis of German interests, emphasising their growth after 1896, Karin Hausen, *Deutsche Kolonialherrschaft in Africa: Wirtschaftinteressen und Kolonialverwaltung in Kamerun vor 1914* (Zürich, 1970).

[17] P. E. Schramm, *Deutschland und Übersee* (Braunschweig, 1950) pp. 251–60; H. W. Debrunner, *A Church between Colonial Powers* (1965) pp. 100–4.

[18] This emerges clearly from commercial estimates published in

for revenue might reach further east – perhaps as far as Great Popo (where French and German merchants shared an export trade worth nearly £50,000), more certainly to Little Popo (or Anecho). Here, the traditional ruling lineage (now headed by Quadzovi) had since 1821 been compelled to share power with the prosperous and strongly pro-British family of Lawson; its new chief, G. A. Lawson of 'New London Palace' (whose 'Prime Minister', W. T. G. Lawson, was a former British colonial employee) was indeed working, against both French and German opposition, to bring about a British protectorate.[19]

This alarmed French and German merchants alike. For many years Fabre and Régis had done profitable trade in the four 'Popo' city-states of Porto Seguro, Little Popo, Aghwey, and Great Popo; the isolated pattern of trade enabled them still to employ their substantial sailing fleets. Recently however the advent of Woermann's steamers carrying German gin and powder, and competition of the Bremen merchants, had made great inroads into their monopoly;[20] the imposition of the British tariff would prove fatal.

[19] On the constitution of Little Popo and its position within Eweland, see D.E.K. Amenumey, 'The Ewe People and the Coming of European Rule, 1850–1914', M.A. thesis, University of London, 1966, pp. 43–5, 118–40.

[20] Figures from *Deutsches Handels Archiv*, loc. cit.:

		Little Popo	Great Popo
Exports	German firms	445,000 Marks	405,000 Marks
	French firms	298,000	525,000
	British firms	169,000	–
Imports	German goods	608,000	279,000
	of which spirits	240,000	120,000
	powder	190,000	25,000
	French goods	121,000	220,000
	of which spirits	75,000	130,000
	salt	40,000	90,000
	British goods	640,000	261,000

According to the Marseille Chamber of Commerce more than eighty French ships were still involved in this trade; (Report of 8 August 1885, in *AE* Afrique 81, M.M.C. to M.A.E., 21 August 1885).

Deutsches Handels Archiv in October 1885 (Copy in ANSOM, Afrique IV/64/a; see note below). While Lome's export of palm produce was estimated at only 167,000 Marks, its imports were estimated at one million marks annually (£50,000). 95 per cent of this figure represented spirits, tobacco and powder, all of predominantly German origin. On the expansion of the Gold Coast, see F. Agbodeka, *African Politics and British Policy in the Gold Coast* (1971) Chap. 3.

In 1881 Fabre had taken the precaution of obtaining letters from the rulers of all four states requesting French protection; but although President Grévy had signed a decree giving effect to this protectorate two years later, nothing had been done to implement it, and by the end of 1883 the French in Little Popo feared that the game had been lost.[21]

Meanwhile the Bremen merchants, though less well organised politically than the Hamburg interest in Kamerun, had also become alarmed. In 1883 the Bremen Senate replied to Bismarck's enquiry by asking for visits by a warship to ensure that German interests in the Popos were respected.[22] This ship, the *Sophie*, reached Little Popo on 30 January 1884, when the British intrigue seemed on the point of success; Captain Stubenrauch was persuaded by the German traders to intervene by physically deporting the leading members of the Lawson family.[23] This vigorous intervention relieved and yet perturbed the French. Bismarck was anxious not to incur French hostility and had no intention of making political claim in an area of interest to them. When he drafted Nachtigal's instructions in May the Imperial Commissioner was expressly ordered to avoid encroaching on French rights at Little Popo, and nothing was said about establishing a German protectorate.[24] But Nachtigal arrived to find Firminger, a Gold Coast official, working actively to secure control of both Lome and Little Popo. Inhibited from direct action at the latter town, Nachtigal was advised instead to work through Mlapa, King of Glidji (or Togo) – an Ewe ruler who, though still acknowledged overlord of Beh Beach and Bagida, had effectively lost his former control over Little Popo since 1850. By signing a protectorate treaty with him on 5 July 1884 and backing his claim to Little Popo, Nachtigal erected a sizeable barrier against the extension of the British tariff.

The establishment of German power in Eweland was even less welcome to the French than to the British, whose hope of eventual continuous fiscal control from Lagos to Accra had already been

[21] *Prelude*, 324–6.

[22] *Weiss Buch:* Deutsche Kolonien, 1 Togosebiet und Biafra-Bai (1884) (W.B.) No. 8270, anlage: Memo of Bremen Senate, 9 July 1883.

[23] Ibid., No. 8274, anlage 2; Stubenrauch to Admiralty, 22 February 1884.

[24] W.B., No. 8274, Bismarck to Nachtigal, 19 May 1884; cf. *Prelude*, pp. 325–8.

ruined by the French reappearance at Porto Novo. Although the Gold Coast government thought the German action 'disastrous to British prestige on this coast', Whitehall preferred the Germans to the French as neighbours and took these events quite coolly.[25] Fabre on the other hand, from his influential office as president of the Marseille Chamber of Commerce, wrote repeated letters urging his government to vigorous protest and declaring that Germans were now talking of occupying the whole Slave Coast, including even Dahomey.[26] Bismarck himself was embarrassed to find he had acquired an unexpected protectorate, in circumstances likely to frustrate his 'wish to appear conciliatory to France in everything which is not Alsace'.[27] For the French government at first shared Fabre's irritation; they published the decree proclaiming their own protectorate over the Popos which Grévy had signed in 1883, and in April 1885 despatched Lieutenant Pornain to try to obtain more satisfactory treaties on which to base their claim.

But this did not prove easy. Local enquiries failed to refute the claims of Germany's *protégé* Mlapa over either Little Popo or Porto Seguro (where Fabre enjoyed a profitable relationship with the ruler, Mensah).[28] By mid-1885 French diplomatists accepted the inevitability of compromise; in December they recognised Germany's right to Little Popo and Porto Seguro, in return for retention of Great Popo and Aghwey (and for the withdrawal of other claims which Nachtigal had intruded on the coast of Guinea).[29] Even this did not eliminate Franco–German friction; with commercial agents of the two nations eyeing each other suspiciously and fearing possible fiscal discrimination, intrigues and conflicts in the hinterland continued until May 1887, when, a

[25] This point is documented in G. E. Metcalfe, *Great Britain & Ghana*: No. 343, Young to Derby, 8 July 1884, No. 346, Minutes by Anderson, Fairfield, August 1884: No. 347, C.O. to F.O., 12 September 1884, cf. W. R. Louis, 'Great Britain and German expansion in Africa 1884–1919' in *Britain and Germany in Africa*, p. 12. It is not clear why Mr. Louis should have interpolated the word 'French' in the quotation on this page.

[26] E.g. AE Afrique 80, Fabre to Ferry, 13 September 1884.

[27] Marginal note, cit. M. Nussbaum, *Togo – eine Musterkolonie?* (E. Berlin, 1962) p. 21. For Nachtigal's report to Bismarck of 9 July 1884 and the text of his treaty, see W.B., No. 8278.

[28] AE Afrique 81, Fabre to Goldschneider, 20 July 1885; Afrique 83, Note pour le Ministre, 22 February 1886.

[29] Hertslet, *Map of Africa* . . . (3rd ed.) II, pp. 653–5, Protocol of 24 December 1885; cf. *Prelude*, pp. 323–8.

frontier having been partially delimited, agreement was reached to operate a uniform tariff, at least for the time being, in all French and German ports to the west of Whydah.[30]

France's difficulties with her African subjects were even harder to solve. Until her power was established in some more permanent manner, even those chiefs who benefited most from the French connection could not afford formally to abate their internal sovereignty. In April 1885 Pornain met spirited resistance to the treaties he proposed from gatherings of local notables at Great Popo and Aghwey; they resisted any weakening of local juris-diction over those 'Creoles' who were the necessary agents of French commerce, any proposal to impose French customs duties, and above all Pornain's attempt to include articles prohibiting slavery.[31] As Captain Pradier, *commandant supérieur* at Gabon, complained in October, French power was little respected by peoples who saw a French warship only every three months or so. To improve matters Pradier suggested sending a garrison of fifty soldiers; but in the absence of any local budget the cost could only be authorised by the French Chamber – which Ministers were most reluctant to approach with any such request.[32] Even Colonel Dorat, the patriotic Resident at Porto Novo, doubted the value of maintaining these isolated footholds and suggested that they might be exchanged with Germany, or simply given up.[33]

Nevertheless – whether because of a continuing dislike of giving things up, or of Fabre's continuing pressure – the French remained, with little profit but considerable risk. In January 1887 there was an alarm at Great Popo; two Africans were shot while resisting attempts to impose custom duties, by Dr. Pereton, the new and hot-headed Resident at Porto Novo, and for a time the tiny French garrison went in danger of attack. Admiral Aube, who cared little for such colonial outposts but much for the honour of his service, exploded with anger at the way French prestige was being point-lessly exposed to risks of humiliation.

[30] *E.D.*, IX, pp. 55–7, Roget reports, 20 July, 5 August 1885; Bayol to S.S.E.C., 9 February 1887; Newbury, *Western Slave Coast* . . ., pp. 114–8.
[31] AE Afrique 81, M.M.C. to M.A.E., 24 June 1885, encl. Pornain, 29 April.
[32] AE Afrique 82, M.M.C. to M.A.E., 29 December 1885, encl. Pradier, 10 October.
[33] AE Afrique 83, De La Porte to Freycinet, 6 April 1886, encl. Dorat, 25 January.

Do we want to stay there, and *in what interest?* [he asked the Foreign Ministry] I do not know. We must ask Parliament for financial support and take action – otherwise it is easy to foresee that we shall be pushed out of these possessions which we cannot defend.

But men with more political experience had no intention either of asking for credits to enlarge West African garrisons, or of hauling down the flag; Augbe was answered with anodyne hopes that 'given vigilance, prudent resolution and judicious employment of our means', all would be well.[34] Failing any stronger decision, the French presence in Great Popo gradually grew. As resources could be scraped together the garrison was slightly enlarged, and a Resident, d'Albeca, appointed – who inevitably began to think of inland expansion. By 1888 he was sending messengers to find Binger at Salaga, with hopes of opening more regular communications with that town.[35] Since German officials had also identified Salaga as their most promising gateway to the rich interior, new dangers of Franco–German friction opened up.

But it was British ambitions which most directly conflicted with German designs on Salaga. Although the British government, desperately afraid of a new military embroilment in Asante, was still trying to limit any extension of its responsibilities, European and African merchants on the Gold Coast hoped to find their eventual escape from the economic depression by northwards expansion; political action to develop the route to Salaga up the Volta valley had long seemed their best chance of doing so.[36] The arrival of the Germans gave new urgency to this vague intention. By the time the Anglo–German frontier on the coastline was fixed at a point two kilometres west of Lome in June 1886, G. A. Krause had already set out on his remarkable (and unofficial) journey through Mossi, and Imperial Commissioner Ernst Falkenthal was pushing political reconnaissances to the north-west with the immediate aim of reaching the banks of the Volta. Early in August 1886 Governor W. Brandford Griffith received a message from

[34] ANSOM, Senegal IV/125/b, Ribell to Aube, 2 March 1887, encl. Bausset, 9 February with annotations by Aube. Charmes to Barbey, 9 August 1887.

[35] Ibid., d'Albeca to S.S.E.C., 27 January 1889 and enclosures.

[36] Cf. above pp. 86–7.

King Kwadjo Deh VI of Crepi reporting the arrival of an African envoy with an offer of German protection.[37]

Although the Ewe of the Lower Volta were still divided into many small states, Crepi had since the early nineteenth century been trying to extend its claims to power over its neighbours, with partial success; it thus occupied a key position in any European struggle to control the Lower Volta.[38] Legally the British position seemed strong; they held that since this state had formerly been under Danish influence, Danish rights there (as also in Akwamu) had been formally transferred to Great Britain in 1850, at the time of the transfer of the Danish forts. But instead of protesting through diplomatic channels Griffith, a white Barbadian who had learned by long service in West Africa how to work discreetly for the extension of British influence, decided to reply in kind. Already, on 27 July, he had conditionally accepted an offer of cession from Akwamu;[39] without informing the Colonial Office he now sent Riby Williams, a District Commissioner, to obtain similar treaties along the Volta – first, with the help of the influential trading family of Ocansey, from some of the smaller states on the left bank; then on 7 October from Kwadjo Deh and a large assembly of Crepi chiefs.[40]

London's response was more hesitant. On the one hand it was appreciated that the German expansion under way might become a cause of friction.

It is safe to assume that the German Government will annex anything which is not claimed by some other power on the ground of prior annexation [wrote Kimberley, briefly acting as Colonial Secretary]. Therefore, we should make up our minds as to any territory we really want and take it at once . . .[41]

But some officials still doubted whether German 'paper protectorates' would jeopardise trade to such a degree as to justify retaliation.[42] They still thought the diplomatic claims inherited from

[37] C.O. 879/25, C.P. African 333, No. 46, Griffith to Stanhope, 11 February 1887.

[38] D.E.K. Amenumey, 'The Ewe People', pp. 38–43.

[39] C.P. African 333, No. 3, Griffith to Granville, 308, 6 August 1886.

[40] Ibid., Nos. 20, 40, 46, 62: Griffith to Stanhope, 432, 17 November 1886; 34, 24 January 1887: 61, 62, 11 February 1887.

[41] C.O. 96/177, Minute of 20 June 1886, cit. Metcalfe, p. 423.

[42] C.O. 96/177, Minute by Fairfield, 10 September, on F.O. to C.O., 31 August 1886.

the Danes in 1850 in Akwamu and Crepi provided sufficient protection against German control of the Volta; Griffith's new treaties
were regarded not only as works of supererogation but as positively 'inconvenient and undesirable'. In plainer words, officials
feared that they might be compelled to take action in ceded territories on the thorny question of domestic slavery, which they now
felt even less inclined to try to abolish than in 1874.[43] Instead of
sanctioning competitive treaty-making with the Germans, the
Colonial Office mildly rebuked Griffith for his secretive initiative.

Even when reports arrived of German action west of the Volta
in the important state of Kwahu, they declined to authorise a new
protectorate; Kwahu had formerly been subject to Asante, with
whom British officials remained desperately anxious to avoid
further conflict.

> . . . we should pause before going further north [wrote Sidney
> Webb]. It would no doubt be inconvenient to have the Germans
> behind our backs at the Gold Coast, but the policy here recom-
> mended involves eventually the annexation of Asante, to say
> nothing of Salagha, and all the other countries of the Upper
> Volta so soon as the Governor for the time being hears a rumour
> that the Germans are going there. The Gold Coast colony has
> cost England some six lives this year alone. Is it worth
> extending?

And Holland, while prepared to authorise a treaty securing Kwahu
against cession to other powers, concluded 'If Ashanti is to be
annexed to any European power, let it be by the Germans'.[44]

For reasons of broad policy also, the British government wished
to avoid African conflicts with Germany. Salisbury, aware of the
central importance of retaining German support in the daily
handling of Egyptian affairs, was already following a deliberately
conciliatory policy in East Africa; Bismarck, preoccupied with
the dangers of Austro–Russian conflict in south -east Europe, was

[43] Metcalfe, *Great Britain and Ghana*, pp. 423–4, Minutes by Hemming,
Herbert, September 1886; C.P. African 333, No. 53, Holland to Griffith,
79, 24 March 1887.
[44] C.P. African 333, Nos. 88, 83, Griffith to C.O., 15 August 1887; Meade
to Griffith, 27 September; C.O. 96/188, Minutes by Webb, 22 August,
Holland, 21 September.

duly grateful.[45] To avoid further tiresome friction in West Africa, the two governments devised a procedure for disposing of complex local issues by remote diplomatic control. In December 1887 Hemming travelled to Berlin and joined Scott, Counsellor of the British Embassy, in working out an agreement which it was hoped would allow both governments to promote the interests of their traders in the interior without danger of political conflicts. Krauel, the German official responsible for colonial affairs, accepted the validity of the British claim to Crepi, and so abandoned his claim to a frontier along the lower Volta, though he made it clear that he would welcome a broader agreement ceding British territories on the left bank of this 'natural frontier'. Pending any such exchange of rights, it was agreed that Commissioners should be appointed to prolong inland the boundary of 1886, on a line which would leave Crepi and Akwamu to the British. Between the northern boundary of Crepi and the confluence of the Daka, the Volta river was to serve as frontier between British and German spheres of influence; north of the confluence, a new expedient was adopted to maintain the possibility of access by both powers to Salaga. Britain and Germany agreed to regard a belt of territory extending north from that latitude as far as the tenth parallel 'as neutral ground, and to abstain from seeking to acquire . . . protectorates or exclusive influence' there. There were also reciprocal pledges not to impose differential duties on transit trade. These recommendations, officially confirmed in March 1888, were intended to ensure 'that neither England nor Germany should go behind the other's territories, so as to leave each nation free to develop its commerce and influence towards the interior'.[46]

Although both governments were acting in good faith, neither could be sure of controlling its agents in Africa, who would try to translate these terms into the realities of the frontier in the most favourable possible way. And unfortunately for British claims, the 'northern limit' of Crepi was by no means clear. After Williams' understanding with Kwadjo Deh in October 1886, British officials used their influence to support the territorial claims

[45] Cf. J. S. Galbraith, *Mackinnon and East Africa, 1878–1895* (Cambridge, 1972) p. 145.

[46] C.P. African 333, Nos. 92, 120; C.O. to F.O., 24 September 1887; F.O. to C.O., 27 January 1888, enclosing 'Joint Recommendations', January 1888.

of their ally. But Kwadjo Deh's authority was bitterly contested by many of his alleged subjects, notably the Tavieves, who had deep grievances of ten years standing. At a further assembly of chiefs at Peki on 15 June, called to acknowledge the British protectorate, Williams noted the absence of representatives from Tavieve, Ho, and other northern districts, which the British recognised as part of Crepi;[47] when in May 1888 a British force tried to enforce Kwadjo Deh's authority on Tavieve it was ambushed, and its commander killed.[48] Crepi, like other frontiers of European influence in West Africa, thus provided ample opportunities for conflict and intrigue.

After making the interim agreement, the Colonial Office agreed to consider the German suggestion for an exchange which would make the Volta the international frontier all the way from its mouth.[49] They believed that the actual interests of British traders on the Trans-Volta littoral were relatively small, and the interest of the colonial government in preventing revenue evasion (which had led to the original extension of jurisdiction) might now be protected by agreement with the Germans. But Griffith, in an intemperate and in parts incoherent despatch, formally approved by his Executive Council, resisted any ideas of recognising further claims in the Volta valley.[50] He again complained about German attempts to capture the trade from Salaga, and reminded the Colonial Office that the Buems, a little-known people who he claimed occupied the left bank of the Volta between the northern frontier of Crepi and the neutral zone, had recently offered to cede their country to Britain.[51] Disregarding the terms of the recent agreement, Griffith admitted that 'My object has been to prevent the Germans from acquiring a hold on the banks of the Volta.' He claimed that any further transfer to Germany of British territories east of the Volta would be resisted both by the Ewe and by the British traders at Keta (who, apart from Messrs. F. & A. Swanzy, were all Africans) and implied that it would have disastrous effects on colonial revenue.

[47] Ibid., No. 86, White to Holland, 249, 11 July 1887.
[48] Agbodeka, *African Politics* . . ., pp. 111, 118.
[49] Ibid., Nos. 121, 122, C.O. to F.O., Holland to Griffith, 15 February 1888.
[50] C.O. 879/28, C.P. African 356, Griffith to Knutsford, Conf., 28 April 1888.
[51] Originally reported in Ibid., No. 7, Griffith to Holland, 96, 28 March 1888.

Griffith's reasoning becomes hard to follow here. As he pointed out in the same despatch, Swanzy and Ocansey (the leading African firm) already did as much business through their branches at Lome as through those at Keta; clearly, they were already content to import consignments of spirits for the Volta valley under the milder German tariff, and could doubtless have learned to work happily under German control at Keta also. As for colonial finance, Griffith's own figures showed that the cost of administering the Trans-Volta district exceeded the revenue collected and he himself seemed to admit that the proposal might be acceptable if it entailed an agreement to raise the German tariff to the British level. From a purely fiscal point of view, this would actually have offered the best solution for the Gold Coast's problems; although, since the Gold Coast revenue depended so heavily on taxes on spirits which represented the staple of Germany's African trade, there might be difficulties in implementing such an equalisation. However, Griffith's real preoccupation seems to have been with the prestige of his government; he showed this by bitterly derogatory comments on German political methods, and his fear that a transfer of British territory might:

> lead the various peoples of this extensive and rapidly developing Settlement to believe that England was no longer a great and powerful country, that she was overshadowed by Germany, and that Germany was the power she should look to in the future.

Rather than bargain away the Trans-Voltan territories, Griffith proposed attempting to induce Germany to withdraw from Togoland altogether.

His hopes of such a bargain had recently been raised during a visit to Accra by Baron von Soden, a Wurtemburger with experience in the Imperial Consular service, who as Governor of Kamerun retained a supervisory responsibility for Togo. After some indiscreet remarks about his subordinate Falkenthal (whom he described as 'suffering from cerebral disturbance'), Soden declared that the German government was dissatisfied with its Togolese colony, which was not meeting its own administrative costs, and would, he thought, 'be very glad to get rid of Togo altogether'. Later the German consul, a trader called Fischer, made similar remarks, both to Griffith and to British mercantile colleagues, hinting that either a sale or an outright exchange might be acceptable.[52]

These were not the first hints that Bismarck, who had not orginally authorised the Togolese protectorate, might be prepared to part with it in return for adequate compensation. On 10 March 1885, during the negotiations for the German withdrawal from Mahin and the settlement of the Kamerun border, Bismarck had declared himself ready to discuss the exchange of Togo either for Walfisch Bay, or for an extension of the Kamerun frontier to the Calabar [i.e. Cross] river; the latter suggestion must have been particularly attractive to von Soden, since Kamerun drew much of its palm oil exports from the Old Calabar region.[53] In March 1885 the British government had been in no mood to engage in wide-ranging discussions with Germany on the basis of phrases communicated by Ambassador Münster, and this hint was not followed up; the Colonial Office did contemplate asking for the 'Togo strip' in connection with British withdrawal from the missionary enclave at Ambas Bay in Kamerun, but such a demand would certainly have been rejected as excessive.[54]

But as Bismarck became occupied with the new crises in eastern Europe, irritated by the many diplomatic conflicts which colonies brought, and disillusioned with their financial position, he became increasingly sympathetic to the idea of rationalising or even partially liquidating the colonial empire.[55] Contemplating the exchange of South West Africa for Heligoland in 1889, his son and Foreign Secretary, Count Herbert von Bismarck, complained of the absence of any German spirit of enterprise directed towards overseas investment: 'Our countrymen prefer to buy unsafe bonds issued by foreign governments than to follow the example of the English, who made their great wealth largely through distant enterprises, and are not deterred from embarking on them by costly initial outlays.'[56] With such attitudes at the top, it was natural that a redistribution of the German empire should seem practical

[52] Ibid., No. 6, Griffith to Holland, Conf., 21 March 1888.

[53] C.O. 879/22, C.P. African 296, No. 58, encl. 3; Granville to Scott, 12 March 1885; cf. Stoecker, *Kamerun . . .*, pp. 79–80.

[54] Rosebery Papers (National Library of Scotland) Box 90, Minute by Meade, 29 March 1885; cf. above pp. 44–5.

[55] D.D.F., 1st series, vii, Herbette to Goblet, 26 January 1889.

[56] *Die Grosse Politik*, iv, No. 952, Herbert v. Bismarck to Count v. Berchem, 21 June 1889.

politics. In May 1888 Vice-Consul Johnston, a great advocate of rationalising the partition by international exchanges, told Griffith that he believed the Germans would agree to withdraw from Togo in return for Walfisch Bay, provided that the offer was made before a large Togolese protectorate had been consolidated.[57]

This was over-optimistic. Even though the opposition from local interests might not have been decisive, German prestige had become involved in Togo; there could be no withdrawal unless the British were prepared to offer some publicly acceptable compensation, either in Africa or in relation to wider aspects of international policy. But Salisbury, while still accepting that imperialist conflicts with Russia and France made it essential to maintain good working relationships with Germany and the Triple Alliance, had no wish to put himself under an obligation to Bismarck by requesting such a substantial favour as the cession of a colony. Despite Salisbury's increasing interest in African questions, in his scale of priorities, the West coast colonies came far below South Africa;[58] this effectively precluded the possibility of a British cession of Walfisch Bay, which would have alienated the politicians of the Cape.[59] Moreover, from about 1888 Salisbury's concern for Egypt began to entail a keen interest in the valley of the Nile, and so in the whole future of East Africa. This meant that Britain might well ask for concessions from Germany in this area in any future colonial exchange – and these would of course require (as they did in 1890) substantial compensation provided by the British. It would have been senseless to add to the objectives to be secured in such a negotiation a demand for Togoland, simply to satisfy local expansionists with unverified expectations about the Volta route.

The balance of advantage might have seemed different if German withdrawal had again made possible the old design of establishing British control of the whole coastline between the Gold Coast and Lagos. In 1888 this was not totally out of the question – the Portuguese had abandoned their protectorate over Dahomey, and the British were about to begin negotiations with France in

[57] C.P. African 356, No. 13, Griffith to Knutsford, Conf., 5 June 1888.
[58] This point is adequately established by Robinson and Gallagher, among others. Cf. R. Oliver, *Sir Harry Johnston* . . ., pp. 136–8; also G. Cecil, *Salisbury*, III, 252–6.
[59] C.P. African 356, No. 46, C.O. to F.O., 1 October 1888.

which an offer to cede the Gambia might just conceivably have secured French withdrawal from the Slave Coast. Such a combination was actually suggested by a naval officer on the coast.[60] But there were too many hypothetical points in the whole calculation to attract British Ministers; no note was taken of the hints about German withdrawal from Togo, and instead the British prepared to go ahead with delimiting the line agreed in principal by Hemming and Krauel.

This process in itself tended to harden the position of the Germans in Togo. While bureaucrats in Europe prepared lengthy papers on the geographical, historical and juridical position of the Volta valley, the situation on the spot was being probed, and so often inflamed, by local agents of both sides, who hoped to discover conclusive evidence on such obscure problems as the full geographical extent of the kingdom of Crepi or its relationship to the strategically important territory of the Buems.[61] The German administration, small though it was, began to thrust northwards more energetically than the British, hoping to profit from Krause's great journey of 1886 by opening an outlet in the direction of the Niger. In February 1888 Captain Kurt von François, a member of a distinguished Prussian military family with previous experience in Leopold's Congo, carried out a remarkable journey through Salaga to Yendi (in Dagomba), Gambaga (in Mamprussi) and into Mossi, where he was finally obliged to turn back.[62] This bold venture placed the German government in contact with sizeable states of the southern savanna at the same time as Binger approached from the north. Although British officials commented cynically on von François's arrival in Salaga in March 1888 with a miserable collection of children's trinkets as gifts for an influential ruler,[63] he was able to obtain a series of treaties which would have seriously inhibited the expansion of the Gold Coast, had they not been nullified by the agreement to establish the neutral zone. Simultaneously Dr Ludwig Wolf (another Congo veteran) founded a government post at Bismarckburg, north-west of Atakpame,

[60] C.O. 879/27, C.P. African 345, Report by Captain G. W. Hand, 7 March 1888, in Admiralty to C.O., 3 April.

[61] C.P. African 356, contains a mass of material on both sorts of activity.

[62] G. Trierenberg, *Togo: die Aufrichtung der deutschen Schutzherrschaft und die Erschliessung des Landes* (Berlin, 1914) pp. 6–7; see also the short biography of von François in *Neue Deutsche Biographie*, iv.

[63] C.P. African 356, No. 8, Griffith to Knutsford, 101, 3 April 1888.

which he made a base for exploration and the conclusion of protectorate treaties among the Kotokoli. In May 1889 Wolf died in
Borgu, where he was pressing towards the Niger through what
would later become French territory.[64] Such daring deeds strengthened the sentimental attachment of Germans to their new
colony. On 27 November 1888 Eugen Richter, a radical Progressive Deputy, ciriticised the administration of Togo in the Reichstag and suggested that the Imperial flag might be withdrawn;
Dr Krauel, replying, asserted that:

> Far from giving up the Togo territory he was of opinion that
> Germany should not hesitate to incur fresh expenditure and risk
> capital in this direction, since trade with her own colonies would
> be more advantageous to her than commercial relations with
> the Colonies of other nations.[65]

In face of such attitudes, a major repartition would require a
deliberate exercise of political will, which neither Bismarck nor
Salisbury thought was merited by the interests at stake in West
Africa.

So it was necessary to implement the Hemming–Krauel agreement. Even this proved more difficult than expected. While Griffith proclaimed his support for the maximum claims of Kwadjo
Deh in regard to the extent of Crepi territory, German agents
produced plenty of evidence that these claims were rejected not
only by the Buems but by such states as Tavieve and Ho. In such
circumstances, to convene a boundary commission of zealous
colonial officers from Togo and the Gold Coast would simply
invite conflict. So Togo *was* included in the comprehensive agreement of 1 July 1890, in which Bismarck's successors made great
concessions in East Africa in return for the cession of Heligoland;
but rather than providing for any German withdrawal this agreement simply spelled out a compromise on the Crepi frontier in a
sense extremely favourable to Germany. Salisbury had soon recognised that to secure gains in the east 'someone must be sacrificed'
and that 'the Volta offers the line of least resistance – neither a
company nor a mission station'. Knutsford, conscious of promises

[64] R. Cornevin, *Histoire du Togo* (1959) pp. 138–43: Trierenberg, pp.
7–9.

[65] Note by H. C. Lowther of Reichstag debate, in C.P. African 356,
No. 197, F.O. to C.O., 6 December 1888.

made to the people, suggested that Germany might still be bought out of Togo altogether,[66] but since no purchase price was available, Crepi had to be sacrificed, despite protests from Governor Griffith and subsequently from many sections of the Ewe people.[67] Here as elsewhere the wishes and natural alignments of Africans were sacrificed not so much in the interests of avarice or of great Imperial purposes as for the sake of other international priorities.

THE CRISIS OF BRITISH GAMBIA

A settlement of Anglo–French disputes in West Africa was a more serious and complex problem than the adjustment of the frontiers of either power with Germany. The points of local conflict were far more numerous, and of longer standing; the interests, and the tempers, of local 'frontiersmen' were correspondingly more sensitive. Moreover, despite the continuing desire of diplomats in both countries to compromise these local disputes in the interests of general policy, the political climate remained unfavourable to any really broad agreement – a West African equivalent to the Anglo–German repartition of East Africa.

Nevertheless there was still one area where Britain had the possibility of making a concession which would require generous compensation from France. French politicians and officials still regarded the Gambia as an anomalous enclave in their Senegambian empire which – like Portuguese Guinea – would one day have to be acquired and assimilated. But though the Gambia was the highest card in the British hand, it was no ace of trumps. Quite apart from the political objections to its transfer, which had become so evident in 1870 and 1876, the strength of the French desire to acquire it was by no means constant. As the French tightened their hold on the Senegambia after eliminating Mahmadu Lamine it seemed less urgent to control imports of arms; British rule in the Gambia looked like an historical anomaly which was shortly bound to disappear. Even the French merchants, though now clearly in favour of transfer, had little left to gain; 'The Gambia

[66] Sal. P. D.32, Salisbury to Knutsford, 22 January 1890; E., Knutsford to Salisbury, 19 February 1890.

[67] Agreement . . . respecting African and Heligoland', Article 4, Hertslet *Map of Africa*, 3rd ed., p. 903. The lines of compromise may be followed briefly in Metcalfe, *Great Britain and Ghana*, Nos. 365–8, and more fully in C.O. 879/31, C.P. African 384; cf. Amenumey, 'The Ewe People . . .', pp. 144–8, 192ff.

is already a French colony, though still administered by the British,' wrote one of their spokesmen.[68]

Since the failure of exchange negotiations in 1876, British policy had indeed been inert. Administrators, well aware that bold and costly political initiatives were more likely to win censure than applause, confined themselves to administering the parochial affairs of Bathurst as economically and equitably as possible, and trying to avoid trouble in its independent settlements – 'British Combo' to the south of the river, the 'ceded mile' on its north shore, and MacCarthy's Island up-river. Towards the African states of the river banks they could only follow a policy of peaceful diplomacy, reinforcing their self-interest in trade by the discreet distribution of small stipends to those leaders who seemed strong enough to give it effective protection. There seems to have been an air of negligent decay about the whole colony; a French visitor in 1882 found that even the liberated Africans, the core of Protestant loyalism in the previous decade, were:

> disheartened by the lack of interest of the colonial administration – and will accept our flag without too much repugnance: already a number of them are trying to learn our language with the aim of finding employment with French firms.[69]

And yet this negative approach to administration could produce very acceptable economic results. The colony was free from public debt; apart from a slight deficit in 1876 its accounts showed a comfortable surplus of revenue over expenditure in each of the ten years 1874–83; and the colonial statistics indicated that market forces were producing a generally rising trend in exports of groundnuts. Throughout Senegambia farmers were responding to the challenge of the market economy by bringing more land into cultivation and by directing resources to the production of this valuable cash-crop. As in other cases, the initial stimulus was not easy to maintain, as alternative sources of oilseeds came into production to meet rising demand; but the evidence seems to suggest that Gambian farmers were able to bargain effectively enough with the traders to maintain their incomes and a generally high level of exports until 1883–4.

[68] AE Afrique 84, L. Prom to Ferry, 24 June 1884.
[69] ANSOM, Senegal VI/13/a, Report by Penfentenyo, 28 February 1882; cf. Gray, pp. 456–7.

At that point, governmental measures designed to promote the groundnut trade became counter-productive. The first impact came with Lat-Dior's resistance to the railway which the French hoped (in the long run correctly) would greatly increase groundnut production in Cayor; the immediate effect was to bring production almost to a halt, and in 1883 Senegal's exports of groundnuts slumped to 9,245 tons – roughly a quarter of the usual figure.[70] French merchants, anxious to maintain their tonnages, greatly increased their purchases in the Saloum area during 1884, offering sufficiently good prices to attract something like 4,000 tons of nuts from the states of Gambia valley. These were transshipped to Rufisque, and exported at the high price prevailing for the better quality nuts of Cayor. [71]

In 1885 French importers ended this particular piece of sharp practice by quoting differential prices according to the origin of the nuts, and so much of the Saloum trade returned to the Gambia. But world oilseed prices had begun to fall, in consequence of the worldwide depression of trade and of high rates of production in India; yet the Gambia traders had to compete to buy a crop reduced by unusually low rainfall, by the effects of recent heavy cropping, and by fighting in Badibu, the principal producing area.[72] As some British officials at least knew, this type of warfare was often a symptom rather than a cause of commercial depression; long-standing antagonisms could be brought to flashpoint

[70] Exports of groundnuts, in shell from Senegal: *1883*, 9,319,078 Kg; *1884*, 36,790,331 Kg; *1885*, 45,061,108 Kg; *1886*, 21,729,088 Kg; *1887*, 35,560,106 Kg; *1888*, 40,342,649 Kg; (*Annuaires Sénégalaises*). On Lat-Dior, cf. above p. 47.

[71] C.O. 87/126, Moloney to Rowe, 354, 13 October 1885. Despite the indications in M. A. Klein, 'The Muslim Revolution in Senegambia' (*JAH*, xiii, 1972, pp. 438–9), we still lack systematic data on world groundnut prices and their relation to buying prices in the Gambia; further indications will however be found in Mr. Mboge's thesis.

[72] C.O. 87/126, Moloney to Rowe, 354, 13 October 1885. Groundnut exports: *1882*, 25,522 tons; *1883*, 23,094 tons; *1884*, 18,396 tons; *1885*, 12,330 tons; *1886*, 6,094 tons; cf. Appendix, Table IV. Badibu provided 4,232 tons in 1882, 4,894 tons in 1883, 5,001 tons in 1884 – not including nuts carried directly to Bathurst – (C.P. African 341, No. 67, Walcott Memo, 13 May 1887). For unsuccessful attempts by traders to maintain profits by offering only 1/- instead of 2/- for a 'bushel' of nuts reduced in size by only 30 per cent, see P.P. (1887) LIX, C.4978, Nos. 11, 13, Carter to Rowe, 24 December 1885, 22 January 1886.

by struggles to control the profits of a diminishing trade, as when Saer Mati and Biram Cissé fought over the latter's chief port of Kau-ur.[73] But Governors unfamiliar with the working of the oil-seed market tended to look for political solutions, trusting that 'the question of the price will no doubt right itself'; it was in hope of restoring order to Badibu that Carter decided to transfer British support from Mahmoud N'Dari Ba to Saer Mati in February 1887.[74]

Since this diplomatic coup provoked the French invasion of April, however, its immediate effect was to intensify the economic plight of both merchants and government. Groundnut exports in 1887 fell to a mere 2,995 tons, and although the situation was partly retrieved by record exports of rubber (which since 1884 had been gathered for export from the forests of Fogni, between the Gambia and the Casamance),[75] about one-seventh of the country's diminished exports were of specie.[76] The effect on the government's financial position was even worse. After ten years during which reserves had accumulated (and it had even become possible to apply some of them to improving the Bathurst water supply) the colonial accounts again showed mounting annual deficits; expenditure exceeded revenue by £4,523 in 1884 (over 18 per cent); by £6,359 in 1885 (over 31 per cent); by £9,120 in 1886 (64 per cent); by £10,543 in 1887 (79 per cent).[77]

First reactions of colonial officials to the Gambia's declining fortunes were predictably orthodox; seeing the crisis as essentially one of colonial finance, they tried to restore solvency by tinkering with the tariff and proposing savings in colonial expenditure, including a withdrawal of the subsidy paid to the British and African Steam Navigation Company in respect of its postal services.[78] The

[73] C.O. 87/127, Hay to Rowe, 125, 24 March 1886; C.P. Africa 341, No. 1, Carter to Hay, 287, 16 July 1886.

[74] Ibid., No. 9, p. 20, Carter to Hay, 15 December 1886, cf. above pp. 82–5.

[75] C.P. African 341, No. 66, Memorial of Bathurst Chamber of Commerce, 6 May 1887, says Fogni supplies 'all the rubber and nearly all the wax' exported from Bathurst.

[76] £12,147 out of £86,933 (*Blue Book* for 1887), cf. Appendix, Table IV.

[77] See Appendix, Table V.

[78] These proposals may be studied in P.P. (1887) LIX, C.4978 and C.5001.

Company then threatened to withdraw its scheduled steamship service to British ports, which would make the Gambia's trade even more dependent upon Marseille and Gorée at the expense of Liverpool and Freetown; the latter connection was particularly vital to African merchants, like J. D. Richards, who not only retained close family links with Sierra Leone but conducted a profitable coastal trade in the import of kola nuts.[79] This inert and negative approach to colonial administration was strongly criticised by James F. Hutton, whose interests in the colony were managed by one of his sons, and by Thomas Brown's former agent, H. H. Lee.[80] Hutton repeatedly called, on behalf of both France and British merchants, for more effective protection of trading operations in the river, and his complaints intensified after fighting resumed in Badibu in 1885; but the Colonial Office remained wary of military involvement.

> These chiefs and their followers are not by any means the mere savages we have to encounter on the Gold Coast, or even in the neighbourhood of Sierra Leone [wrote Hemming]. They can bring large forces, including many cavalry, into the field, and any expedition to deal with them must be on a large scale.

With equal plausibility Britain might have been asked to intervene between Chile and Peru, or even in the American Civil War.[81] Recognising the entrenched inertia of the Colonial Office, Hutton began to discuss with his business associates in the *Compagnie française de l'Afrique Occidentale* that suggestion of an exchange of British rights which he had done so much to defeat in 1876.[82] The French invasion of Badibu in April 1887 reminded the Colonial Office of the need to take decisions, though it did not greatly help them to decide. Hemming's reaction was to bar France's road to the waterside by proclaiming a protectorate over a one mile strip of each bank of the river up to MacCarthy's

[79] P.P. (1887) LIX, C.4978, Nos. 19–20, Rowe to Granville, 9 June, Liverpool Chamber of Commerce to C.O., 1 July 1886, with enclosures.

[80] Ibid., No. 32, Hutton to C.O., 9 Nov. 1886; C.O. 87/134, Lee to Knutsford, 11 October 1888. Cf. above pp. 26–8.

[81] C.O. 87/126, Minute by Hemming, 24 September 1885, on Manchester Chamber of Commerce to C.O., 9 September. For examples of Hutton's complaints, see C.4978, Nos. 3, 4, 6.

[82] C.4978, No. 33, Hutton to C.O., 18 November 1886; cf. *Prelude*, pp. 184, 190–3.

Island.[83] But his colleagues could not yet accept the notion of a
Gambian protectorate – partly because its proclamation might
escalate a conflict with France which they hoped to compound
diplomatically, but also because of its internal implications. If
protectorate treaties were made with the militant Muslim leaders
of the south bank – Foday Kabba, Foday Silla in Combo, Brima
Njie in Fogni – some officials believed that this would mean
legitimising not merely slavery but slave-raiding, and the oppression of peaceful cultivators. '. . . is it wise to attempt to define the
limits of the authority of Foday Silleh and Brima Njie?', wrote
Reginald Antrobus. 'They are adventurers who do not belong to
the country, and with a little encouragement the people might be
able to get rid of them.'[84]

But if Britain relied instead on alliance with those peaceful
cultivators, the responsibility of defending them against insurgent
Islam would hardly be politically acceptable. 'The difficulty of
sending an armed force against Foday Cabba would be very great,
and even hardly possible until we have disposed of the Yonnies,'
wrote Holland in November 1887, when it seemed that such a
course might be called for. Nor did his qualification mean that he
would later be willing to take the logistically simple though costly
course of tranferring de Winton's force to the Gambia after the
defeat of the Yonnies; he was piously hoping that 'If that expedition is successful it may have some effect upon men like Foday
Cabba.'[85]

In the short term, the Colonial Office tried to plug the drain
which the French were threatening to drive into Bathurst's commercial hinterland by the old expedient of treaties of friendship,
binding their African neighbours not to cede territorial rights or
privileges to any foreign power.[86] To this end Rowe, now nearing
mental and physical exhaustion and increasingly obsessed by anti-
Muslim prejudices, took up residence in the Gambia from May
until the end of the year, accompanied by Festing and a Sierra

[83] C.O. 87/130, Minute by Hemming, 6 May, on Rowe, Tel., 5 May
1887.
[84] C.O. 87/131, Minute by Antrobus, 20 October on Rowe, 115, 27
September 1887.
[85] C.O. 87/131, Rowe to Holland, Tel., 22 November 1887; Minutes
by Hemming, Meade, Herbert, Holland, 26 November.
[86] C.O. 879/26, C.P. African 341, Meade to Rowe, 14 April 1887
(printed in Newbury, *British Policy* . . . , II, pp. 11–12).

Leonean secretary, J. W. Lewis. He secured several such treaties with the various rulers of the south bank; on the north bank he worked more circumspectly to strengthen Britain's position (particularly in the district of Nuomi Bata on the borders of Barra) without prejudicing diplomatic moves towards an Anglo–French agreement to respect the *status quo* until a settlement could be negotiated in Europe.

But this was a costly operation (travelling and subsistence allowances for Rowe's party amounted to £2,228, a serious addition to the Gambia's deficit),[87] and Rowe himself had little confidence in the results. Now totally opposed to any alignment with the marabout party, he could see no effective way of protecting 'simple industrious folk' like the Jolas against them. No West African people would acknowledge Queen Victoria, 'except they felt that to accept Her Sovereignty or be under Her protection was the only means by which they could avert some greater evil which was imminent'; unbacked by force, non-alienation treaties were 'not worth the paper they are written on'.[88] Conceivably, British strength might have been reinforced by alliance with Moussa Molo, who seemed disposed to sign a treaty when Rowe met him at MacCarthy's Island in June 1887. But (as Rowe had recognised when Hay made a similar suggestion the previous year),[89] Mousa Molo's known relations with France demanded prudence; if the French had a valid treaty, not only could they invalidate any document the British might sign with Moussa Molo, but they might use him as the agent for extension of their claims on the south bank in the same way that they had used Guedel Mboge in the north.[90]

If Rowe's negotiations could offer only a temporary reprieve to Bathurst's imperilled sphere of influence, and military solutions were still excluded, a diplomatic demarcation might at least separate the danger of French intrusion on the river bank from the problem of organising British authority. Meade and Holland urged this course on the more impatient Hemming.[91] But, as ex-

[87] C.O. 87/133, Rowe to Knutsford, 80, 2 June 1888.

[88] C.O. 879/27, C.P. African 348, No. 7, Rowe to Holland, 131, 22 October, 1887; C.O. 87/131, Rowe to Hemming, 22 October 1887.

[89] See above p. 81–3.

[90] C.O. 87/26, C.P. African 341, Nos. 82, 84, 90, Rowe to Holland, 41, 13 June; 6, Conf., 14 June 1887.

[91] E.g. C.O. 87/131, Minutes on Rowe to Holland, Tel., 10 October 1887.

perience elsewhere showed, negotiations with France could be a lengthy business; not until December 1887 was it possible to conclude even the interim agreement to maintain the *status quo* and avoid further flag-hoisting by either side.[92] Inevitably the question arose whether British rights on the Gambia were worth demarcating, or whether they might be more profitably exchanged for concessions elsewhere; but until late in 1888 Holland refused to make any such offer, for fear of political complications.[93]

This negative decision implied some further steps at least to put the Gambia's affairs in order, and to reassure European and African residents in the colony about its future. One step which they had long demanded was administrative separation from Sierra Leone; subordination to Freetown not only meant that the Gambians helped to subsidise a government from which they derived little benefit, but involved long delays in the despatch of official business, which would become intolerable if the threatened mail service became less regular. In November 1888 therefore the Gambia was constituted a separate colony. This also implied the reconstitution of the Legislative Council, which had already been recently strengthened by the appointment of a second African and a second European member.[94] With the identity of the colony thus strengthened and reaffirmed, Carter, who returned to head the new administration, began to press more confidently for means to carry out a more forthright policy against men like Foday Kabba.[95] Given the indecisiveness of the Colonial Office, their knowledge that the anglophone Africans of Bathurst would struggle to retain a separate identity had proved decisive. Through sheer logic of events the British were going to retain a colony in the Gambia. They now urgently needed to mark out its future boundaries.

TOWARDS NEGOTIATION

The British Foreign Office began serious preparations for a com-

[92] See within, p. 233.
[93] C.O. 879/29, C.P. African 348, No. 28, F.O. to C.O., 16 December 1887.
[94] C.O. 87/133, Carter to Knutsford, Conf., 10 September 1888; cf. the forthcoming book by Florence Mahoney, *The Origins of the Modern Gambia*, Chap. 6.
[95] C.O. 87/135, Carter to Anderson, Pte., 23 April 1889; C.O. 879/29, C.P. African 360, No. 40, Carter to Knutsford, 23 April 1889.

prehensive negotiation over its West African disputes with France
during the summer of 1887. In many ways, the timing seemed
impropitious. Despite Boulanger's exclusion from office in the
Rouvier ministry of 30 May, the political condition of the French
Republic still seemed profoundly depressing to British patricians;
the French government's decision to oppose the Drumond Wolff
Convention was a great disappointment to Ministers who had
hoped that it might lead to an honourable appeasement of Anglo-
French hostility over Egypt. In moments of irritation Salisbury
could see 'a silver lining even to the great black cloud of a Franco-
German war';[96] in this mood he authorised direct counter-
measures against French 'encroachments' at Porto Novo and in
the Gambia which seemed to form part of the same hostile
policy.[97]

In calmer moods, Salisbury favoured patient attempts to work
with the numerous Frenchmen who still shared his desire for
compromise or even co-operation. Emile Flourens, a former
conseiller d'état who had become Foreign Minister on 13 December 1886, remained in office under Rouvier, and until 3 April
1888. He professed conciliatory intentions, and the British Embassy
generally believed him, though they regretted some of the expedients by which, as a non-political Minister, he had to protect himself against political criticism. His constant complaints about anti-
French articles in the British Press, and the necessity for the British
government to humour 'the caprices of the little Parliaments' of
the Australasian colonies did little actual harm, but it was a more
serious matter when Flourens conformed to his colleagues' tactic
of 'irritating public opinion' by ostentatiously opposing British
policy in Egypt.[98] But even if the demands of Republican politics
precluded progress on the major issues of Anglo–French relations,
it might at least be possible to dispose of the minor irritants in
West Africa.

To the Colonial Office, a comprehensive settlement was primarily attractive because reciprocal concessions might make it

[96] Salisbury to Lyons, 22 June 1887; Newton, *Lord Lyons* (1913) II, p. 409.
Chapter 17 of this work is generally illuminating on attitudes in 1887.

[97] Sal. P. D.32, Salisbury to Holland, 3 June 1887. C.O. 147/59,
Minute by Onslow, 13 June, on Moloney, Tel., 10 June. C.P. African
341, No. 92A, F.O. to C O., 4 July 1887; cf. above p. 153.

[98] Sal. P. A. 56, Lyons to Salisbury, 7 June 1887. AE, Papiers Waddington, Flourens to Waddington, 24 February 1887.

easier to settle the complex local disputes in Badibu and Porto Novo – and also on the Ivory Coast border, where renewed French activity was raising contentious issues on which the Boundary Commission of 1883 had reached deadlock.[99] But since late 1886 the War Office had seen a more important interest in the need to eliminate the threat which a French protectorate over Samori would pose to the Freetown coaling station. General Brackenbury's immediate reaction to the revival of conflict at Porto Novo was to suggest that concessions over these 'purely local' interests might secure a frontier which would keep French power at a very safe distance to the north of Sierra Leone.[100] Hence, when in August 1887 Flourens tentatively expressed interest in 'an early understanding . . . about the disputed territories on the West Coast of Africa – and about an exchange if possible of territories',[101] Salisbury at once reacted by inviting the Colonial Office 'to make an attempt to extend the scope of the contemplated negotiations with the French so as to embrace a general settlement of West African questions'.[102]

Rumours were already current that the French were hoping through negotiation to obtain British withdrawal from the Gambia; and the Colonial Office rightly concluded that Salisbury might welcome such a broad exchange. But Meade, Herbert and Holland himself felt 'tolerably certain' that any proposal to cede the Gambia would meet the same strong political opposition as in 1876. Only the Parliamentary Under-Secretary, Lord Onslow, a future Governor of New Zealand who was inclined to treat territorial claims in West Africa seriously, was disposed to take the risk.

> Is it so certain that no such proposal could be got through the House of Commons? [he asked] – the policy of territorial expansion finds lip favour more than it did when the question was under consideration before, and if a 'valuable consideration' could be shown for the cession I am not sure that it would be so difficult to get it through.

[99] Cf. above pp. 89–91.
[100] C.P. African 334, No. 121, W.O. to C.O., 1 July 1887, encl. Brackenbury Note, 27 June; cf. above pp. 185–6.
[101] Sal P. A56, No. 46, Egerton to Salisbury, 5 August 1887.
[102] C.P. African 334, F.O. to C.O., 12 August 1887.

Onslow, though no enthusiast for African territory as such, therefore wished to treat British claims on a broad and rational basis.

> I cannot agree with the policy which tries to keep the French out of every part of the world except France. She is the worst of colonizers, her colonists cost her more than those of any other nation, and if she chooses to weaken herself in Europe by schemes of colonization in deadly climates why should we be so anxious to protect her from her own folly.[103]

But he could not move his superiors; Salisbury was told that there could be no question of ceding the Gambia, although Holland would welcome a comprehensive settlement of other disputes, preferably by a discreet exchange of notes.[104]

Despite hints from Percy Anderson that it might be expedient to respond to Flourens' conciliatory feelers while they lasted,[105] the Colonial Office moved only slowly towards even this more limited negotiation. Given the more central importance of the Sierra Leone frontier, it would be imprudent to open negotiations without fuller information about the treaties which France claimed to have made with Samori; and Festing's mission, which was expected to provide this, could not leave Freetown until January 1888.[106] Meanwhile tempers were still inflamed by the confrontations in the Gambia and at Porto Novo, where even provisional agreements to respect the *status quo* were not reached until 7 December 1887 and 2 January 1888, respectively.[107] In the Gambia, unlike Porto Novo, the French had sufficient local strength to benefit from uncertainty. In November, Rowe's pessimistic reports prompted Hemming and Bramston, the officials most directly concerned with the Gambia, to call for a clear-cut decision by Parliament on the colony's future; the alternatives to exchange, Bramston wrote, were to provide the funds to establish an effective protectorate, or to do nothing and to see such value as Bathurst

[103] C.O. 87/131, Liverpool C. of C. to C.O., 15 July 1887, Minute by Onslow; C.O. 147/62, Minutes by Meade, Herbert, Onslow, Holland on F.O. to C.O., 10 August 1887. On Onslow, cf. above p. 153.

[104] C.P. African 334, No. 175, C.O. to F.O., 29 August 1887.

[105] C.O. 147/62, Minute by Hemming, 31 October on F.O. to C.O., 10 September 1887.

[106] Cf. above pp. 185–7.

[107] Cf. above pp. 153–5.

possessed wither gradually away.[108] Holland was sufficiently impressed by these arguments to request a memorandum on the past history and future prospects of an exchange from Hemming, long its principal advocate; but he was still too terrified by the prospect of political opposition to act on it. The least objectionable course was Bramston's suggestion of organising a permanent sphere of influence on the Gambia; but to avoid political difficulties of another sort Holland deferred acceptance of its essential provision – the request for a Parliamentary subsidy.[109]

In fact, the propitious signs in Paris were soon obscured. The death of Mahmadu Lamine in December removed some of the urgency of France's interest in the Gambia valley; and the government had too many domestic troubles to think seriously about sacrificing even quite limited French interests in order to secure an exchange. During the last months of 1887, the British Embassy's hopes of greater political stability were destroyed by the impact of scandals involving the son-in-law of President Grévy. On 2 December the President's forced resignation removed one of the oldest and strongest opponents of the group of colonial enthusiasts formerly associated with Gambetta;[110] the consequent weakening of governmental authority increased the opportunities for effective pressure by colonial 'hawks'. British diplomatists realised that Flourens though personally 'conciliatory and straightforward' was under increasing pressure from Etienne's Colonial Department. 'He is evidently not master of his office,' wrote Lord Lytton, the new Ambassador, 'and the practical effect of his general assurances is apt to be watered down by the permanent officials.'[111] On the Gambia, Etienne was pressing Flourens to deny all British territorial claims in Saloum and above MacCarthy's Island, hoping thus to squeeze out the British altogether; he also aimed 'to reconstitute the ancient Kingdom of Porto Novo under our protectorate' (thus endorsing Tofa's claims in Egbado), and wished to reject the unratified 1882 Convention on the Sierra Leone bound-

[108] C.O. 87/131, Minutes by Hemming, Bramston, 18 November, Holland, 26 November, on Rowe to Hemming, Pte., 22 October 1887.

[109] C.O.879/27, C.P. African 348, No. 26, C.O. to F.O., 5 December 1887.

[110] C. F. Ageron, 'Gambetta et la réprise de l'expansion coloniale', *RFHOM*, LIX (1972) pp. 173, 189.

[111] Sal. P. A56, No. 58, Lytton to Salisbury, 30 December 1887; A57, No. 10, Lytton to Salisbury, 27 January 1888.

ary on the ground that it left Britain in control of the Isles de Los. To secure concessions on these points, Etienne would offer to settle only the Ivory Coast border in a sense favourable to the British.[112]

The Foreign Ministry still wanted agreement with Britain on the widest possible basis; on 4 January 1888, when formally agreeing to proceed from the two local *status quo* agreements towards 'the collective settlement of this whole group of questions,' Flourens kept open the possibility that this might be 'by means of exchange or otherwise'.[113] But he warned the Colonial Department (which Etienne had temporarily left on the fall of the Rouvier Ministry) that there was little hope of obtaining the Gambia as cheaply as Etienne wished; while it might possibly be worth offering in exchange a *total* withdrawal from the Ivory Coast alone, experience suggested that Britain would demand Porto Novo also. As for Etienne's designs on the Isles de Los,, Flourens preferred to stand by the 1882 agreement, which had been respected in practice for five years.[114] The Colonial Department did not think the Gambia worth such terms and preferred to negotiate a delimitation from their position of local strength. Although the treaties of 1783, 1814 and 1857 entitled Britain to 'possession . . . of the river Gambia', they wished to argue that this referred to the water alone and that British territorial claims were restricted to Bathurst, Albreda and MacCarthy's Island. If the proposed Anglo–French Commission could be brought to accept this position, the Colonial Department's desire to eliminate Britain from the Gambia would become much easier to achieve.[115]

Flourens recognised that this was not a promising bargaining position; he therefore played for time by inviting the British to formulate proposals for a settlement, which might form the starting point for negotiation by Commissioners meeting in Paris.[116]

---

[112] AE Afrique 86, Barbey to Flourens, 10 December 1887.

[113] C.O. 879/27, C.P. African 345, No. 63, Lytton to Salisbury, 4 January 1888, encl. in F.O. to C.O., 24 January.

[114] ANSOM, Afrique VI/66/a, Flourens to Krantz, 13 January 1888.

[115] Ibid., undated note on the negotiations; Krantz to Flourens, 18 February 1888. See also Gallieni's note of 20 January 1888; Senegal VI/19/a.

[116] C.O. 879/27, C.P. African 345, No. 84, F.O. to C.O., 6 March 1888, encl. Flourens to Lytton, 27 February; No. 87, F.O. to C.O., 9 March 1888.

But while he avoided any direct mention of the Gambia, other Frenchmen raised the question unofficially. Bohn, the managing director of C.F.A.O., was anxious to develop the interests which Verminck had established in the Gambia and Guinea in order to establish a firm commercial base in Senegambia – traditionally a preserve of Bordeaux; he now responded to the hints which Hutton had been dropping for some time. On 9 March Bohn, implying that he spoke with government approval, told Hutton that he thought an exchange might be negotiable. While echoing the official view that the market value of British Gambia had so depreciated that the French posts on the Ivory Coast would provide adequate compensation, Bohn suggested that if pressed the government might offer frontier concessions – perhaps agreeing to equalise tariffs between Porto Novo and Lagos or to exchange the Mellacourie against the Isles de Los. On 4 April similar suggestions appeared in the authoritative daily *Le Temps*.

These hints provided Hemming with the opportunity to revive within the Colonial Office the idea of an exchange.[117] By this time both governments were becoming increasingly conscious that, despite their agreements to respect the *status quo* in the different colonies, 'frontiersmen' in Africa were leading them towards dangerous confrontations. In March news of Festing's mission alarmed the French and prompted them to produce their protectorate treaties with Samori and Ahmadu; immediately afterwards Viard's mission to Abeokuta gave the British comparable grounds for complaint.[118] Prudent diplomatists recognised 'the practical impossibility of putting timely and adequate checks upon the acquisitive energies of officers employed in remote and unexplored countries'.[119] In the Africa of the 1880s there were limitless opportunities for enterprising officers of one power to exploit the desire of African rulers to escape from the embarrassing attentions of the rival empire; in the interest of European solidarity some working understanding was needed as to what constituted legitimate treaty rights and legitimate spheres of influence.

[117] Ibid., No. 89, Hutton to C.O., 19 March 1888, encl. Bohn to Hutton, 9 March, C.O. 87/134, Minute by Hemming, 2 April. *Le Temps*, 4 April 1888.
[118] Ibid., No. 100, F.O. to C.O., 12 April 1888, encl. Flourens to Lytton, 30 March 1888; cf. above pp. 156–61.
[119] Sal. P. A57, Lytton to Salisbury, 12 December 1888, quoting Nisard.

Hemming could thus give increasingly powerful reasons in favour of reopening the idea of a comprehensive exchange. Citing Hutton as the best authority for believing that British mercantile opposition would no longer be serious, he agreed that African opposition (which the merchants had used so skilfully in the 1870s) might reappear, but:

the French would, in all probability, be able easily to 'square' them by a small expenditure of money and a liberal one of promises.

Hemming admitted that better terms would be needed than the French feelers suggested;[120] but Bohn, when told this by Hutton, held out some hope that the French might still agree to withdraw from the whole coast between Sierra Leone and Lagos – the opposition of Mantes Brothers and Fabre might be overcome by pressure from other merchants whose main interests were concentrated in Senegambia.[121] Hemming's eagerness for exchange was reinforced by Captain G. W. Hand, a naval officer serving on the West Coast who shared Johnston's enthusiasm for the consolidation and expansion of British power; after arguing specifically for a British protectorate over the Kru coast, and eventually Liberia, Hand suggested that negotiations might secure the withdrawal of both French and German claims between Sierra Leone and the 'Rio del Rey' (in exchange respectively, for the Gambia and Ambas Bay).[122]

Even Meade was now tempted by the possibilities of exchange; pointing out that the essential question turned on the domestic political situation and could only be settled by the Cabinet, he added the reminder that retaining the Gambia would also involve an unpalatable political decision, to request a grant-in-aid. Herbert, more concerned than Meade about the political fortunes of the Conservative government, prophesied opposition in the Commons, apparently less on the basis of available evidence than of memories of his cousin's former discomforture: 'the handful of merchants interested in the settlement would get up a strong

120 C.O. 87/134, Minute by Hemming, 2 April, on Hutton to C.O., 19 March 1888.

121 C.P. African 345, No. 97, Hutton to C.O., 6 April 1888, encl. Bohn to Hutton, 30 March.

122 Ibid., No. 96, Admty to C.O., 3 April 1888 (encl. Hand report, 7 March).

opposition – many Conservative and protestant Liberals would join them – and the Government would have to withdraw the proposal in disgrace.' He did however suggest a possible way forward. The application for a grant-in-aid, Herbert thought, might provide the occasion to appoint a new Select Committee, through which:

> the public could be educated (without political danger to the Government) to understand how much money and how many valuable lives we have sacrificed since 1865 for the limited benefit of our few not very successful traders and merchants, and of the few protestant religionists artificially cultivated at the Gambia; and also would learn what real advantages might be obtained from France in return for the cession.

But the Secretary of State remained apprehensive. His recent ennoblement had entailed the transfer from the Department of the vigorous Lord Onslow; the new Under-Secretary, Baron de Worms, was a political lightweight who reinforced his superior's nervousness. The most that Knutsford would accept was that the exchange might be considered if proposed from the French side during the negotiations which had slowly begun.[123]

Encouraged this far, Hutton moved next through his friend Harry Johnston, just back from the Oil Rivers, whose unexpected social contacts with Lord Salisbury encouraged him to venture into the high politics of African partition. In *The Times* of 22 August Johnston publicised a blueprint for a grand rationalisation of Eurpean territorial claims throughout Africa; as far as the west coast was concerned its main feature was an Anglo–French boundary moving north-eastwards from the Guinea rivers, implying exactly such an agreement as Hutton proposed. This bold scheme, Johnston claimed, would win 'the concurrence of all the great missionary societies, of the steamship companies, of the various trading corporations, and emphatically of the Press'.[124] Salisbury remained a little sceptical about this latent reservoir of imperial enthusiasm; he recalled the Parliamentary opposition to transfer

[123] C.O. 87/134, Minutes by Meade, 3 April, Herbert 4 April, de Worms, 5 April, Knutsford, 8 April, on Hutton to C.O., 19 March; by Hemming, 9 April, Knutsford, 11 April, on Hutton to C.O., 6 April 1888. C.P. African 345, C.O. to F.O., 14 April 1888.

[124] R. Oliver, *Sir Harry Johnston and the Scramble for Africa* (1957) pp. 133–44.

in 1876, feared it would now be reinforced by Irish obstruction-
ists, and concluded that 'neither the French government nor the
House of Commons are in a condition to give a fair hearing to
any external question.'[125] Nevertheless, he and his officials did
want to get the discussions with France moving again on as broad
a basis as possible; Percy Anderson reminded the Colonial Office
of this on 8 October, while warning them that Porto Novo might
prove too high a price to ask for the Gambia.[126]

During the summer of 1888 the merchant community generally,
possibly orchestrated by Hutton, began to support the consolidation of British colonial holdings in West Africa; this was an
important development, given their role in opposing cession in
the 1870s. In July the Liverpool Chamber of Commerce presented
a memorial to the Colonial Office asking for more treaties to
secure British trade and influence against such intrusions as
Viard's at Abeokuta, and for exchange negotiations with France
and Germany, designed to secure an unbroken line of coast under
British protectorates.

> . . . the method of British trading with Africa has been under-
> going a change [wrote the Chamber] . . . instead of proceeding
> from isolated factories, or groups of factories, trade is now
> being carried on by the natives themselves; . . . in many in-
> stances they come to England to be educated and return to
> their own country with sympathy for civilised life and com-
> petent to conduct business with English houses . . . this system
> is greatly on the increase, tending to make African settlements
> permanent and valuable additions to the British Empire . . .

The merchants and shippers of Liverpool, having abandoned
the idea of joining the Niger Company in an extended system
of Chartered government, were thus coming to favour an extension of Crown Colony rule in face of foreign competition; to work
effectively, this would require consolidated control of the coast
and the elimination of rival fiscal systems.[127]

In October, Hutton returned to the specific problem of the

[125] Johnston Papers, i/i/i (Microfilm in Ibadan University Library),
Salisbury to Johnston, 26 September, 25 October 1888.
[126] C.O. 147/68, Anderson to Herbert, Pte., 8 October 1888; C.O.
879/28, C.P. African 355, No. 42, F.O. to C.O., 29 September 1888.
[127] C.O. 879/28, C.P. African 355, No. 14, Liverpool Chamber of
Commerce to C.O., 24 July 1888.

Gambia, with an enthusiasm which does not seem to have been warranted by actual attitudes in Paris. According to his French correspondent, Hutton told Knutsford, it would now be feasible to secure French withdrawal from the whole coastline between Gabon and the Scarcies and a partition of influence in the interior along the sort of line which Johnston had suggested; such an agreement seemed the only way to secure Britain's future in West Africa by guaranteeing 'communication and trade with the tribes of the interior'. He went on to assure the hesitant Minister that the change in merchants' attitudes would reduce political opposition to a mere 'sentimental outcry'. Even in 1875, said Hutton (who was in the best position to know), Manchester merchants would probably not have opposed cession had they understood what advantages were to be secured in exchange.[128] This change of attitudes was subsequently confirmed by direct communications from the Manchester and London Chambers.[129]

These discussions transformed Knutsford's views; his fears of a political storm allayed, he positively welcomed the prospect of getting rid of the troubles of the Gambia. He at once began to press the Foreign Office to resume negotiations and encouraged Hemming once more to expound reasons for favouring an exchange.[130] Arguing that France's provocative actions might have intended to harass the British into abandoning the Gambia, Hemming now indulged in an orgy of expansionist speculation about the 'very material concessions' which might be obtained in return. Once agreement was complete Porto Novo could be brought under British protection, and Tofa pensioned off; Grand Bassam and Assinie could be incorporated in the Gold Coast, whose territory might then extend up to the Liberian border; the Popos could also be taken, and handed on to Germany in exchange for a favourable settlement of the Volta frontier.[131] On the other hand:

[128] Ibid. Nos. 44, 46A: Hutton to C.O. 10 October; Hutton to Knu ford, 15 October, 1888.

[129] Ibid. Nos. 66, 74, Manchester C. of C. to C.O., 28 November; London C. of C. to C.O., 11 December 1888.

[130] Ibid. Nos. 47, 52, C.O. to F.O., 16, 19 October 1888; Sal. P., Box E, Knutsford to Salisbury, 31 October 1888.

[131] C.P. African 355, No. 48, C.O. to F.O., 16 October 1888, and Memo by Hemming, 14 October; C.O. 879/29, C.P. Africa 357, Memo by Hemming, November 1888.

Without the cession of the Gambia it is doubtful whether the French would consent to negotiate at all, and even if they do, we shall have so little to offer them in exchange for the concessions we desire that no really satisfactory or permanent settlement is likely to be arrived at.

Knutsford still thought it might be prudent not to propose the cession of the Gambia but to await the expected suggestion from the French government, but the idea gradually grew on him; by 1890 he could contemplate making an actual offer of cession in return for a settlement of the troublesome Newfoundland fisheries dispute.[132]

Meanwhile, Lytton and his deputy, Edwin Egerton, had established good relations with René Goblet (an ex-Premier of the Left Centre who succeeded Flourens in April 1888) and with Nisard (his Director of Protectorates) and were moving cautiously towards negotiations. When invited to protest against French encroachments into Combo which violated the Gambian *status quo* Lytton (to Knutsford's irritation) declined to do so, for fear of stirring up recriminations from expansionists in the Colonial Department[133] – who were indeed all too ready to make counter-charges.[134] Early in January another dangerous frontier quarrel, arising from the shooting of two French protected persons on the Porto Novo lagoon, was averted by sensible and friendly co-operation locally between Moloney and Beckmann.[135] Despite the agreements to respect the *status quo* such incidents could still arise at any time, so the diplomatists were anxious to press on with negotiations while the attention of French politicians was directed to domestic affairs. Boulanger's triumph at a Paris by-election on 27

[132] C.P. African 355, No. 81, C.O. to F.O., Conf., 22 December, 1888; Sal. P., Box E., Knutsford to Salisbury, 29 May 1890.

[133] C.O. 879/29, C.P. African 360, No. 6, C.O. to F.O. 19 November 1888, No. 14, F.O. to C.O., Conf., 3 January 1889, encl. Lytton to Salisbury, Af. 150, Conf. 20, December 1888; Sal. P. A.57, Nos. 73, 75, 84, 87; Lytton to Salisbury, Tel., 7 December; 12, 20, 26 December 1888; Box E, Knutsford to Salisbury, 13 December 1888.

[134] ANSOM, Afrique vi/73a, De La Porte to Goblet, 2 January 1889; Goblet to De La Porte, 23 January 1889.

[135] C.O. 879/29, C.P. African 365, No. 33, Moloney to Knutsford, 36 29 January 1889, with many enclosures. For a French version, ANSOM, Senegal vi/19/d, Thomas to De La Porte, 405, 17 February, 502, 4 March 1889.

January 1889, his departure for Brussels on 1 April, and the preparation for the general election eventually held under a new electoral law in September, helped divert attention from British iniquities; but if publicised such insults to the French flag might have provided tempting electoral material.

The Quai d'Orsay and the British Embassy accordingly worked out procedures for discreet and business-like negotiations which they hoped would not attract too much attention from politicians and the Press. Adopting the procedure used by Britain and Germany over the Togo border, they agreed to form a small commission of officials qualified to elucidate the complex local issues on the basis of the documentation available in Europe; these men would explore the issues informally before meeting in formal sessions. Although British officials who feared the influence of French colonial 'hawks' would have preferred to leave actual negotiation to the diplomatists, it was finally agreed that colonial experts should be full members of the commission, and this procedure worked satisfactorily. Hemming crossed to Paris to assist Egerton, and on the French side Nisard and d'Estournelles de Constant (a conciliatory diplomatist) were joined by Bayol, who proved to be much more moderate and co-operative than his record of vigorous patriotism in Africa might have suggested.[136]

Although the British Government had decided not to take the initiative in offering to cede the Gambia, Hemming still hoped that the French would be willing to pay generously for it. On 5 March, before leaving London, he drafted two alternative 'Schemes of Settlement', one involving only a balanced adjustment of the various disputed boundaries, the other a territorial exchange. Favouring the latter scheme, Hemming thought that Britain should ask for 'very much larger and more important concessions', larger even than those which Hutton had hoped for; France might be asked, as in 1875, to 'withdraw from the whole of the coastline between the right bank of the River Pongas and the Gaboon' (that is, from Conakry and the Mellacourie as well as from Porto Novo and the Ivory Coast), and to accept a related demarcation line in the interior, which would provide Freetown

[136] C.P. Africa 365, Nos. 13, 20, F.O. to C.O., 22 January, 15 February; No. 24, C.O. to F.O., 22 February 1889. C.O. 147/73, Minute by Meade on F.O. to C.O., 16 March 1889. ANSOM, Afrique vi/73/a, M.A.E. to M.M.C., 12 March 1889.

with maximum protection. If it proved necessary during negotiations however the western end of this line might be moved southwards as far as the Great Scarcies.[137] Accordingly at the first meeting of the commission on 25 April, Hemming and Egerton suggested that the 'French and English spheres of influence' might
be defined by a line following the 10th parallel from the mouth
of the Pongos to 4 degrees West and proceeding thence in a
north-easterly direction to Burrum on the Niger. In accordance
with instructions, there was no formal offer to cede the Gambia,
but the idea was clearly implicit in this proposal, as Egerton
hinted directly.[138]

The French however were no longer tempted. Given their improved military situation in Senegabia, they were confident of
eventually controlling the economy of the whole Gambia. 'There
is no need at present to open discussion about the cession of the
Gambia', the Colonial Department decided, 'This river will become French through force of circumstances, like Ziguinchor in
the Casamance.'[139] And, as the British Embassy feared, the influence of the Colonial Department was growing. When Tirard
formed his government in March 1889 he apparently intended
to establish an independent Colonial Ministry under Etienne; and
although he subsequently decided not to approach the Chamber
for the necessary funds, the Department was transferred from the
control of the Ministry of Marine to the laxer empire of the
Ministry of Commerce. As Under-Secretary, Etienne acquired
increased status within the government hierarchy, including the
right to attend Cabinet meetings.[140]

Etienne had no intention of trading any of France's prospects
of empire in West Africa for the wasting asset of British Gambia.
In 1888 his department had been prepared for concessions on the
Ivory Coast, though not necessarily *of* the Ivory Coast; but Binger's
journey had put this colony into a new perspective.[141] Indeed,

---

[137] C.P. African 365, No. 31; Memo by Hemming, 5 March 1889. See
Map 5, p. 250.

[138] C.O. 879/29 – C.P. Africa 360, No. 34, F.O. to C.O., 30 April
1889, encl. Egerton to Lytton, 25 April.

[139] AE Afrique 128, Note aux Affaires Etrangères, 25 April 1889.

[140] F. Berge, *Le Sous-Secretariat* . . . , pp. 57–65; C.O. 147/73, Egerton to
Hemming, Pte., 15 March 1889.

[141] ANSOM, Afrique vi/66/c, M.A.E. to M.M.C., 16 November 1888;
Afrique vi/73/a, Etienne to Spuller, 25 April 1889.

the stakes were in process of being raised as Anglo–French rivalry extended northwards into Gyaman. Over a year before Treich-Lapleine's treaty of November 1888 King Agyeman had accepted a British flag from an African corporal, Van Dyke; in March 1889 the French learned that a British officer, Captain Lethbridge, had used this to justify the removal of the tricolour from Bonduku and the signature of a new treaty. Etienne, egged on by Binger, reacted fiercely, denying that treaties made by African agents had any validity;[142] but the Quai d'Orsay, anxious to save the negotiations, insisted that the incident 'should be reduced to as small dimensions as possible' in order to avoid any risk of Parliamentary discussion.[143] But clearly there was now no possibility of Etienne agreeing to withdraw from the Ivory Coast; the best the Commissioners could do was to settle the southern section of the frontier and leave the fate of Gyaman for subsequent negotiation.

At Porto Novo, the prospects of French withdrawal were no better. Although French prestige locally was badly damaged when Tofa fled from the supposed Dahomean invasion in April, Etienne was determined to restore it, and to make Porto Novo the base for a thrust towards the Niger. His nomination as Commissioner of Bayol, who had been closely identified with Tofa's claims, reflected this concern. Etienne's intentions were reinforced by Father Planque's hopes of reviving connections with Abeokuta and Oyo, and by continual pressure from Fabre (in numerous letters, and at least one meeting at Marseille station).[144] Clearly, the Quai d'Orsay could not have persuaded Etienne to sacrifice even a small part of what Britain was demanding without a political storm. But even with a more amenable Colonial Under-Secretary, the political uncertainty would have made it dangerous to conclude an ambitious exchange of territory requiring Parliamentary ratification. In this crisis of the Republic no government could risk another rebuff such as that experienced over the Sierra Leone boundary agreement of 1882.

Any possibility that the British proposal might tempt the French

---

[142] ANSOM, Afrique vi/73/c, Etienne to Spuller, 17 June 1889 (drafted by Grodet on notes of conversation with Binger), cf. above p. 91.

[143] AE Afrique 125, Note pour le Ministre, 28 June 1889.

[144] AE Afrique 125, Planque to Etienne, 25 April 1889. ANSOM, Senegal iv/124/b, Fabre to Etienne, 13 May 1889. Cf. above pp. 168–9.

was finally destroyed by Hemming's decision to ask for a north-ward extension of the Sierra Leone/Guinea boundary, instead of conceding the slight southwards movement to the Scarcies which Hutton's friends in C.F.A.O. had suggested. For the French as well as the British regarded this as a critical area. Apart from the interest of the merchants, the Sudanese military had, through Gallieni's initiatives, become very interested in securing a route from Benty to Futa Jalon through the upper valley of the Scarcies. Their actual position was much weaker and more vulnerable than the British realised. In March 1888 the Colonial Office had ac-cepted the French claim to a protectorate over Futa Jalon at face value, and their main objective became French recognition of the commercial rights conferred by old British treaties; although Hemming expressed hopes of including Futa Jalon in the British sphere during the Paris negotiations, in practice he made no serious effort to do so.[145] In fact, the French government doubted whether either Bayol's treaty of 1881 or Oberdorf's of 1888 could be com-pletely relied upon; the problem of making their occupation effec-tive still remained to be faced.[146] And even in the coastal area the limits of French authority had been illustrated by the humiliating Fourichon affair of November 1888.[147]

The colonial authorities therefore hoped to strengthen their position by obtaining the Isles de Los, and access to the Great Scarcies; had the British revealed their willingness to bargain over these territories Etienne would certainly have been interested, though he would never have agreed to the compensation required. But there could be no question of weakening French prestige by abandoning territory to the British. The Foreign Ministry, aware of their vulnerability, thought it safe to reaffirm the unratified frontier of 1882 than to expose their position in Guinea to any extended scrutiny in the context of a major distribution of terri-tories.[148] So, at the second session of the commission, Nisard and

[145] C.O. 267/373, 13 April, on W.O. to C.O., 5 April 1888; C.O. 267/372, Minute by Hemming, 25 November, on Hay 326, 1 November 1888; C.O. 267/379, Minute by Hemming, 22 March, on F.O. to C.O., 21 March 1889. Inter-departmental correspondence on the subject may be studied in C.P. African 318 and 377

[146] AE Afrique 122, Etienne to Spuller, 14 May 1889; Note pour le Ministre, 21 June 1889.

[147] See above pp. 197–8.

[148] AE Afrique vi/73/b, M.A.E. to M.M.C., 8 March 1889.

Bayol, having invited their British colleagues to mark their proposed demarcation line on a map, commented that they would prefer to discuss the various frontiers *seriatim,* and 'endeavour to arrive at a settlement of the disputed points', rather than embark on discussions involving a great exchange of territory.[149]

Thereafter the outcome was more or less inevitable. The British delegates had feared a possible French argument that Britain's old treaty rights in the Gambia referred to the waterway only – as indeed the French colonial 'hawks' claimed. But on 5 May Bayol conceded that these rights implied control of the river banks within the limits of navigation – and the boundaries of a narrow Gambia protectorate began to take shape on the map.[150] The British thereupon agreed to withdraw from Ketenou and part of Appa, and accept a frontier at Porto Novo, which they believed (somewhat hopefully) to represent 'a plain geographical and ethnographical division.[151] Elsewhere it was essentially a matter of drawing similiarly compromised lines on maps, affecting territories which only Bayol, of the Commissioners, had ever seen. The British ensured that the French would halt their advance towards Freetown before Falaba, in the region of the tenth parallel, while the French kept open their route to the north from the Ivory Coast, by a vague formula which left the frontier in Gyaman to be 'fixed in accordance with the various treaties which have respectively been concluded by the two governments with the natives'. By 10 August the Commissioners had completed and signed a detailed agreement. This laid down frontiers for the Gambia, at a distance of approximately ten kilometres to the north and south of the river; confirmed and further defined the settlement of the Sierra Leone/Guinea frontier along the lines agreed in 1882 (thus confirming French possession of Futa Jalon); and sketched out boundaries on the Ivory Coast and Porto Novo as far north as the ninth parallel.[152]

[149] C.P. African 360, No. 35, encl. Egerton to Lytton, 20 April 1889.

[150] Ibid., No. 39, encl. Egerton to Salisbury, 57 Af, 5 May 1889, and memo by Hemming.

[151] C.P. African 365, No. 75, encl. Egerton to Salisbury, 64, 10 May 1889.

[152] Hertslet, *Map of Africa,* 3rd ed., ii, pp. 729–37. Records of the Commissioners' proceedings may be found in AE Afrique 128, and in C.O. 879/29, C.P. African 360 and 375.

ILLUSORY EQUILIBRIUM

Given the assumption that colonies once established would continue to exist, the agreement of August 1889 was a sensible piece
of horse-trading, which does not seem to represent much 'vicarious
generosity' by the British.[153] True, the French Foreign Ministry
drew up a summary claiming great successes on all fronts:
security in Saloum, Rip and Bondou; the definitive exclusion of
British influence from the Guinea rivers; a clear route from Assinie
to the northern Ivory Coast; and at Porto Novo such an access of
strength as would secure France's future influence in Dahomey
and on the route to Mossi.[154] Yet only at Porto Novo were the
perils said to have been averted real, and even here the establishment of Germany in Togo had removed any real incentive for the
British to squeeze out the French. Britain's sense of weakness had
not been fully appreciated in Paris; what London had feared was
that Bathurst or Freetown might be strangled by French establishments on the lower Gambia or at Porto Loko, and these dangers
at least were finally averted. The French memorandum was
clearly written to provide ammunition against political critics who
might understand what Britain had gained. Both Foreign and
Colonial officials remembered the vicissitudes of the 1882 agreement, and later agreed that this one should be ratified by presi-
dential degree, rather than submitted to 'the inconvenience of
re-opening a political discussion upon questions which the Plenipo-
tentiaries have only been able to resolve with the help of their
professional experience, and to the danger of exposing to possible
failure the results of negotiations that have required several years
of study.'[155]

Salisbury and the Foreign Office doubtless hoped that this sensible bit of diplomacy had disposed of the troublesome problems

[153] Robinson and Gallagher, 'The Partition of Africa', *New Cambridge
Modern History*, xi, p. 611. Compare this very British view with Kenneth
Vignes, 'Étude sur la rivalité d'influence entre les puissances européenes
en Afrique equatoriale et occidentale depuis l'acte général de Berlin
jusqu'au seuil du XXᵉ siecle', *RFHOM*, 48 (1961) p. 47.

[154] AE Afrique 128, Résumé de la Situation Respective de la France
et de l'Angleterre à la Côte Occidentale d'Afrique avant et apres
l'arrangement définitif signé le 10 août 1889.

[155] Ibid., Note pour le Ministre, December 20 1889; see also correspondence in ANSOM, Afrique vi/73/a.

of Anglo–French relations in West Africa, and that they could now concentrate on more important problems in other quarters of the continent, or in other continents. But the equilibrium achieved proved illusory. The temper of French colonial policy was about to change; indeed, Britain was fortunate to have concluded this agreement before Etienne became fully entrenched in his new appointment. Etienne, encouraged by his contentious *sous-directeur* Albert Grodet, seems to have accepted the terms negotiated by the Commissioners with some reluctance, especially as regards territories north of Sierra Leone; he complained petulantly that the Foreign Ministry (now under an old Gambettist ally, J. Spuller) had not kept his newly autonomous department fully informed and seemed reluctant to recognise 'if not the existence of its autonomy, at least its duration'.[156] Etienne would shortly match this sensitivity about the status of his department by a new imperialistic vigour in action.

The development of this new French imperialism, both within the political life of the Third Republic and on the frontiers of the African empire, was to provide the major theme of West African history during the next five years. Bayol, his negotiations hardly completed, returned to Porto Novo with an increased status, and with instructions which provided him with ample scope to provoke a conflict with Dahomey through the imprudent exercise of patriotic initiative.[157] On the Ivory Coast, Treich-Lapleine was appointed as Resident, and he set to work to build up a genuine autonomous colonial administration around the coastal territories whose prospects of future expansion had just been so greatly enlarged.[158] At the same time Etienne gave substance to other British fears by contemplating the occupation of territories previously regarded as Liberian.[159] In Guinea, the consolidation of

[156] ANSOM, Afrique vi/73/a, Etienne to Spuller, 4 July, 25 July, 14 August 1889.

[157] AE Afrique 125, Etienne to Bayol, 13 August 1889. (Draft instructions communicated to Spuller for approval on 5 August; cf. Spuller to Etienne, 12 August.)

[158] Cf. Atger, *La France en Côte d'Ivoire*, Part iii.

[159] AE Afrique 121, Etienne to Spuller, 16 April 1889; cf. C.O. 879/27, C.P. African 345, No. 96, Admiralty to C.O., 3 April 1888, enclosing report by Captain G. W. Hand, 7 March 1888; C.O. 879/29, C.P. African 357, Memo by Hemming, November 1888. This subject will be treated in Volume ii.

French control, under Bayol's direction, would shortly begin to affect the prosperity of Sierra Leone. Meanwhile in the Sudan, Archinard was preparing to launch the full-scale military advance which in a few years' time would bring his command into closer contact with the British and begin the long-expected 'contest for the middle Niger'.[160] All these new departures were increasingly sustained by pressure-groups inside France; soon the growing acceptability of imperialist doctrines would mean that politicians no longer needed to pursue colonial adventures furtively and apologetically but could present them as patriotic work of national interest. The future course of the European partition in West Africa would be largely determined by the fact that France became ready to undertake aggressive policies there some five years before their British rivals were fully prepared to do so.

[160] F.O. 84/1787, Minute by Anderson, July 1886, cf. above p. 98.

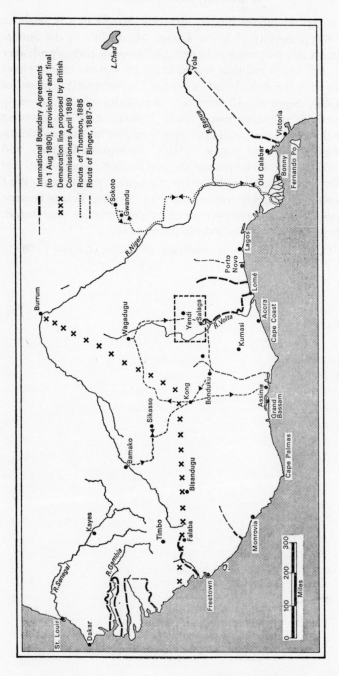

International Boundary Agreements
(to 1 Aug 1890), provisional and final

××× Demarcation line proposed by British
Commissioners April 1889

.... Route of Thomson, 1885

–·–·– Route of Binger, 1887-9

5 Exploration and Partition, 1885–90

Appendix:
Some statistical indications

Theories of imperialism often imply correlations between political expansion and economic relationships. In general, the more sophisticated the theory, the more difficult it becomes to measure the relevant relationships. To attempt a precise calculation of all transactions between different European states and the various regions of independent West Africa, or to measure the extent to which Europeans or Africans had become dependent upon such transactions, would involve methodological difficulties which the author feels quite incapable of resolving. However, it will be apparent to readers of this work that there were many points at which the behaviour of colonial governments was determined by considerations of trade and revenue; and on such matters relevant figures are normally available in the statistical returns which colonial governments were required to keep. So long as there were alternative ports where Europeans could trade with Africans without the supervision of colonial custom officials, these figures can not be expected to provide comprehensive data about the imports and exports of a region. But, besides demonstrating the commercial and financial problems as perceived by colonial governors, they do provide statistical indices by which we can assess the relative importance, as precipitants of change, of changing prices on international produce markets, local political conditions, variations in rainfall, and new scales of colonial tariff.

First, as an index of the movement of world prices for oil-seeds, it may be useful to register the average prices of imports into the U.K., from all world sources, of these staples of African trade. For palm oil, this can be derived from the figures for quantity and value of British imports given in the annual *Statistical Abstract of the U.K.* Unfortunately, the *Abstract* does not give separate figures for palm kernels, groundnuts, and other crops, but only

TABLE I: ANNUAL IMPORTS TO U.K.

	PALM OIL			NUTS AND KERNELS		
	Quantity (cwts.)	Value (c.i.f.)	Price (per ton)	Quantity (tons)	Value (c.i.f.)	Price (per ton)
		£	£		£	£
1876	879,824	1,529,360	34.77	31,471	469,275	14.91
1877	897,264	1,598,166	35.62	28,806	427,107	14.83
1878	670,797	1,167,161	34.80	32,557	513,507	15.77
1879	881,329	1,344,788	30·52	34,366	521,770	15·21
1880	1,083,823	1,519,701	29·43	49,635	748,814	15.08
1881	826,891	1,202,571	29.09	38,173	508,906	13.33
1882	813,870	1,240,866	30.49	57,962	726,428	12.53
1883	749,422	1,315,559	35.11	61,262	872,129	14.24
1884	841,012	1,408,753	33.50	69,331	1,026,645	14.81
1885	905,439	1,217,816	26.90	55,820	730,796	13.09
1886	1,004,419	1,050,459	20.92	52,894	595,529	11.26
1887	968,227	943,126	19.48	56,894	624,348	10.99
1888	953,799	945,896	19.83	62,932	713,061	11.17
1889	1,031,440	1,091,922	21.17	61,857	684,635	11.07
1890	873,923	1,000,535	22.90	47,526	603,569	12.70
1891	1,018,420	1,186,705	23.30	62,830	827,270	13.15
1892	1,058,580	1,169,490	22.10	55,492	676,653	12.19

(Sources: P.P. (1890–1) LXXXIX; P.P. (1895) CIV.

consolidated totals for 'nuts and kernels used for expressing oil'; as uses as well as sources of supply were different, the resulting index has only limited value. Nevertheless, these figures do suggest that prices of 'nuts and kernels' held up somewhat better than those for palm oil to the depression of the mid-1880s, and recovered more quickly; also that the volume of demand increased more rapidly.

Supplies and prices in Africa were affected by local conditions of production and marketing as well as by the international terms of trade. Figures drawn from colonial Blue Books (on which the returns in the *Statistical Abstract* for the colonies was based) often show local prices not only running below European levels (which is to be expected since freight charges are excluded) but fluctuating at their own pace. Table II, based on figures for the exports of Lagos, raises interesting problems concerning the relative effect of political conditions and of market incentives in determining supply. It is difficult to establish any constant relationship between changes in price and changes in quantities exported. Possibly the fall in oil exports after the record figure of 1886 may be a delayed

TABLE II: ANNUAL EXPORTS OF LAGOS

	I	II	III	IV	V	VI
	Palm-oil exported (Gallons)	Value (f.o.b.) £	Calculated price (per ton) £	Kernels exported	Value (f.o.b.) £	Calculated price £
1877	3,304,967	239,134	21.15	30,875	335,591	11.52
1878	1,570,638	139,093	26.55	27,873	317,950	11.40
1879	2,469,418	208,795	25.35	26,839	319,444	11.90
1880	1,526,423	133,225	26.20	29,632	346,147	11.69
1881	1,807,296	147,423	24.45	20,801	221,634	10.65
1882	2,637,326	219,521	24.90	28,592	261,184	9.13
1883	1,971,359	186,637	27.60	25,821	278,303	10.78
1884	2,382,656	225,558	28.40	29,773	327,347	10.99
1885	2,657,775	218,410	24.60	30,805	282,393	9.17
1886	3,097,538	213,194	20.15	34,812	255,422	7.34
1887	2,506,146	151,167	18.00	35,784	266,960	7.46
1888	2,446,706	123,368	15.00	43,525	314,885	7.23
1889	2,349,011	133,723	17.10	32,715	239,987	7.34
1890	3,200,824	190,657	17.85	38,829	319,276	8.22
1891	4,204,835	252,958	18.00	42,342	341,349	8.04
1892	2,458,260	137,743	16.80	32,180	260,109	8.08

Sources: P.P. (1890) LXXVIII; (1895) CIV. *Statistical Abstract for the Several Colonial and other Possessions of the U.K., 1875–89, 1880–94.* Checked with annual Blue Books.

reaction to the collapse in prices which began in 1885, but the figures for kernels do not behave similarly. But neither do these figures sustain the view of contemporaries that the Yoruba wars were destroying the produce trade. The outbreak of the Kiriji war in 1878 may help to explain some of the poor figures in 1878–81, but thereafter the course of hostilities seems to have had no more drastic effect than to retard a general tendency for exports of palm produce to increase (cf. pp. 133–4 above). The poor figures for 1892 however were probably affected by the British invasion of Ijebu. Possibly the weather may have affected supply more strongly than either price or politics. In 1888 rainfall was only 50 inches, compared to an average figure of 72 inches; this may explain the setbacks in both oil and kernels in 1889.

Figures for the exports of Sierra Leone similarly cast doubt on the contemporary belief that 'tribal war' was the greatest deterrent

TABLEI III: ANNUAL EXPORTS OF SIERRA LEONE

	1877	1878	1879	1880	1881	1882	1883	1884
Total exports* (f.o.b.)	£388,530	£391,646	£391,080	£375,986	£365,861	£420,017	£442,373	£337,055
Total value, four principal African exports	£232,841	£202,988	£200,158	£220,656	£234,902	£270,602	£224,474	£177,044
Kola nuts – Packages exported	1,573	2,288	2,447	2,331	2,458	2,388	3,172	3,420
Price	221/-	220/-	193/-	209/-	221/-	213/-	199/-	233/-
Value	£17,725	£25,482	£23,859	£24,442	£27,169	£25,547	£31,161	£40,001
Palm Oil – Gallons exported	348,500	347,265	440,175	292,306	391,372	562,614	250,734	261,305
Price	2/5	2/-	1/10	1/9	1/9	1/8	1/8	1/4
Value	£39,472	£36,921	£41,195	£26,343	£35,143	£47,217	£21,953	£17,773
Palm Kernels – Bushels exported	514,020	404,909	513,258	363,318	388,915	300,858	193,077 cwt.	194,133 cwt.
Price	5/8	5/-	4/5	5/9	5/4	6/7	8/6 per cwt.	7/-
Value	£145,280	£112,675	£113,993	£107,221	£104,941	£101,164	£81,578	£68,377
Rubber – lb. exported	609,728	687,134	379,220	829,636	956,394	1,388,150	1,083,269	810,198
Price	1/-	10d	1/1	1/6	1/4	1/4	1/8	1/3
Value	£30,364	£27,910	£21,111	£62,650	£67,669	£96,674	£89,782	£50,893

	1885	1886	1887	1888	1889	1890	1891	1892
Total exports (f.o.b.)	£326,931	£325,352	£333,516	£339,042	£319,719	£349,318	£477,655	£420,451
Total value, four principal African exports	£161,881	£172,247	£174,076	£199,849	£183,620	£200,324	£292,566	£263,311
Kola nuts – Packages exported	3,224	3,072	3,616	7,191 cwt.	8,907 cwt.	6,991 cwt.	9,183 cwt.	11,213 cwt.
Price	201/-	144/-	116/9	94/3 per cwt.	70/3	[82/3]	94/-	86/4
Value	£32,400	£22,139	£21,111	£23,940	£31,275	£28,790	£43,004	£48,421
Palm Oil – Gallons exported	307,154	227,478	231,864	262,566	227,696	263,825	288,972	243,401
Price	1/9	1/-	10d	11d	1/-	[c1/-]	1/-	1/-
Value	£27,048	£11,791	£10,396	£12,285	£11,379	£13,600	£14,369	£12,959
Palm Kernels – Bushels exported	200,745 cwt.	236,096 cwt.	219,500 cwt.	276,278 cwt.	310,540 cwt.	317,960 cwt.	395,940 cwt.	379,400 cwt.
Price	7/7	7/4	7/3	7/-	6/9	[c6/9]	8/-	7/6
Value	£76,802	£86,364	£76,884	£97,177	£105,963	£107,827	£157,456	£141,491
Rubber – lb. exported	479,984	857,991	10,018 cwt.	11,301 cwt.	6,930 cwt.	8,979 cwt.	13,361 cwt.	10,772 cwt.tt
Price	1/-	1/3	191/1 per cwt.	110/6	106/9	[c114/3]	116/-	114/-
Value	£25,631	£51,952	£65,685	£66,447	£37,003	£50,102	£77,737	£61,440

(Source: Annual Blue Books)
*Freetown being an entrepot, this figure included a large element of re-exports.

TABLE IV: ANNUAL EXPORTS OF THE GAMBIA

	All exports Total Value £	GROUNDNUTS			RUBBER		
		Quantity (tons)	*Price* £	*Value* (f.o.b.) £	*Quantity* (lbs.)	*Price* @ c	*Value* (f.o.b.) £
1877	125,051	15,939	@ 7	111,573	841	(1/1)*	45
1878	204,300	23,996	8	191,970			
1879	207,364	22,890	8	183,120			
1880	138,983	13,824	8	110,944			
1881	140,423	16,958	(7)*	118,712			
1882	254,711	25,522	9	229,701			
1883	208,120	23,094	7.7.4	170,164	52,003	2/4	6,048
1884	199,483	18,396	(7.13.9)*	141,389	257,285	(1/9)*	23,212
1885	119,385	12,330	(7)*	87,108	42,178	(1/3)*	2,670
1886	79,516	6,094	(6.6)*	38,401	154,550	(1/6)*	11,376
1887	86,933[1]	2,995	(8.14.0)*	26,001	190,177	(1/4)*	12,848
1888	118,188	10,207	(7.6-8)*	74,877	48,834	(1/4)*	3,277
1889	167,599	19,648	(7.3-6)*	140,083	55,548	(1/3)*	3,469
1890	164,374	19,260	(6.15.0)*	129,846	154,737	(1/4)*	10,144
1891	180,052	19,702	7	142,933	246,690	1/- (sc1/3)	15,451
1892	172,197	21,281	7	150,206	51,614	1/- (sc 1/1)	2,920

[1]Including specie exports £12,147
*calculated
(Source: Annual Blue Books)

to production. Over the years 1877–92 the most striking feature is perhaps the tendency of exports of palm oil to decline, roughly in step with the declining world price. But quantities of palm kernels exported remain relatively stable, despite falling prices. Rubber – a commodity where world demand for industrial purposes was buoyant – shows a generally expanding tendency, although there are setbacks in 1879, 1885 and 1889; these may represent reactions to falls in price during the previous year, although in 1885 it may well be that wars in the Yonni country and the Scarcies did interfere with the tapping of the wild vines. Finally kola nuts show a fairly gradual and steady increase in export values. This was a long-established trade, and the demand of African consumers provided a steady market and a fairly constant price; the main exception is in 1886–7, when the crisis in the Gambia reduced the incomes of African traders there.

Finally, the figures for the Gambia demonstrate the effects of

TABLE V: EXPORTS AND PUBLIC FINANCE IN THE GAMBIA

	Value of total Exports £	Revenue £	Expenditure £
1874	180,094	21,380	20,787
1875	147,465	22,700	19,565
1876	86,216	19,787	21,489
1877	125,057	26,585	21,381
1878	204,299	25,731	19,807
1879	207,364	28,505	20,639
1880	138,983	24,553	19,926
1881	140,423	24,451	22,116
1882	254,711	26,265	22,964
1883	208,120	28,866	23,982
1884	199,483	24,959	29,482
1885	119,385	20,236	26,595
1886	79,516	14,233	23,353
1887	86,933	13,377	23,920
1888	118,188	20,986	21,355
1889	167,599	26,281	21,566
1890	164,374	30,573	22,759
1891	180,052	31,038	27,697
1892	172,197	30,977	28,739

(Sources: C. W. Newbury, *British Policy towards West Africa; Select Documents 1875–1914*, pp. 612–22; P.P. (1895) CIV; *Statistical Abstract for the several Colonial and Other Possessions of the U.K., 1880–1894*, pp. 34–5).

variations in price and in political conditions on a colony which was already becoming a classical 'mono-crop' economy.

Here the catastrophic fall in groundnut exports in 1886–7 is clearly related to political disorder in Badibu; but a full explanation of these fluctuations must be somewhat more complex (cf. pp. 224–6 above). The variations in the supply of rubber are somewhat more difficult to explain; the large yield of 1884 may be related to the high price offered the previous year.

Other products made only small contributions to the colony's exports (in 1880, for example, wax accounted for £4,432, hides for £3,759, and palm oil for £2,133). Hence the particularly direct and drastic effect of the variations in the groundnut trade upon colonial finance.

Index